D1614763

Fantasy and the Real World in British Children's Literature

This study examines the children's books of three extraordinary British writers—J.K. Rowling, Diana Wynne Jones, and Terry Pratchett—and investigates their sophisticated use of narrative strategies not only to engage children in reading, but to educate them into becoming mature readers and indeed individuals. The book demonstrates how in quite different ways these writers establish reader expectations by drawing on conventions in existing genres only to subvert those expectations. Their strategies lead young readers to both evaluate for themselves the power of story to shape our understanding of the world and to develop a sense of identity and agency. Rowling, Jones, and Pratchett provide their readers with fantasies that are pleasurable and imaginative, but far from encouraging escape from reality, they convey important lessons about the complexities and challenges of the real world—and how these may be faced and solved. All three writers deploy the tropes and imaginative possibilities of fantasy to disturb, challenge, and enlarge the world of their readers.

Caroline Webb is a Senior Lecturer in English at The University of Newcastle, Australia. Her current research focuses on fantasy literature, especially children's fantasy. She has published articles on a range of authors including J.K. Rowling, Terry Pratchett, and Diana Wynne Jones. She is currently Secretary of the Australasian Children's Literature Association for Research.

Children's Literature and Culture

Jack Zipes, *Founding Series Editor*
Philip Nel, *Current Series Editor*

For a full list of titles in this series, please visit www.routledge.com

Fantasy and the Real World in British Children's Literature
The Power of Story

Caroline Webb

Routledge
Taylor & Francis Group

NEW YORK AND LONDON

First published 2015
by Routledge
711 Third Avenue, New York, NY 10017

and by Routledge
2 Park Square, Milton Park, Abingdon, Oxon OX14 4RN

*Routledge is an imprint of the Taylor & Francis Group,
an informa business*

© 2015 Taylor & Francis

Library of Congress Cataloging-in-Publication Data

Webb, Caroline, 1961– author.
  Fantasy and the real world in British children's literature : the power of
story / Caroline Webb.
      pages cm. — (Children's literature and culture ; 101)
  Includes bibliographical references and index.
  1. Children's literature, English—History and criticism. 2. Fantasy fiction,
English—History and criticism. 3. Narration (Rhetoric) 4. Reality in
literature. 5. Storytelling in literature. 6. Rowling, J. K.—Criticism
and interpretation. 7. Jones, Diana Wynne—Criticism and interpretation.
8. Pratchett, Terry—Criticism and interpretation. I. Title.
  PR990.W43 2014
  823.009'9282—dc23
  2014015791

ISBN: 978-0-415-72271-1 (hbk)
ISBN: 978-1-315-85811-1 (ebk)

Typeset in Sabon
by Apex CoVantage, LLC

Printed and bound in the United States of America by Publishers Graphics,
LLC on sustainably sourced paper.

Contents

Acknowledgements

I am grateful to The University of Newcastle, Australia for the award of a Career Enhancement Fellowship to support my research and my conference participation in 2012, and to its School of Humanities and Social Science for provision of marking relief and research assistance in 2013. Thanks to Emma Hamilton for providing that assistance. The Faculty of Education and Arts also arranged research workshops that have been very useful. I am grateful to Bronwyn Hemsley and Trisha Pender for organising and the Faculty for supporting the "It's a WRAP" research group that has helped me maintain an active research programme during the academic year.

It has given me great pleasure to discuss the work of these writers with fellow scholars at a number of conferences in recent years, including those of the Australasian Children's Literature Association for Research and the Children's Literature Association. Thanks to Christine Moon for sending me her unpublished ACLAR conference paper. The Diana Wynne Jones conference in Bristol in 2009 was particularly stimulating. I apologise to its participants for not giving space here to more of their, and my, favourite novels.

I have had much helpful feedback on my work from academic staff and postgraduate participants in the Ourimbah Humanities Research Seminar Series and the Writing Cultures seminar series at The University of Newcastle, Australia. Hugh Craig has been a wise advisor. I am particularly grateful to members of my writing circle: Lyndall Ryan, Jill Bough, and especially Wendy Michaels. Wendy's enthusiasm and critical energy have been unflagging. Thanks also to Jenny, Neville, and Susan Webb for their unfailing support.

Finally, I cannot sufficiently thank Barry Hodges for the rich engagement, the endless patience, and (in the best sense) the critical mind with which he has attended to this project by day and by night.

Small portions of Chapters 1 and 3 have appeared in articles published in *Papers: Explorations into Children's Literature*. See Webb, "Abandoned," and Webb, "Change," respectively, in the Works Cited list.

I am grateful to the Blair Partnership, agents for J.K. Rowling, for permission to quote from the Harry Potter sequence:

Harry Potter and the Philosopher's Stone: Copyright © J.K. Rowling 1997
Harry Potter and the Chamber of Secrets: Copyright © J.K. Rowling 1998
Harry Potter and the Prisoner of Azkaban: Copyright © J.K. Rowling 1999
Harry Potter and the Goblet of Fire: Copyright © J.K. Rowling 2000
Harry Potter and the Order of the Phoenix: Copyright © J.K. Rowling 2003
Harry Potter and the Half Blood Prince: Copyright © J.K. Rowling 2005
Harry Potter and the Deathly Hallows: Copyright © J.K. Rowling 2007

Extracts from *The Spellcoats*, *Cart and Cwidder*, and *The Crown of Dalemark* by Diana Wynne Jones are reproduced by permission of the original publishers, Oxford University Press.

Quotations from the following works are reprinted by permission of HarperCollins Publishers Ltd. [UK]:

Power of Three © 1976 Diana Wynne Jones
Howl's Moving Castle © 1986 Diana Wynne Jones
The Dark Lord of Derkholm © 1998 Diana Wynne Jones
Charmed Life © 1977 Diana Wynne Jones
The Lives of Christopher Chant © 1988 Diana Wynne Jones
Witch Week © 1982 Diana Wynne Jones
Fire and Hemlock © 1985 Diana Wynne Jones
Conrad's Fate © 2005 Diana Wynne Jones
Hexwood © 1993 Diana Wynne Jones
The Game © 2008 Diana Wynne Jones

Quotations from the following works are used by permission of Harper-Collins Publishers [US]:

Power of Three text copyright © 1976 by Diana Wynne Jones
Howl's Moving Castle text copyright © 1985 by Diana Wynne Jones
The Dark Lord of Derkholm text copyright ©1998 by Diana Wynne Jones
Charmed Life text copyright © 1977 by Diana Wynne Jones
The Lives of Christopher Chant text copyright © by Diana Wynne Jones
Witch Week text copyright © by Diana Wynne Jones
Conrad's Fate text copyright © 2005 by Diana Wynne Jones
The Crown of Dalemark text copyright © 1995 by Diana Wynne Jones
Cart and Cwidder text copyright © 1995 by Diana Wynne Jones
Hexwood text copyright © 1993 by Diana Wynne Jones
The Spellcoats text copyright © 1995 by Diana Wynne Jones

I am also grateful to the Laura Cecil Agency, agents for the Diana Wynne Jones Estate, for permission to use:

Extract from *The Power of Three* © The Estate of Diana Wynne Jones, 1976 (HarperCollins)

Permission granted by the Estate of Diana Wynne Jones

Extract from *Fire and Hemlock* © The Estate of Diana Wynne Jones, 1985

Permission granted by the Estate of Diana Wynne Jones

Extract from *The Crown of Dalemark* © The Estate of Diana Wynne Jones, 1985

Permission granted by the Estate of Diana Wynne Jones

Extract from *The Crown of Dalemark* © The Estate of Diana Wynne Jones, 1993

Permission granted by the Estate of Diana Wynne Jones

Extract from *Cart and Cwidder* © The Estate of Diana Wynne Jones, 1975

Permission granted by the Estate of Diana Wynne Jones

Extract from *The Spellcoats* © The Estate of Diana Wynne Jones, 1979

Permission granted by the Estate of Diana Wynne Jones

Extract from *Hexwood* © The Estate of Diana Wynne Jones, 1993 (HarperCollins)

Permission granted by the Estate of Diana Wynne Jones

Extract from *The Game* © The Estate of Diana Wynne Jones, 2007

Permission granted by the Estate of Diana Wynne Jones

Extract from *The Tough Guide to Fantasyland* © The Estate of Diana Wynne Jones, 1996

Permission granted by the Estate of Diana Wynne Jones

Introduction

Children's fiction has been both criticised and celebrated for over a century now for its role in shaping children's lives, although the actual effects of this shaping are still little known. Early seen as a way to provide models for child behaviour, as in the moral stories of the Victorian Julia Horatia Ewing, children's fiction developed in many directions. Charles Kingsley's *The Water Babies* (1863) also seemed to have a moral impulse: it addresses itself to a child reader and instructs that reader—who is clearly identifiable in both class and gender terms—in a proper understanding of the society he is to grow up to govern. However, Kingsley's novel predicates that understanding on an attempted fusion of Christianity with mid-nineteenth-century scientific theories of evolution. It thus presents its protagonist allegorically, using fantasy, as medieval Christians did, to represent the journey of the soul as he understood it. Although Kingsley's goals were practical, fantasy offered him a way to instruct his reader that realism could not offer. George MacDonald's *The Princess and the Goblin* (1872), like his fairy stories, similarly deployed what we would now call fantasy, in this case as a vehicle rather for mystical than for theological or practical moral messages.

Lewis Carroll's extraordinary Alice stories (1865, 1872) extend fantasy to the apparent randomness of a real dream rather than, as in MacDonald's novels for adults, framing a fantastic narrative as a medieval dream vision. Carroll's stories nevertheless reflect on the real problems of a real Victorian child of the educated classes, negotiating the peculiarities of etiquette and the English language as well as the sometimes contradictory expectations of a child to be at once a "big girl" and a child who should be seen and not heard. The idea of presenting a child with a child's view of the world— or at least an adult's idea of that view—can be seen in E. Nesbit's early realist novels *The Story of the Treasure Seekers* (1899) and *The Would-begoods* (1901); Nesbit's later and more celebrated fantasy stories carry such real children into fantastic situations in ways that make the fantasy plausible. Moral and social messages—notably relating to the social inequities of Edwardian England—emerge as it were interstitially in a novel like *The Story of the Amulet* (1906), in which the reader's engagement with the children's adventures and their quest to restore the Amulet is primary. In

Nesbit's fiction, as in Carroll's, engagement of the child reader seems more powerful than any instructional purpose, and fantasy becomes the path to that engagement.

Social rather than religious concerns can be seen to provide the moral energy behind much children's fiction in recent decades. Children's fiction has been seen, especially in the US, as a way in which adults can redress imbalances in society through engagement of child readers with their concerns. Stories about the disabled, about members of ethnic minorities, and most visibly about girls as heroes push against the social and literary conventions that have ignored or denigrated members of these groups. Other fictions depict the horrors of war or of the Holocaust to assist children's understanding of and reflection on—and rejection of—the activities that have produced social and individual suffering. This powerful awareness of concerns in the real social world is reflected in the mode of writing: for much of the past few decades, realism, rather than fantasy, has been seen as the appropriate mode for social and moral engagement. Nevertheless, fantasy fiction has continued to gain both critical acclaim and, through library purchases and teacher recommendations as well as publishing, a considerable readership. Many of the most celebrated UK children's novelists of the past few decades—Alan Garner, Susan Cooper, Diana Wynne Jones, Philip Pullman, J.K. Rowling, Neil Gaiman, Terry Pratchett—have written fantasy, and its prominence in popular culture in the English-speaking world has increased considerably, perhaps reflecting a recognition that the problems of the "real world" extend to its representation as well.

Yet adults continue to worry over what children read, especially if they read fantasy, because fantasy is seen as fuelling another form of escapism, more subtle and more complex in its effect than simply the act of being absorbed in fiction. This version of escapism involves the reader mistaking what is said in the book: believing that it is true. To fall into this trap need not involve accepting the story as literal truth, although that is a possibility. Rather, the reader may be misled by the pattern of the story, especially by reading stories with similar patterns, into believing that certain solutions to problems are inevitable. Fantasy involving magic is a typical target here, as its critics expect that readers will believe in the magical solution of problems. Colin Manlove has pointed out, however, that one element largely missing specifically from English children's fantasy is "the idea of magic as a gift with which to increase one's wealth or status" (*From Alice* 197)—an idea typically associated with fantasy as escapism. The wider problem of narrative patterning is not unique to fantasy, but the nature of the pattern, and its generally "happy" conclusion, is perhaps of particular concern within this genre. Readers who accept this pattern may fail to take possible actions in their own lives because they think that their lives will be shaped by the automatic movement of the world-narrative. The orphan boy must turn out to be a lost prince; the neglected child will be celebrated as a hero or heroine. Good will triumph over evil, and virtue will be rewarded. Such assumptions simplify the complexities of our human experience; more significantly, they encourage passivity, as the reader waits for rescue—and possibly for a more dramatic life—rather than engaging with whatever difficulties are posed by their actual situation.

It is not my purpose in this book either simply to attack the view that fantasy is escapist or to demonstrate how other forms of writing, including apparently realist fiction, can generate patterns that may influence reader expectations of literature or of life. Such a demonstration was arguably a major project of Modernism—Virginia Woolf's *Jacob's Room* (1922), for example, can be seen as an anti-realist novel in these terms. The significance of fantasy, including children's fantasy, in commenting on the world around it, meanwhile, has been discussed by various scholars. Ann Swinfen's 1984 book *In Defence of Fantasy: A Study of the Genre in English and American Literature Since 1945*, for instance, demonstrates the concerns of a number of fantasy novels—all in fact fantasies for children or young adults, although Swinfen does not highlight this—and shows how works in the various classes of fantasy she identifies comment on particular issues. Manlove's 2003 study *From Alice to Harry Potter: Children's Fantasy in England* has examined the ways in which English children's fantasy over the previous century and a half shared certain preoccupations from phase to phase and observed how those preoccupations reflect developments in its contemporary society, although this reflection is rarely didactic in impulse.

In this book I examine the work of three prominent English writers of children's fantasy—J.K. Rowling, Diana Wynne Jones, and Terry Pratchett—and demonstrate how these writers deploy fantasy neither as mere escapism nor as a mask for didactic moralising, but instead make manifest the ethical power of fantasy and the imagination itself. Although these three authors appear very different from each other, they share a common interest in the power of story, an interest visible in different ways and at different levels of their writing. As they demonstrate, engagement with fiction can be immensely powerful, as readers of story can not only learn about the world but can imagine new ways in which to grapple with that world, new possibilities: "Change the story, change the world," as Pratchett's Granny Weatherwax puts it (*A Hat* 338). This study investigates the sophisticated use of narrative strategies by Rowling, Jones, and Pratchett not only to engage children in reading, but to educate them into becoming mature readers and indeed individuals. What is most significant here is the marriage in the works of these writers between literary self-consciousness, a self-consciousness that largely distinguishes them from their contemporaries as it emerges through deployment and subversion of formal and thematic elements common in genres of children's fantasy, and a profoundly ethical impulse. Of other writers, Philip Pullman arguably shares this literary self-consciousness, but most of his fiction repeats rather than subverting existing genre models, and—with the obvious exception of the theological and moral drive in *His Dark Materials* (2002), which has been extensively discussed—does not seem impelled by an ethical impulse beyond that already associated with those existing genres. I demonstrate how in quite different ways Rowling, Jones, and Pratchett establish reader expectations by drawing on conventions in existing genres only to subvert those expectations, compelling young readers to evaluate for themselves both the power of story to shape our understanding of the world and the values and qualities needed for ordinary life. In so doing, these writers extend and validate the traditional uses of fantasy writing not only to entertain but to provide opportunities for critique and speculation about alternative possibilities for living.

Rowling's Harry Potter sequence (1997–2007) has been credited on the one hand with "turn[ing] a generation into lifelong readers" (Tyler) and stigmatised on the other for apparently haphazard and uninventive borrowing of elements from earlier fantasy fiction (Pennington), conservative and otherwise problematic politics (Mendlesohn, "Crowning"), and poor writing (Bloom), as well as for its notorious and allegedly unchristian praise of witches—the negative views mostly emerging well before the completion of the sequence in 2007. The somewhat hyperbolic claims for the unique attractiveness of the sequence to readers might suggest that the sequence is in some way *sui generis*; in fact, little scholarly work has yet appeared comparing Rowling's fiction with that of her contemporaries. A notable exception is Sarah Fiona Winters's essay "Good and Evil in the Works of Diana Wynne Jones and J.K. Rowling," which appeared in 2002 and therefore focuses on the early novels. However, several critics, including Winters, have identified Harry Potter's debts to the school story tradition, and it has been compared to the work of earlier writers, such as Enid Blyton, in attempts to analyse its power to engage.

Scholars writing during and after publication of the last novels in the sequence have taken a range of approaches, examining such matters as gender roles, philosophical attitudes, symbolism, adaptation to film, and the depiction of heroism, to look no further. In addition to numerous essay collections, there are several full-length studies, notably Sunan Gupta's *Re-Reading Harry Potter*, which examines the theoretical approaches of various earlier scholars and highlights the flaws and contradictions in these approaches as tested against the sequence, as well as offering his own text-to-world and world-to-text commentary on it. At the other end of the spectrum, Manlove's *The Order of Harry Potter: Literary Skill in the Hogwarts Epic* focuses closely on Rowling's writing and demonstrates not only the echoes within the sequence of a wide variety of literary predecessors, but also both the thematic concerns specific to each of the seven books of the sequence and the narrative methods that reflect those concerns. Manlove's treatment of the sequence demonstrates its deep coherence and in so doing argues powerfully for its literary significance, a matter somewhat taken for granted by many of the scholars who have focused on various elements of its operation.

Harry Potter and the Philosopher's Stone (1997; published in the US as *Harry Potter and the Sorcerer's Stone*) was J.K. Rowling's first published novel; in addition to the sequence itself, she has published several short works that are essentially appendices to it—*Fantastic Beasts and Where to Find Them* (2001) and *Quidditch Through the Ages* (2001), both purporting to be books consulted by Harry in the course of the early novels, and *The Tales of Beedle the Bard* (2008), a collection of fairy tales referred to and quoted from in the final novel of the sequence, the publication of which it closely followed. We shall see later in this chapter the significance of Rowling's treatment of the fairy tale in *Harry Potter and the Deathly Hallows* (2007). Since the sequence concluded Rowling has written three novels for adults, *The Casual Vacancy* (2012) and, as Robert Galbraith, *The Cuckoo's Calling* (2013) and *The Silkworm* (2014), the former largely grim realism, the latter two versions of the "gumshoe" detective narratives of an earlier era that manifest her awareness of literary genre as well as her willingness to manipulate genre conventions. All these novels display ethical concerns. In this study, however, I shall focus on the Harry Potter sequence as Rowling's master-work for child readers and shall explore how Rowling evokes the narrative energies of certain genres and concepts to ethical ends.

Unlike Rowling, whose first novel appeared in 1997, Jones and Pratchett are writers of long standing. Jones's first novel appeared in 1970, and she wrote no fewer than thirty-six fantasy novels originally or subsequently marketed to children, besides gaining attention among fantasy scholars for her satire on formula quest fantasy, *The Tough Guide to Fantasyland* (1996), before her death in 2011. Several of her novels have gained literary awards, notably *Charmed Life* (1977), winner of the 1978 Guardian Children's Fiction Prize; *The Crown of Dalemark* (1993) and *The Dark Lord of Derkholm* (1998), both winners of the Mythopoeic Award for Children's and Young Adult Fantasy; and *Howl's Moving Castle* (1986), which was awarded the 2006 Phoenix Award by the Children's Literature Association. Many of her early novels have been republished by HarperCollins in the past decade. Although her writing has not received the extensive academic attention devoted to Rowling's, its importance has been recognised in two collections of essays—*Diana Wynne Jones: An Exciting and Exacting Wisdom*, edited by Teya Rosenberg, Martha P. Hixon, Sharon M. Scapple, and Donna K. White (2002), which included Winters's essay, and an issue of the *Journal of the Fantastic in the Arts* (21.2, 2010)—and in Farah Mendlesohn's noteworthy study *Diana Wynne Jones: Children's Literature and the Fantastic Tradition* (2005), in which Mendlesohn examines Jones's fiction as deploying and subverting the conventions of various subgenres of fantasy that Mendlesohn herself was later to outline in her *Rhetorics of Fantasy* (2008). Charles Butler also included Jones as one of the objects of study in his *Four British Fantasists: Place and Culture in the Children's Fantasies of Penelope Lively, Alan Garner, Diana Wynne Jones, and Susan Cooper* (2006), a valuable study of the concerns of four closely contemporary fantasy novelists. Scholars agree on the challenges Jones's novels pose to readers—not only to child readers—and on the consequent importance of her writing as intellectually and morally educative.

Although Jones has published some novels that fall into groups, notably the Chrestomanci or Related Worlds novels (1977–2006), the Dalemark quartet (1975–1993), and the "moving castle" novels (1986–2008), these are not "series" novels in the narrow sense. The Dalemark quartet is drawn together as a sequence only in the final novel, *The Crown of Dalemark* (1993), written well over a decade after the other three, and the Chrestomanci novels, while sharing a universe, are held together only by the presence of Chrestomanci himself, who is rarely a central character and who appears at various stages of his life. Only the last Chrestomanci novel, *The Pinhoe Egg* (2006), and an intervening short story, "Stealer of Souls" (2000), can be described as direct sequels in the usual sense—following the subsequent experiences of central characters—to the first published Chrestomanci novel, *Charmed Life*, written nearly thirty years before *The Pinhoe Egg*. Sophie, Howl, and Calcifer, central characters in *Howl's Moving Castle* (1986), also appear in *Castle in the Air* (1990) and *House of Many Ways* (2008), but are not central characters, let alone focal as Sophie was in *Howl's Moving Castle*. *The Merlin Conspiracy* (2003) is set in the same universe as *Deep Secret* (1997), a set of parallel worlds between which individual magic users can move, like the Chrestomanci universe, but monitored in this case not by a single guardian enchanter but by a group of Magids operating under the direction of an Upper Room, only some members of which are human. But whereas *Deep Secret* is largely set on Earth and is very much concerned with the activities of a Magid, *The Merlin Conspiracy*, though featuring an Earthly narrator who also appeared in *Deep Secret*, is set almost entirely on other worlds, and merely alludes to the existence of Magids. Mendlesohn has discussed the complicated time-scheme of *The Merlin Conspiracy*, analysing it in terms of Series A and Series B timelines (*Diana* 61–68); this operation subverts what would otherwise be in Mendlesohn's own terms a portal-quest fantasy, as in this case the Earthly narrator, Nick, discovers that he himself has caused many of the problems to which in typical portal-quest fantasy his arrival would provide a solution. Rupert Venables, the Magid who is one narrator of *Deep Secret*—a novel comparatively uncomplicated in its time-scheme—also discovers that his well-meant actions have precipitated some of the apparently unrelated violence on Earth and on other worlds; as often in Jones's fiction, it is the underlying thematic concern that unifies Jones's related novels rather than any obvious connection in the plot. The variability of Jones's apparently related novels reflects the complexity of her literary approach.

Terry Pratchett has been writing comic fantasy for several decades, beginning with *The Carpet People* (1971). He gained popularity in Britain and elsewhere through his continuing Discworld series of novels, which have been marketed simply as fantasy. These novels, beginning with the thin and somewhat clumsy *The Colour of Magic* (1983), gradually moved away from simple satire of fantasy tropes to develop a coherent, complex, and rich vision of a flat planet "right on the edge of reality" (Pratchett, *Witches* 8) in which each novel presents a complete and engaging story in a generally comic style while at the same time commenting, sometimes seriously, on literary and/or social concerns from Western culture.[1] At one point it was claimed that one in ten books currently being sold in England was by Pratchett; whether or not this is true, there is little doubt that he is a very successful novelist. He was diagnosed with a form of Alzheimer's in 2007, but has continued to write and publish since then, and several of his Discworld novels have been filmed for television and a number of others adapted for radio in the past few years.

In addition to the Discworld novels themselves, Pratchett has written several novels in a simpler voice that seem directed at children, notably the Nome Trilogy, or Bromeliad (1989–90), a wainscot fantasy that I discuss in Chapter 3, and the Johnny Maxwell novels (1992–96). The latter are set in our own world, but in each case that world takes a peculiar turn, rendering them fantastic. All three Johnny Maxwell novels offer insight into concerns in contemporary Britain, ranging from wry comments on how divorce is seen to affect children—and how it actually does—and the prizewinning but shoddy architecture of government housing projects to a more focused consideration of, respectively, how television represents real violence, how contemporary society treats its own past, and how small decisions can have far-reaching consequences. All three novels expand these local concerns to engage with broader metaphysical and ethical concepts. Pratchett's more recent children's novel *Nation* (2008) has a somewhat fantastic frame, being apparently set on an alternative version of Earth; it also engages closely with issues such as racism, colonialism, and, even more prominently, belief in God (or gods).

Although the Discworld novels generally can and have been read by younger readers, in the past decade Pratchett has published books set in the Discworld marketed specifically to child readers. The first of these, *The Amazing Maurice and His Educated Rodents* (2001), won the Carnegie Medal; he has since written a sequence of novels featuring Tiffany Aching, a child from the downlands of the Disc who wants to be a witch. Both *The Amazing Maurice*, which I discuss below, and the Tiffany Aching sequence highlight the power of story in interesting ways; I discuss the Tiffany Aching sequence in Chapters 1 and 4.

Somewhat surprisingly, there has been comparatively little scholarly publishing on Pratchett's writing. The most notable work so far is *Terry Pratchett: Guilty of Literature*, a somewhat uneven essay collection edited by Andrew M. Butler, Edward James, and Farah Mendlesohn. Several articles considering Pratchett's witches have, however, appeared in the last few years, and *Discworld in the Disciplines: Critical Approaches to the Terry Pratchett Works*, edited by Anne Hiebert Alton and William C. Spruiell, is being published in 2014. Of the three novelists I am discussing, Terry

Pratchett most visibly concerns himself with the power of story; Nickianne Moody has pointed out the extent to which narrative causality structures the Death sequence of Discworld novels. Indeed, several of Pratchett's plots explicitly revolve around the nature of story—most obviously the Discworld novel *Witches Abroad* (1991)—and his characters frequently contemplate its operation.

THE POWER OF STORY IN PRATCHETT'S *THE AMAZING MAURICE AND HIS EDUCATED RODENTS*

Pratchett's first Discworld novel marketed to children, *The Amazing Maurice and His Educated Rodents*, makes very clear his engagement with the problem of fiction. On the one hand, stories generate dreams, even ideals, through which people can imagine and construct a better future; on the other, taken too literally, they can produce false expectations, with dangerous results when readers trust to the happy ending of fairy tales to bypass the power of actual evil. The story of *The Amazing Maurice* holds both ideas in tension. It offers a beguiling story, or set of stories—the story of two children outsmarting a gang of thieves, aided by a cat and some rats; the story of a homeless boy and a homeless family, who happen to be rats, finding places to live—but at the same time it critiques the conventions of story and asks pertinent questions about how we not only think about but think with and through stories to shape our lives.

The novel's premise seems to answer one of Pratchett's characteristically faux-naïf questions: if you pay someone to remove rats, isn't it in his interest to make sure there are always rats to take away? Thus we are introduced to a young traveller whose bags contain a clan of intelligent rats—or, as they prefer to be known, educated rodents (Pratchett, *The Amazing* 87)—whose role is to provide the impression of a rat plague that the young man, known for the first part of the novel simply as "the kid" (12), can then triumphantly remove from each town by playing his pipe. The absurd rightness of this scenario is heightened when the reader realises that the brains of this operation is a cat, the amazing Maurice, who magically gained intelligence at the same time as the rats, but whose cat instincts for making the most of a situation remain well to the fore.

As is characteristic in Pratchett's work, the ideas presented and indeed the structure of the opening pages of the novel are highly significant to his project. In this case, the novel's opening highlights the extent to which *The Amazing Maurice* is "a story about stories" (10). First, we are presented with an epigraph drawn apparently from a children's book called *Mr Bunnsy Has an Adventure*.[2] Second, the opening lines echo Browning's famous poem, "The Pied Piper of Hamelin": "Rats! They chased the dogs and bit the cats, they—" (Pratchett, *The Amazing* 9). The reader is immediately, and doubly, projected into story, whether the imitation Beatrix Potter of the epigraph—the fictional source text of which turns out to be significant to the plot—or the quotation from Browning. However, the narrator interrupts his own sentence, commenting "But there was more to it than that" (9) before quoting, this time, the title character himself—"As the amazing Maurice said, it was just a story about people and rats" (9)—and observing, significantly, that "the difficult part was deciding who the people were, and who were the rats" (10). The final one-sentence paragraph before we are introduced to the central characters underlines the metafictional aspect of what we are reading: "But Malicia Grim said it was a story about stories" (10).

This layering and contrasting invites readers to keep in mind several ideas in reading the novel: that we are reading a story that may be interpreted in different ways; that the story may provide a comment on story itself, as underlined by the epigraph and quotation as well as Malicia Grim's assertion; and, importantly too, that it may involve a confusion between good and evil, distinguishing the "people" from the "rats." This Orwellian difficulty is explored in the later stages of the novel, but it is intriguingly literalised in the opening pages. The reader discovers that some of the "squeaky voices" heard by the coachman belong not to humans but to rats—but rats who are definitely "people" (10). The novel at one level imitates the many children's stories featuring animal characters, but this is not simply naturalised; through Pratchett's initial use of the coachman as focaliser, the reader is left guessing the identity of the "voices." Pratchett thus introduces us to the world of the novel, in which animals are not expected to have voices—but may turn out to—and in which not only the characters but the narrator may conceal information from the reader.

This element suggests an ethical dimension to the novel that is further established in the immediately following action. The "fair-haired young man" (10) who is the only person the briefly focalising coachman can see, asks, "Maurice? [. . .] You don't think what we're doing is, you know . . . *dishonest*, do you?" (11),[3] and is fobbed off with the unseen Maurice's glib arguments. The young man's awareness that "some of those towns looked pretty poor" (12) generates an argument about the nature of the group's activities that is ironically punctuated by a more explicit theft than the scam the characters are clearly running, as the coach is held up by a highwayman. Only when the highwayman is in turn attacked by beings that "ran up your trouser legs [. . .] Typical rat trick" (16) does he, and the reader, realise that the hidden Maurice is a cat—and that the other speakers, apart from the young man, are rats. We, like the now vanished coachman, and the highwayman who enquired whether his intended targets were wizards, witches, vampires, or werewolves but did not think of intelligent rats or cats, have been deceived, and our awareness of this deception is focused by the continuing discussion. Clearly we are reading not only a story about stories, but a story that will constantly engage with questions of right and wrong—and with judgements less between good and evil than between the greater and the lesser evil. After all, no one expects the heroes of a story to be rats.

The Amazing Maurice highlights two approaches to fiction. In the first, an individual may lose sight of the world—and his or her place in it—through belief in the literal truth or the universal applicability of a story. The rats, who have taught themselves to read after suddenly becoming intelligent, believe in the reality depicted in *Mr Bunnsy Has an Adventure*. Malicia Grim, meanwhile, has immersed herself in stories; she is fully aware that the stories she reads are fiction, but her admiration for story results in her endeavouring to turn everything she encounters into the shape of a story. People turn around to watch her being inconspicuous (112). As a result, although Malicia sees a lot more than do the townsfolk around her, she misses seeing some obvious facts because she is convinced that she knows how the story ought to go. Importantly, the human beings she meets do not behave as she expects they will, as when the villainous rat-catchers beat up her and Keith, the kid—who does not bounce back displaying superhuman powers—and shut them in a prison that lacks an obvious escape route. The rats, on the other hand, have been using *Mr Bunnsy* as their guidebook: they believe there must already be a place where people and rats relate to each other as described in *Mr Bunnsy*.

Both views misinterpret the ways in which stories can tell the truth. Stories do not provide the literal truth about events. What good stories do, as the rat Darktan eventually recognises, is to provide "a map of . . . where we are and where we're going" (Pratchett, *The Amazing* 227). *Mr Bunnsy* does not describe the world as it really is; it is, as Malicia points out, a rather silly story that ignores not only social realities, such as the enmity of humans and rats, but physical possibilities, as it depicts a snake wearing a collar. But just as Darktan could use the idea of a rat in a jacket, depicted in *Mr Bunnsy*, to invent something that is not a jacket but is a version of a jacket that might be useful to a rat—a harness of straps and pockets—so he and the other rats can use the idea of a place where animals and humans can live with and help each other to start to make that happen. In the novel's denouement, the intelligent rats negotiate a way in which they can cohabit with the humans to the benefit of both. Malicia, too, turns out to have learned at least some useful things from stories—she is able to manipulate hairpins to open locks because she has practised this storybook skill, and her decision to provide the villainous rat-catchers with the same emetic as fake antidote that they have been given as fake poison is, as she observes, "narratively satisfying" (214). And Keith, the "stupid-looking kid" (31) who initially claims that he just wants to be allowed to play music, but by the end has not only helped to track down the villains but also been clever enough to defeat and then do a deal with a real rat piper, is last seen speculating about how long it might take to become mayor. Keith, who expressed scepticism about story in his discussions with Malicia, has also learned from story by the end of the novel, in this case about the possible future of a boy who arrives in a town with a clever cat. The rats and Keith, as well as the humans of the town, have used story to imagine and to begin to construct new ways to live their lives.

The Amazing Maurice, like a number of Pratchett's novels, highlights both the inevitable falsity of stories and their power. At the end of the novel Malicia's father, the town's mayor, remarks, "Stories are just stories. Life is complicated enough as it is. You have to plan for the real world. There's no room for the fantastic"; the response " 'Exactly,' said the rat" (313) underscores the extent to which this practical conclusion is emerging within a fantastic scenario. Stories in this novel turn out to be more than "just stories," and planning for the real world entails an idea strikingly akin to Sir Philip Sidney's suggestion that "her [Nature's] world is brazen, the poets only deliver a golden" (216). The "golden world" only available through art becomes an exemplar for real life to follow. Pratchett's story simultaneously warns against a simplistic investment in the literal truth of story and provides what might seem a wonderfully escapist fantasy that in fact educates its readers in how to learn from what they read.

BOOKS AND CLEVERNESS IN ROWLING'S HARRY POTTER SEQUENCE

The first six novels of the Harry Potter sequence refer to many books, but what all of those books have in common is that they are, or purport to be, factual. It is striking that Rowling, author of an enormously successful series of fantasy novels, nowhere depicts Harry or any of his classmates—even the book-loving Hermione—reading fiction; there is just one passing reference to a pile of adventure comics in Ron's bedroom, in *Harry Potter and the Chamber of Secrets* (1998). Yet a fairy tale, a fantastic narrative, lies at the heart of *Deathly Hallows*, the culmination of the fantasy sequence. Consideration of the operation of that fairy tale is vital to understanding the functionality of fiction as Rowling sees it.

Whereas Pratchett's literary reflexivity is explicit and well known, discussions of Rowling's work generally do not recognise the self-consciousness of her engagement with story. Paradoxically, this oversight is particularly evident in scholarly discussion of the relationship of Harry's experience to fairy tale. M. Katherine Grimes carefully maps characters in *Philosopher's Stone* against their counterparts in traditional European fairy stories, but her argument focuses rather on the ways in which this recapitulation of traditional roles appeals psychologically to child consumers of narrative than on what this repetition suggests about Rowling's manipulation of tradition itself. Maria Nikolajeva's 2003 observation that the novels do little to depict Harry's development or interiority, resulting in a fairy-tale-like simplicity of reading experience ("*Harry*" 134), has recently been countered by Anne Klaus, who provides an example of interior dialogue (26)—significantly, drawn from the penultimate novel in the sequence, published later than Nikolajeva's essay.[4] However, despite Klaus's acknowledgement at the end of her essay that "Rowling even consciously plays with the reader's 'fairy tale' expectations" (32) she does not speculate on the implications of Rowling's decision to play with fairy tale in the first place. In Chapter 1 we shall see the implications of Rowling's deployment of the "Cinderella" plot in the first few chapters of *Philosopher's Stone* for her representation of Harry's agency, but I wish here to contend that the literariness of Rowling's activity is an important element in her writing.

Rowling's embedding of literary material from prior sources in her work has, of course, not gone entirely unnoticed. Manlove's *The Order of Harry Potter* includes not only comparative study of the sequence in relation to other works such as Enid Blyton's, but also examination of, for example, a passage in *Deathly Hallows* that seems closely similar in situation and idea to one in Charles Williams's *The Place of the Lion* (1931). The emphasis in Manlove's study of the thematic coherence of the sequence and the ways in which each novel contributes a separate idea to it points to its manifestation of intelligent construction and literary awareness. Like Manlove, Veronica L. Schanoes perceives the powerfully educative element in Rowling's writing, in an early, and masterly, acknowledgement of the significance of Rowling's engagement with books as a concept. Schanoes argues persuasively for the complexity of Rowling's written narrative as repeatedly educating the reader in the avoidance of stereotype through its construction of good and evil.

What interests me here is the extent to which Rowling not only draws on earlier forms of story such as the fairy tale and the school story, but uses those forms to engage the child reader in particular ideas of agency. The sequence emphasises the extent to which literature, and art more generally, can be functional within heroic action and even within daily life; it is neither mere decoration nor distraction. This functionality is visible from Harry's first arrival at Hogwarts, when he discovers not only that the people in paintings on the wall are moving, speaking, and looking at him, but that they form part of the structure of the school as an institution. Thus the painting of the Fat Lady admits students to Gryffindor Tower, swinging open when they give the correct password; later, in *Harry Potter and the Prisoner of Azkaban* (1999), Harry can descend into a passage from Hogwarts to Hogsmeade by tapping the statue of a witch, and in *Harry Potter and the Goblet of Fire* (2000) he learns how to tickle a painted pear in order to gain access to the Hogwarts kitchens. Finally, in *Deathly Hallows* a portrait in a pub in Hogsmeade opens a tunnel through which Harry can enter the school itself undetected. In each of these instances, an artwork turns out to enable access, legitimately or otherwise, to something otherwise unavailable, metaphorically suggesting the value of art within human action.

The importance of the specifically literary in Rowling can be gauged in part by her treatment of books within the narrative. Critics have observed that Hermione Granger's deep respect for books is undercut by the somewhat contemptuous attitude of Harry, the focal character, to her enthusiasm;[5] nevertheless, books and reading play an important part in nearly every novel. Harry is depicted as absorbed in his school textbooks following his trip to Diagon Alley, and although the secret of the Philosopher's Stone is found not in the library but on a Chocolate Frog card, Hermione's prompt production of an account of the Stone and its maker, Nicolas Flamel, validates her belief in the library as a resource not just for classroom success but for adventure. In *Chamber of Secrets* Harry is again able to draw on her effective deployment of this resource when he finds her notes in her Petrified hand. In both novels what is demonstrated is the importance not just of reading but of comprehension: the books are to be treated not as static compendia but as resources that may contribute to successful deduction and detection. The teachers are pleased and the other children awed by Hermione's parrot-like repetition of her reading, but it is her ability to make sense of what she reads—in turn informing Harry's own powers of deduction, as in her note about the Basilisk—that makes her an important companion in Harry's quest. While Harry remains the focal figure and potential model for agency, Hermione becomes a model for the reader in the role of reader.

Counterparts to the library books in *Chamber of Secrets* are Professor Lockhart's textbooks about himself, which turn out to be based on lies; readers are reminded not to trust absolutely in the literal truth of what they read.[6] It is noteworthy that Hermione surrenders her enthusiasm for the conceited and ineffectual Lockhart only belatedly, as to the physical charm that acts on her as a heterosexual female—and not on the boys as heterosexual males—is added admiration for his productivity as an author as well as a hero. In the same novel, however, both Ginny Weasley and Harry himself are also beguiled by a book, Tom Riddle's diary, and in Ginny's case especially it is clear that the attraction is the amelioration of her loneliness, "*It's like having a friend I can carry round in my pocket*" (Rowling, *Chamber* 333). Harry believes he can learn otherwise undiscoverable facts from Riddle's memories; in this case the problem is more subtle than the simple lies of Lockhart's books, as Riddle's perspective on events is carefully edited to show Harry only what Riddle wants him to see. As Schanoes has observed, "Rowling complicates her reader's trust in her narrative project" (143). The episode of the diary reminds readers that novels too are written from the perspective of a single person, and indeed that they may be focalised through a deceptive or merely fallible perceiver—in the case of this novel, Harry himself.

It is significant that in both the last two novels of the sequence Harry again invests his energies in belief in books. In *Harry Potter and the Half-Blood Prince* (2005) he becomes fascinated by his idea of the clever writer of the annotations to his Potions textbook. Due to the helpfulness of the notes, Harry imagines the writer not only as a clever but as a generous boy, overlooking the fact that the Half-Blood Prince's annotations appear only in his own copy and do not seem to have been shared with, for example, his Potions teachers, who might have revised their instruction. In this case the warning is against misreading, in particular the misreading that imagines the writer as concerned with Harry, the accidental discoverer of the private notes. But Rowling's meditation on the importance of books and their relationship to living emerges most clearly in *Deathly Hallows*. Although Harry has left school and is travelling around the countryside, he is preoccupied almost throughout first with a book, Rita Skeeter's biography of Albus Dumbledore, and second with a story, "The Tale of the Three Brothers."

The biography of Dumbledore is important to *Deathly Hallows* on three levels. First, it is important to the plot: it provides Harry with information not only about Dumbledore's childhood in Godric's Hollow and connection to Bathilda Bagshot, which gives Harry a reason to visit the village, but also with an image of Grindelwald he can connect to Gregorovich's memory of the theft of the Elder Wand and with information about Ariana and especially Aberforth Dumbledore that turns out to be useful when Harry returns to Hogsmead. Second, it is important to Harry emotionally, as an irritant and a magnet, because it purports to provide access to Dumbledore's private life. The fact that Dumbledore is dead is crucial here: Harry resents being deprived of Dumbledore's personal presence and compelled to resort to Rita Skeeter's collection of material. Third, it contributes to the novel's moral message by replacing Harry's, and the reader's, image of Dumbledore as the stereotypically benevolent as well as omniscient mentor figure with a portrait of human complexity. Harry's eventual recognition that Dumbledore's misplaced idealism in his youth does not vitiate his subsequent actions and advice to Harry, and that goodness is a process rather than a fixed and absolute state, is crucial to the novel's lesson to the reader as well as to Harry.

Early in *Deathly Hallows* Hermione is surprised to receive, as a legacy from Dumbledore, an old copy of *The Tales of Beedle the Bard*. Dumbledore's will expresses the hope that she "will find it entertaining and instructive" (Rowling, *Deathly* 106), in a noteworthy echo of Sidney's suggestion that literature should teach and delight (Sidney 217). However, despite Hermione's contempt for Rufus Scrimgeour's attitude to Harry's Snitch-shaped birthday cake—"Oh, it can't be a reference to the fact that Harry's a great Seeker, that's way too obvious [. . .] There must be a message from Dumbledore hidden in the icing!" (Rowling, *Deathly* 108)—she nevertheless takes the same approach to the fairy tales herself, seeking to decode them, via her study of runes, rather than to read them for content. This is another form of misreading against which Rowling warns her readers.

As with the biography of Dumbledore, *The Tales of Beedle the Bard* operates within the novel on several levels. The tales are, after all, fairy tales; Harry's scepticism at the content of the key fairy tale—"Sorry, [. . .] but *Death* spoke to them?" (Rowling, *Deathly* 330)—reflects his expectation that books will contain literal truth. When Xenophilius Lovegood expounds his belief that the three objects in "The Tale of the Three Brothers" really exist, he offers a different view of truth: "That is a children's tale, told to amuse rather than instruct. Those of us who understand these matters, however, recognise that the ancient story refers to three objects, or Hallows, which, if united, will make the possessor master of Death" (313). Rather like Hermione's initial response to the gift of the book, Xenophilius's view is hermetic: the story contains truth, but a veiled one, accessible only to those already informed. Hermione even rejects this version of truth in the tale, arguing that "it's just a morality tale" (336), thereby providing for the first time in Rowling's sequence an explicit suggestion that fictional writing can contain moral messages. At the same time, however, Rowling acknowledges that different readers find different messages within stories: Hermione's confident assertion that "it's obvious which gift is best, which one you'd choose—" (336) is promptly undermined by the simultaneous choice by Ron, Harry, and herself of different Hallows. Ron, seeking always the obvious path to victory, chooses the Elder Wand that can defeat any opponent; Harry, burdened not only by the longstanding loss of his parents but by more recent losses including that of Dumbledore, chooses the Resurrection Stone that can revive the dead. Only Hermione chooses the Invisibility Cloak, the one object whose choice in the fairy tale is depicted as bringing success. As Rowling indicates, even a simple fable with an obvious moral may be misread by readers with their separate concerns and desires, underlining the importance of reading with a mind open to what the text can offer rather than focused on personal needs.

Rowling's deployment of the fairy tale in *Deathly Hallows* highlights her approach to the power of story. "The Tale of the Three Brothers" is crucial to the plot of the novel because, as Xenophilius argued, it does contain an allegorised version of the facts: the three Hallows do exist. Harry's subsequent obsession with them, however, his belief that "You've got to find out about them for yourself! It's a Quest!" (351), locates his approach to the story as one of wish-fulfilment; as Hermione points out, "this isn't a game, this isn't practice!" (351). Harry is temporarily beguiled by the idea of the magical objects into seeing his adventure in terms of heroic quest; we shall see in Chapter 2 how Rowling elsewhere undermines the conventions of heroic quest fantasy. Like a child who finds in *Philosopher's Stone* the promise that they too may be magically rescued from an unpleasant or simply tedious suburban life, Harry initially takes from the fairy tale the message that there are magical objects that can conquer his apparently insuperable enemy. Only belatedly does he recognise that Hermione is right, first in her identification of the actual object of their journey—destruction of Voldemort's Horcruxes—and second, at the end of the novel, in her identification of the only Hallow worth keeping. Within the action of *Deathly Hallows*, the moral truth contained within "The Tale of the Three Brothers" turns out to be no less important than the literal truth of the Hallows—and the rules of wandlore are more important to the defeat of Voldemort than any magical quality in the Elder Wand.

Fiction, Rowling tells her readers, does refer to and even provide a guide for reality—it can be functional, despite its fantastic appearance—but it is most valuable in its capacity to provide moral instruction in the form of

entertainment. Her reflection on this capacity within *Deathly Hallows* makes manifest her engagement across the Harry Potter sequence with the power of story.

ART, LANGUAGE, AND PLAY IN DIANA WYNNE JONES

While Rowling represents art as functional within the world, Diana Wynne Jones's fiction shows a fascination with its potential to generate that world. Following Deborah Kaplan's analysis of the importance of story-telling in *Witch Week*, Debbie Gascoyne has discussed Jones's preoccupation with the performative power of language. This power extends in *The Spellcoats* (1979) to woven words or signs, as Tanaqui discovers that the evil mages weave statements of their achievements into their coats and that those woven statements are the spells that make their achievements real. Observing that the mages' weaving is loose and crude by comparison with her own fine weaving, Tanaqui concludes that "My weaving is a performing too. [. . .] I know I am a greater weaver than they" (Jones, *The Spellcoats* 185–86)— and since she is weaving her story into the spellcoats, this statement too turns out to be true. Moril's cwidder can make even mountains move, provided he plays it with the right thoughts (*Cart and Cwidder*, 1975). Indeed, even thoughts by themselves can affect reality, as the children in "The Plague of Peacocks" (1984) confidently anticipate that the four-year-old Daniel Emanuel will solve the problem of their annoying neighbours for them—and he does, producing hundreds of peacocks that drive the Platts away when he perceives Mr Platt as a peacock and Mrs Platt as a peahen. In Jones's fiction, the human imagination is more powerful than the world around it, and can be used either directly, as by young Daniel Emanuel, or indirectly, through human creations such as language and art, to change the world.

Jones is also profoundly interested in myth, which represents the ways in which earlier peoples saw their world as shaped. In *Eight Days of Luke* (1975), the protagonist, David, realises that the mysterious boy Luke whom he can summon by striking a match is in fact the Norse god Loki, and that the various people who are seeking Luke are other Norse gods who appear on their own days of the week. *The Game* (2007) features a child who discovers that her whole family are beings from mythology, and goes out joyfully to explore the "mythosphere" where myths mutate along strands (30). The endpapers of *The Game* instruct child readers in the mythological sources for the characters and invite them to solve simple puzzles about these myths. But these novels also demonstrate Jones's profound ethical impulse: David's actions are influenced by loyalty, while Hayley's adventures in the mythosphere enable her not only to locate her own parents, Sisyphus and Merope, but also to find a way to defeat the domineering Uncle Jolyon/Jupiter. In these as in so many other of Jones's fictions—most notably

Black Maria (1991; published in the US as *Aunt Maria*)—the children must learn to develop their own agency in order to escape oppression. David's contest with Mr Wedding (Woden), like Hayley's journeys in the mythosphere, involves development of his own will through conflict with beings that mythologically represent mastery. These children learn both about their own individual desires and about their capacity for action through a literal engagement with the forces of story.

Nikolajeva has noted how Jones's fiction operates metaphorically to destabilise expectations, arguing that this postmodern process in Jones's work depicts adolescent confusion ("Heterotopia" 27). But Jones draws on fantasy to create metaphor in a range of ways; her work is often metafictional, as several scholars have pointed out. I have argued elsewhere (Webb, "False" 229–30) not only that the Chrestomanci novel *Conrad's Fate* (2005) uses the protagonist's training as a servant at the Stallery estate as a correlative for his development of identity, but that Jones's depiction of Stallery as a beautiful mansion surrounded by gardens can be taken as an image of pastoral, a genre that suppresses labour. Both the novel's realist demonstration of the human labour needed to sustain the appearance of Stallery and its fantastic depiction of Stallery's ruined counterparts, which the butler/owner Mr Amos is seeking to avoid by desperately "pulling the possibilities" (Jones, *Conrad's* 18), point to the labour involved not only in writing—Mr Amos's construction of the house—but also in reading. Fiction may tempt readers with the appearance of escape into a story with an inevitable and satisfying ending, but too easy a conclusion will, like the pastoral, belie the realities of human experience.

A work that richly brings together Jones's concerns with the power of language and of story in negotiating the real world is her 1985 novel *Fire and Hemlock*, which Akiko Yamazaki has described as "the most densely intertextual of her works" (108). Charles Butler ("Now Here") and Martha P. Hixon have both observed how this novel works metaphorically, while Mendlesohn points out that "*Fire and Hemlock* is constructed of *mise en abyme*, in which each element of intertextuality [. . .] reflects, reproduces, or comments on aspects of what we might call the primary narrative or story" (*Diana* 159). Jones's own essay "The Heroic Ideal" makes very clear her attention to literary and mythic sources in constructing the novel: not only do two old ballads play an important role in the plot, but Jones incorporates a range of other references from T.S. Eliot's "Four Quartets" to the myth of "Cupid and Psyche."

What is important about this intertextuality is the extent to which for Jones the literary interacts with the mundane, and indeed empowers the heroine, Polly Whittacker, in her engagement with ordinary life, as René Fleischbein has pointed out, enabling her finally to play "the best role, the one she created: herself" (244). Tom Lynn, the novel's other central character and prisoner of the fairy queen referred to in the ballads "Tam Lin" and "Thomas the Rhymer," sends parcels of books to Polly, and instructs her that "only thin, weak thinkers despise fairy stories. Each one has a true, strange fact in it" (Jones, *Fire* 171). This advice is not only directly applicable to his own situation, as Polly belatedly realises, but acts also as a message to the reader: *Fire and Hemlock* itself is a fairy tale, though a highly complex one, and, as Hixon argues, it teaches the importance of the creative imagination. Central to the novel is Tom's and Polly's joint creation of a story that turns out, magically, to interact with their real experiences; Tom insists throughout on the importance of consistency and accuracy in their construction of this world and rejects Polly's attempts to imitate other stories.

That Jones's concern here goes beyond the literary to creativity more generally can be observed through consideration of one of the novel's many buried motifs: play. I have counted at least twenty separate forms of play mentioned or enacted in the text. At various times characters play with toys, play games, play sport, and play musical instruments—or play recordings of music. On at least two occasions Polly acts roles in pre-scripted plays or pantomime. What each of these activities turns out to involve is both the need for serious attention and some degree of risk, whether that be simply the risk of failure, or of boring one's audience, or the more complex risks involved in Tom's and Polly's creation of "hero business" (Jones, *Fire* 78), the extended narrative they develop in which they are respectively the hero Tan Coul and his apprentice Hero. Creativity in *Fire and Hemlock* takes labour, but it does so because it matters. Tom plays the cello professionally, earning a precarious living by it, and "hero business" itself is not just what Polly's mother scornfully calls "One of your make-believes" (73) but a fantasy narrative with its own coherence that turns out to be deeply implicated in Tom's and Polly's actual experience. Their shared construction of the hero narrative helps Polly understand the true nature of Tom's plight, and validates their relationship.

Polly eventually manages to rescue Tom from Laurel, the fairy queen, by complying with the queen's "chilly logic" (Jones, *Fire* 392): Laurel too is playing a game with its own complex but rigid rules. Polly realises that she has to surrender her affection to Tom and leave him, paradoxically, helpless in order for him to win in Laurel's final challenge. *Fire and Hemlock* concludes with a somewhat puzzling "Coda" in which Polly and Tom confront each other following the departure of the queen and her court; Polly remains aware that she "had to go on meaning [her rejection of Tom], or it would all be to do again" (391–92), but nevertheless ends by holding her hands out to Tom and declaring "if it's not true nowhere [that they can be together], it has to be somewhere. We've got her, either way" (393). Critics have speculated on this conversation and its implications for Tom's and Polly's future. I agree with Mendlesohn (*Diana* 164) that what Polly has to keep rejecting is romance, or romanticism—the "Sentimental Drivel" that informs both the early draft of her story (Jones, *Fire* 263) and the story of fatal illness with which Laurel enchants her into giving up her relationship with Tom. The ending of the story is happy, in that Tom survives and he and Polly seem to be working out a way to be together, but their relationship will continue to be complex as relationships are in the real world, not simple as conveyed by the common fairy-tale ending "happily ever after."

Story in *Fire and Hemlock* is enormously powerful, but Jones reminds us that that power can be limiting if it is not properly engaged with. On the one hand, the act of reading stories enables understanding, as when Polly ferrets out the truth of her own hidden memories with the aid of a book and learns from the ballads what steps she must take to save Tom. On the other, it is also potentially limiting, as when the complexity of reality is reduced to simplistic sentimentality. Jones suggests that readers must not rest content with the formulaic pattern of narratives, but be alert to the "true, strange fact[s]" (171) that they convey about the world. In this way story is liberating: it enables readers to read past their assumptions about the world and imagine new possibilities. Above all, it is the creative play of imagination that, for Jones, enables real growth and the development of worthwhile relationships. Reading and understanding Jones's own novels requires intellectual and emotional labour, but the reward of that labour is found both in the pleasure of that understanding and in a fresh view of our own potential as agents in the world.

CHAPTER OUTLINE

The apparently simple surface of Rowling's fiction, especially in the early novels of the Harry Potter sequence, has, as I have said, discouraged critics from recognising the strategic and self-conscious nature of her work. Where Pratchett overtly addresses the idea of story as central to the plot as well as the concerns of his novels, and Jones's fictions deploy a complex and frequently subversive structure that challenges readers, Rowling's writing appears to engage readers comparatively simply and may seem unreflective by contrast with the other two. In Chapter 1 I point out the ways in which Rowling and Pratchett posit different readers in the first novels of the Harry Potter sequence and the Tiffany Aching sequence respectively. Each of these novels provides an important introduction to the concerns of the respective sequence, and their location of readers is therefore crucial to their writing strategies. Both *Philosopher's Stone* and *The Wee Free Men* (2003) deploy fairy-tale plots across part or all of their narratives; the situation of their protagonists in relation to those plots is central to the initial characterisation of those protagonists and therefore to their reception by readers. Harry Potter and Tiffany Aching differ dramatically in their levels of agency and apparent maturity within their communities, with Harry located very forcefully as a child while Tiffany functions at least to some extent as an adult; importantly, Tiffany herself manifests a sophisticated awareness of fairy-tale conventions. I explore the implications of these characterisations for the strategies taken by these two novels in engaging their readers. As we shall see, moreover, Rowling's narrative changes stylistically where Pratchett's does not; the novels present contrasting approaches to the education of the child reader.

Chapter 2 examines the idea of heroic fantasy as practised and critiqued by Rowling and by Jones. We shall see how Rowling's sequence shifts from school story to heroic fantasy, but also how her depiction of Harry within his changing context suggests the inadequacy of the values and practices of the hero in formula heroic fantasy to the difficulties of ordinary life, or even of heroic struggle itself. Jones's critique operates differently: although the novels of the Dalemark quartet seem in some ways to draw on elements of the fantasy tradition, its conclusion *The Crown of Dalemark* at once obtrudes and departs from key practices, while *Hexwood* (1993) jumbles and confuses conventional fantastic elements. Her later novel *The Dark Lord of Derkholm*, meanwhile, appears to parody fantasy tropes, but also engages critically with the assumptions of fantasy and offers a markedly critical perspective on the ethics of the fantasy world as conventionally depicted. Jones's fiction, like Rowling's, highlights the inadequacy of conventional heroic fantasy to lived experience; in *Dark Lord* she goes further, indicting formula fantasy for promoting an exploitative approach to the world.

Chapter 3 continues the examination of how these writers draw on genre conventions by considering the ways in which Pratchett and Jones treat wainscot fantasy. In wainscot fantasy, the everyday world is imagined to be concealing miniature societies, which may consist of animals or small humans. Inevitably, fantasies dealing with wainscot societies other than the animal must take account of the reader's knowledge, or at least assumption, that no such societies have been heard of; various wainscot fantasies posit different explanations for our human ignorance of these societies. A celebrated example of such a fantasy is Mary Norton's Borrowers sequence, which is an important precursor to Pratchett's Nome Trilogy, or Bromeliad, and which directly addresses the fact that humans are ignorant of the borrowers' existence. Pratchett's sequence is superficially very similar to Norton's, but provides a very different explanation for that ignorance. His solution to the problem relates not only to the time of his writing the trilogy—nearly forty years after most of Norton's sequence—but also to the messages he conveys about the limitations imposed by relying on conventional assumptions and the importance of recognising cultural diversity. Jones's early novel *Power of Three* (1976) also develops messages about cultural tolerance and resistance to racism, but in quite different fashion, as she initially conceals the fact that her focal characters are living as a wainscot society on Earth. *Power of Three* operates by initially deceiving its readers; like the Bromeliad, it requires readers to critique their own assumptions. Both Pratchett and Jones therefore deploy the concept of the wainscot society to convey important ethical messages to the reader, although in contrasting ways.

In Chapter 4 we shift focus from genre to content, focusing on the traditional stereotype of the witch or crone. Jones's *Howl's Moving Castle* deploys the figure of the witch/crone to subvert expectations about fairy tales, as Sophie Hatter finds herself liberated from her own constrained ideas of her future by suddenly becoming a crone. Jones's own narrative method endorses the potential of the creative imagination to break down limits. Chapter 4 also concludes my discussion of Pratchett's Tiffany Aching sequence as it represents various facets of the concept of the witch, stereotypically a negative figure, and explores how reconsideration of these elements can generate a powerful version of identity. Each of Pratchett's Tiffany Aching novels considers a different aspect of the problem of stereotype and proposes ways in which that stereotype can be manipulated and challenged. Like Jones, Pratchett also implicitly invites readers to take his own narrative method as a model as he exploits the attraction of magical adventure while critiquing both escapist and simplistic approaches to reading and living.

Agency remains the focus of Chapter 5 as I investigate the ways in which Jones and Rowling engage with tropes of destiny within their fiction. The Harry Potter sequence has been the site for a number of scholarly discussions of philosophical attitudes to determinism. In this chapter we shall see how Rowling engages with ideas of destiny in passages that explicitly discuss the idea, and encourages her reader to move away from a reliance on what is fated to a belief in the centrality of personal decisions and personal responsibility. This ethic is also very visible in Jones's Chrestomanci novels. These novels are set in Related Worlds that posit parallel universes; I discuss the implications of this concept and of Jones's treatment of it. Despite the implication of fixed identities posited through the concept of personal analogues, Jones resists the notion of a controlling fate or destiny. Her characters learn to face the consequences of their actions. Moreover, in *The Lives of Christopher Chant* (1988) Jones even demonstrates how a reading child can use expectations taken from books about how life ought to go to project her own possible future.

Thus each of these five chapters discusses works by two of the three authors I am examining here, although all three can be considered in these terms. As we have seen, Jones's *Fire and Hemlock*, though not the first of a sequence, is a novel of growth structured according to fairy tale; the Harry Potter sequence takes place largely in a form of "wainscot" world, although not of the same type as those I consider in Chapter 3, and features witches, though less interestingly for the purposes of this study than does Pratchett's Tiffany sequence or Jones's *Howl's Moving Castle*. Pratchett engages with ideas of choice and destiny especially in *Johnny and the Bomb* (1996), and many of his adult Discworld novels, notably *Guards! Guards!* (1989) and *Wyrd Sisters* (1988), parody or subvert notions familiar from heroic fantasy—although this is less true of his children's fiction. My purpose in this book is not, however, to undertake a comprehensive comparison between these three writers—which would in any case involve discussion of a range of other features that connect and distinguish them, as well as of their other writings—but to demonstrate their attention to the power of story as it emerges in key ways and in key texts, and the ethical visions that shape their deployment of that power. Likewise, I do not engage with sociological literature on stereotype, for instance, as my purpose is to examine how these authors conceive of such issues and their function. My Conclusion therefore focuses particularly on the intellectual and moral messages that can be learned from these writers as they have emerged through my examination of their works. As we shall see, Rowling, Jones, and Pratchett all explore, exploit, and critique the power of story across their writing.

NOTES

1. Jacqueline Simpson, in the course of a perceptive discussion of Pratchett's *The Wee Free Men*, has commented that "on one level—a very important level—all but the earliest of Terry's books are realistic works, not fantasies" (14).
2. The inclusion of fictional epigraphs to all chapters also featured significantly in Pratchett's earlier Nome Trilogy, as we shall see in Chapter 3.
3. Material in quotations, including ellipsis and emphasis, is that of the quotation's author unless otherwise indicated.
4. Nikolajeva's analysis in fact indicates considerable sophistication in Rowling's writing.
5. Schanoes has pointed out that this deprecation of Hermione tails off quickly in the early books of the sequence (139).
6. Christine Moon has pointed out Rowling's attention to the unreliability of the spoken as well as the written word.

1 Harry Potter and Tiffany Aching

The 1997 publication of *Harry Potter and the Philosopher's Stone* marked the beginning of a publishing phenomenon. The popular reception of Rowling's Harry Potter books, and the Harry Potter films that followed, has been tremendous: Elizabeth E. Heilman claimed before completion of the sequence that "Harry Potter is present in most of the public and cultural spaces in which we live" (Introduction 1). A series credited, at least by its publishers, with "turn[ing] a generation into lifelong readers" (Tyler) almost by definition has no contemporary peer; passing observations of the relationship of Rowling's school for wizards to Ursula K. Le Guin's much earlier depiction of such a school in *A Wizard of Earthsea* (1968) or to the teaching of magic in Diana Wynne Jones's Chrestomanci series (1977–2006) (for example by Pat Pinsent) mostly functioned merely as reminders that some of Rowling's concepts were not in themselves original.

But there have been other recent "publishing phenomena" with which it is in fact useful to compare Rowling's work. Terry Pratchett's series of Discworld novels (1983–present) had dominated British publishing for years prior to the arrival of Rowling's novels. In 2003, Pratchett published his second Discworld novel for children, *The Wee Free Men*, which featured characters from his Discworld witches novels in cameo appearances, and focused on the experience of a child choosing to become a witch—a topic he had already glanced at in *Lords and Ladies* (1992). *The Wee Free Men* became the first of a series of four novels featuring young Tiffany Aching and her friends the Nac Mac Feegle, the clan of small blue-stained "pictsies" who had previously appeared in the witches novel *Carpe Jugulum* (1998). Moreover, the series became what can be described as a sequence. That is, like Rowling's Harry Potter novels, the four Tiffany Aching books do not merely feature shared settings and characters, but represent a trajectory of development with a recognisable beginning and ending. That ending is less rigidly structured than the Harry Potter novels, with their explicit and narrow goal of Voldemort's defeat; ending for Tiffany has more to do with attainment of maturity and stability, as we shall see later in this chapter and in Chapter 4. Like the Harry Potter sequence, Pratchett's sequence features a child with magical talents developing to adulthood across a span of seven years. Pratchett's Tiffany is nine when we first meet her, and "sixteen, more or less" at the conclusion of *I Shall Wear Midnight* (2010 [397])—exactly two years younger than Harry Potter at the beginning and ending of the Harry Potter sequence, in fact.

My argument in this chapter is that comparison of the two novels that begin the sequences, Pratchett's *The Wee Free Men* and Rowling's *Harry Potter and the Philosopher's Stone*, foregrounds the literary strategies at work in both Rowling's and Pratchett's fictions. Comparison of Pratchett's and Rowling's novels points to the very different concerns highlighted within each sequence and thereby demonstrates the nature of their underlying strategies. In particular, I focus here on the ways in which both these first novels locate their protagonists as heroes within fairy tales. The particular fairy tales evoked here, and the resulting constraints placed on the child protagonists, produce strikingly different images of agency. These establish the nature of the protagonist's trajectory in each sequence; they further indicate the nature of the appeals made to Rowling's and Pratchett's readers, with concomitant implications for character and reader development across each sequence. As we shall see, Pratchett's novel foregrounds analytic capacity and the ability to critique cultural convention; his protagonist demonstrates maturity in her capacity for independent vision and action, if not for social engagement. By contrast, Rowling's positioning of her reader, as well as her protagonist, as initially passive and childish prepares for a subtle development of her story even at the level of language that belies its apparent simplicity. Both writers thus demonstrate a coherent and sophisticated vision of the function of their stories and the relationship of character and reader. Pratchett's fiction emphasises its own literary framework, inviting a comparatively sophisticated response from a reader implied to be consciously intelligent and analytical, whereas, as we shall see, Rowling's story implicitly appeals to a range of readers who can identify or empathise with the initial passivity of a child just learning the possibility of independent action.

THE CHILD IN FAIRY TALE

Both *The Wee Free Men* and *Harry Potter and the Philosopher's Stone* draw on fairy tales, although the particular fairy tales that structure these stories situate their protagonists in sharply contrasting ways. In the case of *Philosopher's Stone*, the hero's first appearance as an infant being deposited on an unsuspecting foster-parent's doorstep immediately suggests fairy tale, and this evocation is supported by the action of the immediately following chapters. Alison Lurie, among others, has remarked that Harry Potter is "in the classic Cinderlad situation" at the start of the sequence (114),[1] and M. Katherine Grimes discusses the operation for their readers of the early Harry Potter books as fairy tales, identifying characters as fulfilling particular fairy-tale roles. Although Grimes's analysis refers repeatedly to

"Cinderella," it could be argued that the "Cinderella" story is present as a psychological structure rather than a literary one in *Harry Potter and the Philosopher's Stone*: that is, it provides not allusion to fairy tale, but an appeal to the common childish fantasy of being recognised as special—a fantasy that informs many children's novels. As Grimes remarks, "Child readers are satisfied to affirm their perception that adults do not always treat them fairly [. . .] These children look forward to the day when everyone notices that they are special, like Cinderella and Harry Potter" (98).

But the connection between Harry Potter and Cinderella is closer than this. Julia Eccleshare's remark that "from the opening scene [sic] of *Harry Potter and the Philosopher's Stone* where they make him cook the breakfast and treat him as an unpaid drudge, Harry fits neatly into the Cinderella tradition" (16) indicates the extent to which the details of Rowling's portrayal, not only its psychological shape, locate Harry as Cinderella in the opening chapters. In the suburban contemporary world of Privet Drive, the kitchen is not a despised region out of the purview of its aristocratic inhabitants, as in "Cinderella," but an ordinary part of the family's household world generally inhabited by its mistress, Aunt Petunia. Nevertheless Harry, who like Cinderella has lost his real parents, is found in the second chapter living literally below stairs, absurdly relegated by his foster mother to the cupboard that is all that remains of the traditional servants' domain, emerging when he is called to the kitchen to mind the frying pan. He is thus established as occupying Cinderella's place physically as well as psychologically. In Charles Perrault's story, Cinderella's fairy godmother appears, announces Cinderella's true state, transforms her clothing and provides her with transport to the ball; in Rowling's, the giant Hagrid bursts into the house where Harry is lying miserably on the floor, tells him of his own true nature as a wizard, and takes him to Diagon Alley to buy robes, and supplies him with his ticket for the Hogwarts Express.[2] Once Harry gets to Diagon Alley, he is met with the acclaim and awe that traditionally greet the revealed Cinderella, as the witches and wizards in the Leaky Cauldron come forward to shake his hand and identify him not just as magical, like the rest of his society, but as special within it, a princess among ladies as it were. When Harry leaves the Dursleys at King's Cross he is challenged by the ticket barrier that admits only the magically gifted, acting as a kind of Cinderella slipper to exclude the unworthy, before recognition of his distinguishing scar ensures that he is not only accepted but celebrated by his schoolmates. Chapters 2–6 of the novel thus provide a complete "Cinderella" story—although already in the sixth chapter this story is modulating into a quite different narrative, as Harry makes friends with Ron Weasley and starts to engage in the social dynamics of his school.

The "Cinderella" story is noteworthy for the lack of agency required of its hero. The displaced child is restored not through his or her own activity but through that of guardians and through the recognition of those in high places of the rightness of his or her actual status. Indeed, Harry arguably has even less agency than Cinderella, who manifests her true condition bodily when she outshines other women at the ball and bedazzles her prince. Harry, by contrast, is already known to be a wizard's child not only by Dumbledore and Hagrid but by the entire magical world, and Hagrid claims that "[h]is name's been down [for Hogwarts] ever since he was born" (Rowling, *Philosopher's* 68). Although we later discover from Neville Longbottom that even wizards' children cannot attend Hogwarts if they lack magic, Harry's own magical acts in childhood—growing his hair, jumping onto a roof, freeing a snake—are inadvertent and are represented as confirmation of what is already known rather than providing a necessary moment of recognition: "Harry looked back at Hagrid, smiling, and saw that Hagrid was positively beaming at him. 'See?' said Hagrid. 'Harry Potter, not a wizard—you wait, you'll be right famous at Hogwarts'" (68). The agency here is that of the fairy godmother asserting "You *shall* go to the ball," not of the nascent hero. Despite his struggles with his Uncle Vernon to get one of the many letters sent to him by the magical authorities, Harry has no agency in his own eventual rescue: Uncle Vernon successfully carries him off to a remote island—itself a classic villain ruse—from which he can be rescued only because the good guys have magical powers. Indeed, prior to his arrival at Hogwarts Harry's own magical interventions are accidental and often self-destructive.

The implications of Rowling's choice of this particular fairy-tale structure to engage readers in her sequence go beyond the rapid movement from neglect to centrality experienced by Harry in what is after all a few short chapters of his seven-book maturation. In exploring these implications, it is instructive to turn to Pratchett's Tiffany, who lives through a complete fairy tale in the first novel of her four-book sequence—but one of a very different kind from "Cinderella." In *The Wee Free Men*, young Tiffany, a child living on the Chalk or downland of Pratchett's Discworld, discovers a fairy-tale monster in the stream by her parents' farm. After attacking it, she seeks information about it, encountering the witch Miss Tick, who tells her that Tiffany's world is being invaded by the parasitic Fairyland. In the course of their conversation Tiffany reveals that she wants to be a witch herself. Spurred on by the disappearance of her little brother, Tiffany sets out to invade Fairyland and get him back. She is aided in her quest by Miss Tick's familiar, a toad, and by a rowdy gang of small blue men, the magical Nac Mac Feegle, who declare her to be the witch of her district and whose matriarch offers her advice. Tiffany seeks out the entry to the fairy realm and invades it armed only with an iron frying-pan; she negotiates its hazards, which include razor-toothed hellhounds and, more insidiously, dreamscapes generated by creatures called "dromes" kept by the Queen of Fairyland (Pratchett, *Wee* 192), and discovers Roland, the twelve-year-old son of the local Baron, who has been lost for a year. Helping rather than helped by Roland, Tiffany locates her little brother Wentworth. She confronts the Queen, who attempts to break her will by pointing out her character flaws, but Tiffany reassesses these and takes ownership of them. She identifies the Queen's weakness in her turn and engineers what she hopes will be an escape from Fairyland based on a dream of her own, but in the process mislays Wentworth and the Feegles, and is brought back to face the Queen again. This time Tiffany draws on the strength of the land itself, and expels the Queen from her world. Although the adults decide that the older and presumably more competent Roland must have saved Tiffany, Roland and Tiffany know the truth—and Tiffany's status as a witch is confirmed by Miss Tick and two senior witches.

This is a very different story from *Philosopher's Stone*, and the fairy tale implicit in the first section of the latter is thrown into sharp contrast by consideration of the fairy tale structuring *The Wee Free Men*. The rescue of a person who has been stolen by the fairies is a plot that, though less individually famous than "Cinderella," appears in various forms in European fairy tale including the Grimms' "The Worn-Out Dancing Shoes," the well-known Scots ballad "Tam Lin," the tale "Kate Crackernuts," also originally Scottish but widely disseminated in England following the publication of Joseph Jacobs's *English Fairy Tales* (1890), and the English tale of "Childe Rowland," likewise included in Jacobs's collection. In such stories a person has been abducted or seduced to Fairyland and must be retrieved, sometimes against his or her own will, by the rescuer protagonist. The rescuer must be determined, like Tam Lin's Janet, who must hold onto him even when he is in the shape of a snake, a bear, or an ember; she must also be clever, like Kate Crackernuts, who adds the right words to the prince's cry in order to be admitted to the fairy mound, delays reporting on his situation in order to get what she wants, successfully eavesdrops, and uses her nuts to lure the fairy baby away from the items she needs to cure both the prince and her own sick sister. Pratchett's Tiffany Aching is both determined and clever.

Pratchett is an enthusiastic student of folklore (see "Imaginary Worlds"), and *The Wee Free Men* makes visible his debt to the folktale tradition. Tiffany's adversary, like Janet's, is the Queen of Fairyland; when Tiffany is attempting to escape from Fairyland she cries to Roland that he must "Crack . . . the . . . nut" (Pratchett, *Wee* 244), evoking Kate; Roland's name evokes Childe Rowland, who like Tiffany, is in search of a sibling rather than like Janet or Kate an actual or potential lover.[3] Also stressed here is the difficulty in entering the dangerous realm—in Childe Rowland's and Kate's cases, a green mound where the prisoners are held—and the injunction against eating fairy food within the mound, which both Tiffany and Childe Rowland almost break. Unsurprisingly, Pratchett also emphasises the deceptive nature of the fairies, traditionally known for their guile, as the Queen uses creatures called dromes to generate dreams in which trespassers will fall. Tiffany, using a dream sword based on her actual iron frying pan, cuts off the head of a drome that is pretending to be Roland and has disguised Roland as itself. Her gesture recalls both Janet's persistence in identifying Tam Lin in his changed forms and the injunction on Childe Rowland to "out with your father's brand [sword] and off with [the] head" of everyone who speaks to him in Elfland before he finds his sister.[4]

But Pratchett also rewrites details, supplying Tiffany with an army of rebel fairies in the form of the Nac Mac Feegle as her Proppian magic helpers, and it is the Feegles who live in a mound in the "ordinary" Discworld of the novel. The Feegles not only assist Tiffany to enter Fairyland by explaining its rules, but also warn her how to deal with at least some of the fairy dangers and emerge, if a little belatedly, to prevent her eating during the fairy ball and, from the nut, in time to distract the Queen and fight her supporters. In return for their aid, as in many fairy tales, Tiffany finds herself, even before her quest begins, promised in marriage to the Feegles' leader, Rob Anybody Feegle; she gets out of the problem of marrying, at age nine, someone six inches high by "naming the day" as an impossible one whose details themselves recall fairy tales, demonstrating characteristic folktale agility.

Pratchett's choice of such a tale to provide the plot of his novel highlights the activity and competence of his child protagonist. Where, as Ximena Gallardo-C. and C. Jason Smith have observed, Rowling genders male the subject of what they call a "girl tale"—indeed, a tale often taken to underscore the passivity expected of women in the Western European fairy tale tradition—Pratchett's nine-year-old Tiffany recalls two of the most active female characters in European folk tale in her heroic quest to rescue her brother from the Queen of Fairyland. Pratchett's construction of Tiffany as a modern Kate Crackernuts proffers a model of independent agency for the child reader—especially, but not only, the female child reader. Following her conversation with Miss Tick, Tiffany learns to negotiate with and even command the unruly Feegles, successfully enters the elusive Fairyland and learns to manipulate its rules, and defies the Queen of the Fairies, turning the tables on her by naming the Queen's weaknesses even as the Queen had sought to demean Tiffany.

Reading Pratchett's story here involves engaging with the activities of an intelligent, stubborn child who refuses to accept that she must be sentimental about her little brother any more than that she herself is, like Harry in Privet Drive, a helpless child. Fairy tales traditionally take small account of human emotions beyond the most basic ones of love, hate, jealousy, and fear. Pratchett foregrounds the sense of duty that implicitly inspires Kate Crackernuts to leave home with her transformed and helpless stepsister and Childe Rowland to seek out and rescue his lost sister without reference to their own personal cost. Thus Tiffany declares "*I have a duty!*" (Pratchett, *Wee* 282), adopting as her own her grandmother's avowed sense of responsibility for the sheep she herds and for "*those who don't have voices*" (43). For Tiffany, this sense of responsibility for the land she inhabits grounds her selfhood. Once she understands this relationship, she can reject as unimportant the Queen's allegation of her heartlessness (277).

Whereas Tiffany is confident at least in part because her abilities as a dairymaid have already been recognised and accepted within her community,

Harry is initially passive because he is both unvalued and as far as he knows incapable of influencing the world around him—as is true for many children. His discovery that he is special, a wizard, is therefore interesting in its retroactive effect. Hagrid's revelation transforms not only his present but also his past: "the very last time Dudley had hit him, hadn't he got his revenge, without even realising he was doing it? Hadn't he set a boa constrictor on him?" (Rowling, *Philosopher's* 68). Within the context of the fairy tale, as I have already indicated, Harry is passive here in his situation as a Cinderella confronted by her fairy godmother; but his own perception of himself is significantly changed. He is now, if only retrospectively, a hero in his own eyes, the Boy Who Got Revenge.

Rowling thus establishes Harry doubly through the first novel's initial fairy tale. He is the passive Cinderella thrust first, an unknowing infant, into the misery of Privet Drive and then into the as yet unknown magical world, but he is also the child who discovers not merely his special status but his potential for action. Both elements speak importantly to Rowling's idea of her reader: this is a broader readership than Pratchett's Tiffany invites. The reader of Tiffany Aching's adventures is invited to identify with her literacy, her intelligence, and her insight as well as her agency. Readers who do not believe themselves at least potentially to share these qualities may admire her, but are also likely to reject her—to find her, in the Queen's words, "cold and heartless" (Pratchett, *Wee* 277). Rowling's construction of Harry encourages a variety of different readers to take an interest in Harry's fortunes. Not only, as Grimes has pointed out, do his adventures take multiple shapes in genre terms that may appeal to audiences of different ages and stages of reading, but his initial position is framed in terms that would make some kind of positive response, whether empathetic or sympathetic, available to a wide range of readers. His structural passivity is offset by the fact that Harry, unlike Cinderella, is both aware of his situation and, within its constraints, resistant. When his brutish cousin Dudley threatens him with a traditional high school initiation, he is ready with a response: " 'No, thanks,' said Harry. 'The poor toilet's never had anything as horrible as your head down it—it might be sick' " (Rowling, *Philosopher's* 40). Although Harry then "ran, before [his cousin] could work out what he'd said" (40), Harry's smart reply to Dudley's bullying has established him as more than a coward, and the narrator's explanation of his running leaves the joke firmly on Dudley. This is a Cinderella with a mind and tongue of his own, pitiable because of his situation but admirable because of his wit, and therefore potentially appealing to different groups of readers.

Tiffany Aching is even more forthright than Harry in responding to threats. Pratchett's fairy tale structure, which requires agency of the protagonist, is underpinned by his characterisation of her as intelligent, level-headed, curious, and proactive. She not only recognises the monster Jenny Green-Teeth who appears in a nearby river, but quickly works out a plan to destroy it—a plan that, as Miss Tick's toad familiar realises, involves "using her *brother* as *bait*" (Pratchett, *Wee* 22). In the course of her identification she also takes the trouble to measure the soup plate to which Jenny's eyes are compared in her book of fairy tales, revealing herself to be detached and analytical as well as able to observe details during a crisis. In their early conversation, the witch Miss Tick commends the complex reasoning by which Tiffany works out that "a witch coming here would know about the Baron [who hates witches] and so she'd wear the kind of hat that everyone knows witches don't wear" (32); recognises the sharpness of her powers of observation (42); and confesses to being "slightly impressed" when Tiffany's response to being told, "Something bad is happening" is " 'Can I stop it?', not 'Can anyone stop it?' or 'Can we stop it?' " (43). Pratchett offers explicit analysis of Tiffany's conversation and actions through the authoritative Miss Tick; that Tiffany can hold her own in their dialogue, which matches her against an adult rather than, as in Harry's encounter with Dudley, against another child, underscores her capabilities. Not only does the plot locate her as an active figure, unlike Harry's initial "Cinderella" situation, but she is forceful, analytical, and proactive in her own right. The empathy she invites from readers therefore depends on those readers being willing to admire and identify with an extraordinary and precocious child rather than, as Nikolajeva among others has observed of Harry, an ordinary one ("Harry" 131).

THE CRITICAL CHILD

Above all, Tiffany Aching is critical of the givens within her culture. Her own awareness of the conventions of fairy tale has been manifest from the first, not only in her recognition of Jenny Green-Teeth, but in her interrogation of the toad: "Were you a handsome prince?" (Pratchett, *Wee* 81). The toad's admission that he was transformed by a fairy godmother, "Never cross a woman with a star on a stick, young lady. They've got a mean streak" (81), mocks the conventions of fairy tales. But Tiffany herself has already done this in her critique of *The Goode Childe's Booke of Faerie Tales*, in which she observed not only the stereotypes that eliminate brown-haired girls like her from adventures,[5] but also the power of such stories within the real world: "all the stories had, somewhere, the witch. The *wicked old witch*. And Tiffany had thought: Where's the *evidence*? [. . .] It was enough to be *called* a witch" (37). What people *call* each other has a very real effect on their lives: Tiffany is well aware of the fate of Mrs Snapperly, suspected of witchcraft, whose house was burnt down and who died in the snow. "I think she was a sick old lady who was no use to anyone [. . .] She just looked like a witch in a story" (47–48). Tiffany's refusal to accept stereotype, her insistence on seeing "what is really there" (140), is an important aspect of her agency that, somewhat paradoxically, conforms to her role as the heroine who, like Janet of "Tam Lin,", can see past the deceptions of fairyland.

Tiffany's critique of the function of story is crucial to an understanding of Pratchett's moral as well as his literary agenda across the sequence.[6] While Tiffany rejects the crude stereotypes established in *The Goode Childe's Booke of Faerie Tales*, it is clear that her rejection relates to its simplistic reduction of human complexity rather than to its status as a merely literary object: "The stories *weren't real*. But Mrs Snapperly had died because of stories" (Pratchett, *Wee* 63). Later, she will similarly resent the attempts made by the Queen and her dromes to manipulate her intelligence. Such manipulation, as Tiffany recognises, denies her agency: the reader who accepts the stereotypical vision proffered by *The Goode Childe's Booke of Fairy Tales* surrenders the capacity to see, as Tiffany can see, "what's really there" (243) and can do unthinking damage to themselves and others. Tiffany's critical capacity is contrasted with that of Roland, who explains "Well, there was this fine lady on a horse with bells all over its harness and she galloped past me when I was out hunting and she was laughing, so of *course* I spurred my horse and chased after her and . . ." (225–26). Roland's unthinking "of course" inadvertently admits his surrender of agency to the obvious distraction of the Queen. On the next page Tiffany enquires "You don't think she's trying to feed you up before she bakes you in an oven and eats you, do you?" to which he replies " 'Of course not. Only wicked witches do that.' Tiffany's eyes narrowed" (227), underlining the connection between Roland's seduction by the Queen—a seduction described in terms straight out of fairy tale—and his submission to the givens of fairy tale itself and thus to their harmful consequences. That Tiffany herself had questioned the plausibility of the oven story to the extent of measuring Mrs Snapperly's oven when the villagers suspected the old woman of doing away with Roland locates her both as forensic detective and as literary critic.

Yet Pratchett's story, much more visibly than Rowling's, itself takes the structure of a fairy tale. In a last throw of the dice, the Queen of Fairyland attempts to unsettle and thereby conquer Tiffany by pointing to the extent to which she may have internalised the conventions of fairy tale herself: "*You*, especially, dream all the time. [. . .] You had this dream about Brave Girl Rescuing Little Brother. You thought you were the heroine of a *story*" (Pratchett, *Wee* 276). Ironically, of course, that is just what Tiffany is. The trope is one familiar to readers of Pratchett: he deploys the structure and evokes the conventions of a genre even as his narrator and characters comment on the absurdity of those conventions—as in his Discworld novel *Guards! Guards!* By contrast with the more subtle nature of Rowling's embedding of fairy tale structure, Pratchett's is explicit and metatextual in its operation. Like Tiffany, he is a literary critic, one who recognises the power of literary tropes and does not disdain deploying them for the entertainment and edification of his readers. He transforms existing patterns, giving them new and surprising shapes, such as the dromes who enforce the Queen's will by trapping trespassers in Fairyland in dreams, or the Nac Mac Feegle themselves. The fate of the toad operates similarly: he is eventually discovered to be a former lawyer, and hired as such by the Nac Mac Feegle without being transformed to either human or Feegle.

Tiffany herself is an example of Pratchett's transformative activity. She is neither a stereotypically passive beautiful princess nor an unthinking hero on an obligatory quest but a modern child wandering Alice-like in a magic landscape determined to "remember what's real" and, ultimately, secure in her own identity:

> Yes! I'm *me!* I am careful and logical and I look up things I don't under-stand! When I hear people use the wrong words I get edgy! I am good with cheese. I read books fast! I *think!* And I always have a piece of string! That's the kind of person I am!
>
> (Pratchett, *Wee* 264)

In this list of character traits, Tiffany's references to "get[ting] edgy" at hear-ing wrong word usage and "always hav[ing] a piece of string" refer back to her early conversation with Miss Tick about the nature of witches, but along with her reading, thinking, and logic they also affirm her sense of herself, and the reader's sense of her, as not only highly intelligent—and, significantly, literate—but also highly capable, a person who controls her environment rather than letting it control her. The fairy tale established in the opening of Harry Potter, by contrast, appears to locate Harry as very thoroughly the object of control; we shall see later how Rowling modifies this picture. Pratchett's portrait of Tiffany is itself a comment on what we tend to mean by "fairy tale"—Kate Crackernuts is far less well-known than Cinderella. There is little room in the traditional European fairy tale for a girl who not only reads but critiques what she reads.

GROWING UP

In Tiffany's list of her characteristics, the statement "I am good with cheese" may appear intrusive, an amusing reminder that she is, after all, only a child who is not quite as good at abstraction and categorisation as she thinks—momentarily inviting the reader to feel superior and indicating that there is more to growing up than reading the dictionary. However, the statement in itself also speaks to an important part of Pratchett's characterisation of his protagonist. Not only is Tiffany curious, adventurous, intelligent, and capable; she is also a worker with her own skills, skills valued in the com-munity in which she is growing up. Unlike Harry, who at almost eleven can be commanded to "look after the bacon" but given the warning "don't let it burn" (Rowling, *Philosopher's* 26) and is otherwise seen as a useless expense within the Dursley household (85), Tiffany is not just *a* but appar-ently *the* dairymaid, left alone not out of neglect but because she does not need either monitoring or care to be provided by her already busy family

(Pratchett, *Wee* 16). Her capacity to function as an adult has already been established within her community, itself of course a simpler and more practically oriented one than that likely to be experienced by Pratchett's readers.

Tiffany's status as worker, no less than her fairy-tale role as active protagonist, provides a sharp contrast to Rowling's portrait of Harry Potter. It is easy to overlook Harry's positioning as a child, since that position is so common within his Western readership, but it is in fact an important feature of his characterisation and of Rowling's appeal to her reader that Harry is the child undergoing schooling—not merely, as is obvious, the hero of a school story. Tiffany is a working child of a type more common in England a century or more ago than now. Growing up in a rural area visited only rarely by wandering teachers, she takes education where she can find it, whether that be from a teacher in a tent with a misspelled sign charging a carrot for instruction or from her own experiences. This image of the protagonist, with its implicit appeal to the long history of children participating in the working life of a farm as soon as they are old enough to be of help, casts into relief Rowling's more contemporary portrait of Harry attending first a primary school where he risks being bullied by Dudley and his friends and subsequently his magical boarding school. Many scholars (for example Alton, Smith, Steege) have commented on Hogwarts' debt to the history of the school story, which is so powerfully the history of the boarding school. Such schools were founded initially because of the scattered nature of feudal communities and the need to bring together the small group recognised as potential students.[7] Ironically, it is Tiffany, not Harry, who belongs to this notably unsuburban tradition.

Following the resolution of the "Cinderella" narrative, the major experience of *Philosopher's Stone* is, as Colin Manlove notes (*Order* 66), not so much the confrontation with Voldemort as Harry's and the reader's discovery and enjoyment of life at a magical boarding school. Harry is exposed to a range of new subjects of study and makes new friends (and enemies), relationships that draw him into various actions such as defying a bully on behalf of his classmate Neville and seeking out the bossy Hermione in the girls' bathroom to warn her of a danger of which she is ignorant because of her distress over rejection by Harry and his friend Ron. Despite these acts, it should be noted that, as a student undergoing schooling, Harry is again placed in an essentially passive role. He is at school to be instructed, and the largely traditional representation of his teachers as authority figures, all known as Professor, underlines this—even if, as Elisabeth Rose Gruner points out, he actually learns more successfully on his own (224). Further, Harry's own engagement with activities within the grounds of the school—which is to say, most of his actions in the first six novels—is consistently framed in relation to the rules of the school, whether he obeys these or not.

Pratchett's portrait of his nine-year-old protagonist highlights the extent to which Rowling locates the eleven-year-old Harry Potter as a child. Unlike Tiffany, whose situation as working girl making daily decisions independently of adults is comparatively unusual within the contemporary England of Pratchett's and Rowling's readership, Harry is the child subject to the orders and ordinances not only of his foster parents, but also of his beloved Hogwarts. His first notably heroic act is explicitly framed as disobedience: he takes to the air to confront Draco Malfoy over the theft of Neville's Remembrall, despite the reminders of his classmates that they have been expressly forbidden to fly during Madam Hooch's absence. His second such act, the decision to seek out Hermione in the bathroom he and Ron believe has been invaded by a troll, also involves deliberate breach of a recent injunction, in this case to follow the prefects back to the dormitory without deviation. The fact that both acts are in effect rewarded by the school authorities—Professor McGonagall identifies Harry as a potential Seeker and arranges to exempt him from the ban on first-years participating in House Quidditch teams; she gives him and Ron points for dealing with the troll even while condemning their disobedience—points not only to a disturbing degree of favouritism comparable to Snape's treatment of the Slytherins, as several critics have remarked, but also to the extent to which even heroism is in effect part of the school system. Dumbledore's awarding of points specifically to Harry and Neville at the end of *Philosopher's Stone* likewise locates moral strength as a quality within the purview of the school authorities, as Harry is commended for "pure nerve and outstanding cour-age" (Rowling, 328) and Neville for being brave enough to stand up to his friends (329).

Where Pratchett's Tiffany is constructed as unusual, then, Rowling's Harry has the appeal of an everychild within Rowling's contemporary England. It is also noteworthy that when confronted with the choice to act or not, Harry experiences his decisions as inevitable. Challenged to a duel, he feels that "this was his big chance to beat Malfoy, face to face. He couldn't miss it" (Rowling, *Philosopher's Stone* 169); learning that the troll has gone to the girls' toilets where an insulted Hermione is weeping, the narrator observes that going there "was the last thing [he and Ron] wanted to do, but what choice did they have?" (190). Harry even experiences agency as constraint on agency. Chapter 5 explores the complexity of Rowling's depiction of choice especially in relation to ideas of destiny. It is in any case clear in the first novel that while Harry admirably takes action where others do not, he does so largely because of a somewhat unimaginative focus on what needs to be done. However, it is central to the reader's perception of him as hero that this focus frequently emerges from a sense of responsibility as powerful as Tiffany's.

Harry's eventual defeat of Quirrell/Voldemort depends in part on his single-mindedness about the task at hand as he looks in the Mirror of Erised, a single-mindedness that Dumbledore much later rather grandly describes as "pur[ity] of heart" (Rowling, *Half-Blood* 478). Given Rowling's well-paced representation of this moment as the climax of his adventure, however, Harry's focus does not surprise the reader. Dumbledore's explanation of the other element in Harry's success, the villain's inadvertent evocation of his mother's protection "in [his] very skin" (Rowling, *Philosopher's* 321), inverts Harry's heroic achievement at the beginning as well as the end of the novel: it is his mother's power that protects him, not his own. That he does not outwit Quirrell/Voldemort is made evident by his uncertainty, on waking in the hospital wing, that he has achieved anything at all. Here, he more resembles Roland, to whom his Fairyland experience "all seems. . . . like a dream" (Pratchett, *Wee* 296), than Tiffany, who reminds herself that "*it's all true*" (297) and goes on to treat the important witch Mistress Weatherwax as an equal, earning her respect. Tiffany herself enunciates her discovery of the nature of the witches' school she had wished for, demonstrating the value of her practical education: "This is the school, isn't it? The magic place? This world. Here. And you don't realize it until you look" (303). Harry, by contrast, remains the schoolchild, dependent on the much-admired Professor Dumbledore for explanation and resolution here as in all six subsequent novels.

The Harry Potter sequence develops a definite and articulated goal—the final defeat of Harry's enemy, Lord Voldemort. As Rowling constructs it, this defeat eventually requires Harry to achieve some degree of emotional maturity. It is important to the effect of the final volume that Harry understands exactly what is required of him, and that this requirement appears as the culmination of a slowly unfolding series of revelations about his own relationship with Voldemort. Growth for Harry Potter involves a move to autonomy; we shall see in the next chapter how that development is related to Rowling's own critique of genre, in this case that of heroic fantasy. Harry himself experiences growth as the need to expand beyond the confines of school rules and expectations established in *Philosopher's Stone*. In *Harry Potter and the Order of the Phoenix* (2003) he constantly chafes not only against the authority of the new headmistress, Dolores Umbridge, but even against Dumbledore, whom he resents for neglecting him. It is significant that Umbridge is characterised as particularly repellent through her infantilisation of her now fifteen-year-old students; Harry's main complaint from the start of *Order of the Phoenix* is that most of his guardian adults, especially Dumbledore, are failing to acknowledge the maturity he feels he has earned through his experiences in the previous novels. In *Harry Potter and the Deathly Hallows* (2007), not only are the last of Harry's guardians stripped away, but he questions even Dumbledore's own character as he travels about the countryside far from what has been the safety of Hogwarts. As we shall see in later chapters, however, this movement toward self-sufficiency is not a move toward unfettered agency. Rowling's depiction of mature action includes the importance of accepting constraints on choice.

As we might expect, the Tiffany Aching sequence operates quite differently. *The Wee Free Men* establishes that Tiffany, like Kate Crackernuts and Janet of "Tam Lin," has both agency and autonomy from the beginning—if anything, as the Queen insinuates (Pratchett, 277), her autonomy is almost too complete. In dealing with other people she relies primarily on her memories of her grandmother, who negotiated with both the physical and the social environment on her own terms and who has left Tiffany with a pronounced sense of responsibility to what she perceives as her world. In this first novel, Tiffany acts more or less as a solitary agent, leaving the deserted farm on a quest in which her assistants are a clan of miniature pictsies and a toad. Although Pratchett depicts Tiffany's home as a working farm, and her memories of Granny Aching extend to interactions within a feudal village, we see Tiffany herself operating in isolation to save Roland and her little brother Wentworth. And far from having to overcome her own weakness, in this novel she claims it as a strength, consciously turning selfishness—typically a negative trait in fairy tales, especially when manifested by girls[8]—into a weapon in order to defeat the Queen.

The subsequent novels, then, complicate both the social world in which Tiffany operates and the security of her moral stance. Where Harry's world gradually extends beyond Hogwarts to include such things as awareness of the politics of the earlier revered Ministry of Magic, yet forces him to rely less and less on mentors and more on his own personal strength, Tiffany confronts an ever increasing complexity in her social environment that requires her to develop a richer understanding of her relationships with individuals and to recognise her own limitations. In the second novel, *A Hat Full of Sky* (2004), she leaves her home on the Chalk to be apprenticed to Miss Level,[9] a witch in a small village in the mountains, and, as we shall see in Chapter 4, she must learn to distinguish the importance of the less exciting duties of a witch to the wider community as opposed to the glamour of magic advocated by a senior apprentice, Annagramma, and her mistress Mrs Earwig. She is compelled, too, to accept that there are limits even to her ability to atone for her own misbehaviour. In *Wintersmith* (2006), the witch Miss Treason with whom she is now working dies, and Tiffany must not only manage the social complexities of a witch's funeral but also help Annagramma, who takes over Miss Treason's cottage, understand the nature and social dynamics of Annagramma's new role. Finally, in *I Shall Wear Midnight*, we see Tiffany as an adult witch responsible for her own community back on the Chalk. In this novel she deals not only with the villagers but, like her grandmother, with the feudal hierarchy—now represented by Roland, briefly her love interest in *Wintersmith* but now engaged to a girl of his own baronial class—and even travels to the city. Notably, although the final novel ends with a heterosexual romance, Tiffany ends up not with the unintelligent Roland, whom the fairy tale structures of *The Wee Free Men* and *Wintersmith* have designated her "Hero" (Pratchett, *Wintersmith* 346), but with a young man who shares her ethic of service to the community and her love of words, and who respects her acumen and supports her actions without attempting to take over leadership. Pratchett concludes the sequence by allowing Tiffany to choose her partner, as she has chosen her career, unconstrained by the stereotypes of traditional fairy tale—but constrained by the habits and tastes of her own distinctive personality.

As Tiffany's social world widens, the nature of her enemies changes too. The Queen of Fairyland's attack is straightforward: she is ruler of a land that Tiffany recognises is parasitic, seeking to steal a warmth and colour the Queen herself cannot provide from the ordinary world. Tiffany's defeat of her involves recognising the Queen's own weakness, her inability to create and her craving for the humanity provided by real children such as Roland and Wentworth. The danger in *A Hat Full of Sky* is posed by a "hiver," an age-old entity who is also parasitic on humanity but, more insidiously, invades by taking over the mind of strong creatures. Tiffany herself is captured by the hiver when she is playing with the ability to leave her body, which she does out of vanity. Horrified by the hiver's exploitation of her own worst desires during its mastery of her, she must acknowledge her own limitations as she discovers its weakness—the lack of secure identity, the fear that makes the hiver prey on the strong. In *Wintersmith*, Tiffany foolishly steps into the Morris dance that summons the elemental bringer of winter, and is mistaken by him for the Summer Lady, his complement. The wintersmith's attempts to woo Tiffany move from comedy, as when he crafts snowflakes in her image, to potential tragedy as the winter deepens. Somewhat similarly to the Queen and the hiver, the wintersmith craves humanity, mistakenly trying to become a man through mechanical means in order to be Tiffany's lover.

In both of these novels, Tiffany's self-sufficiency fails: she needs the help of the Nac Mac Feegle and a senior witch to escape the hiver's control, and the help of Roland, equipped as Hero by the Feegles, to defeat the wintersmith, as he brings the Summer Lady to her while she herself melts the wintersmith with a kiss. More significantly, perhaps, she is mentored not only by Miss Level, Miss Treason, and Mistress Weatherwax, but by the knowing Nanny Ogg, who advises her in the management of heterosexual relationships. It is unsurprising then that in the sequence's final novel, *I Shall Wear Midnight*, the emphasis is social and plural. The enemy is the Cunning Man, a force of hatred who stirs up prejudice and fear of the kind Tiffany rejected at the beginning of *The Wee Free Men*, and whose emotional power can make even Tiffany start to doubt and fear herself. He is unwittingly evoked by Roland's jealous fiancée Letitia, herself a nascent witch, and Tiffany must work with Letitia and other witches and members of the community to combat the hatred that sets Roland, among others, against her. Where Harry Potter must learn to act independently, if increasingly informed by the history of his tangled relationship with his opponent, Tiffany Aching learns how to engage fully with others without surrendering the autonomy she possessed at the start of the sequence. Her growth is measured not by her ability to move beyond the crude assumptions of fairy tale, but by her increasing ability to recognise and engage with the complexities of real human beings.

ENGAGING CHILDREN

As we have seen, the fairy-tale structures of *The Wee Free Men* and *Harry Potter and the Philosopher's Stone* generate very different protagonists. Tiffany Aching is portrayed as in many ways already mature as an agent, although her emotional and social development is limited in ways that the remainder of the sequence will remedy. The Tiffany sequence begins at a level of critical sophistication, as both Tiffany and the text encourage the reader to interrogate convention and stereotype. Harry Potter, on the other hand, is portrayed as a child constrained by his circumstances, whose latent capacities for active heroism must be structured and fostered within, and initially by, the school environment. As is common in school-story series novels, the emphasis will be on the protagonist's growth through his adventures. What Rowling adds to that, however, is a corresponding and sophisticated emphasis on the development of her posited readership.

Where Tiffany's youthful self-sufficiency allows the Queen to label her hard-hearted, Dumbledore's understated admission to Snape, belatedly revealed in *Deathly Hallows*, effectively summarises the most important feature of Harry as we see him at the start of the sequence: "I find him an engaging child" (Rowling, *Deathly Hallows* 545). Harry's qualities as Rowling constructs them through his adventures, as well as his Cinderella plight, make him engaging. Reading Harry Potter's first adventure as a fairy tale—an extended "Cinderella" in which the hero somewhat belatedly demonstrates his moral worth—highlights the extent to which the narrative works to draw in a potentially broad group of readers. This strategy of engagement also makes sense of some of the peculiarities of the novel's initial situation. Farah Mendlesohn, in a scathing critique of the ideology of the first four novels, has pointed out among other things the unlikelihood both of the Dursleys' extreme treatment of their nephew and of Harry's being, in these circumstances "almost incomprehensibly" ("Crowning" 38), a nice child. Mendlesohn does not link these observations to her further critique of the wizarding authorities' decision to abandon him to the Dursleys without "provid[ing] financial support for their care of Harry" despite Harry's inheritance of a substantial fortune (172); but all three details cohere if they are considered, not from the position of the analytic adult critic, but from that of the implied child reader of what Mendlesohn recognises is a fairy tale. In such tales moral positioning is often crude: as Tiffany Aching observes, the reader is invited to accept the tale's implicit and explicit assertions of good and evil without evidence. What the child reader is asked to recognise in the "Cinderella" narrative is the initially downtrodden position of the hero both physically and emotionally, the alignment providing the maximum emotional charge for the unreflective reader targeted by this strategy.

The cartoonish depiction of the Dursleys—which Rowling in fact modifies subtly though not completely across the sequence—is essential to this black-and-white portrait of Harry as suffering Cinderella. The potential inconsistency of this behaviour with their concern for the attitudes of their neighbours, noted by Mendlesohn, is less important to the child reader postulated by the narrative than is the hero's plight itself. Moreover, any indication that the Dursleys were receiving recompense for their guardianship would considerably complicate this picture. It seems almost inevitable that guardians who were being compensated for their task would be, however resentful of the source of their compensation, more physically generous to him than the Dursleys are: he might be better fed and clothed, he might not be relegated to a cupboard. If they were not thus generous, Harry's discovery of the compensation would be emotionally distracting, taking energy away from his Diagon Alley experience of delight as a simple dramatic contrast to his prior situation—"How often had [the Dursleys] complained about how much Harry cost them to keep? And all the time there had been a small fortune belonging to him" (Rowling, *Philosopher's* 85). But if they *were* more willing to provide physical comforts, the reader would need to accommodate a more complex understanding of Harry as physically comfortable but emotionally isolated and miserable, as in fact we find him at the beginning of the following novel. At the start of the sequence, Rowling on the surface eschews complexity, simplistically aligning Harry's physical and emotional plights in fairy-tale fashion and eliding the kind of interrogation that analytic readers like Mendlesohn, or Pratchett's Tiffany, would provide.

Later in the sequence Rowling offers some corrective to the points made by Mendlesohn and others about the morality implied in such details of the early books, including some of the financial and political details Mendlesohn queries. These may be seen as responses to criticism, but are generally sufficiently integral to the action of the sequence as to suggest an emerging narrative strategy. So seen, these details cohere with other changes, including in the representation of the Dursleys themselves. In *Deathly Hallows* the thuggish Dudley registers an inarticulate sympathy for Harry that may be the result of increasing maturity or, as Harry jokingly suggests, of a change in his personality induced by the Dementors (40), but may also be a novelistic acknowledgement that most individuals are not simply and naturally evil. Aunt Petunia is discovered to be emotionally sensitive to the threat of Voldemort's return (Rowling, *Order* 47), and is belatedly revealed, via Snape's memory, to have been deeply jealous of her sister (Rowling, *Deathly* 537), a jealousy that can be read on one level as characteristic of the fairy-tale Ugly Sister jealousy but on another as providing a psychological explanation for her explicit hatred both of Lily and of Harry.

The extent to which *Philosopher's Stone* can be read as written to engage the reader in the most simple of ways has suggested to Manlove that the viewpoint here and later is Harry's own:

> What if the nature of the first book was Harry's own picture of the Hogwarts world rather than one to be taken simply at face-value? Suppose

the first book expressed Harry as he was aged eleven? Might it not be that its absurd fantasy portrayed the exaggerated responses to life of an eleven-year-old? And then if that were so, might not each book work the same way? [. . .] In such a case the picture of the Dursleys in *The Philosopher's Stone* would be quite other than a lapse or an aberration. It would be a picture made by the boy hero, not simply by the author. This would be the way the boy saw them, to deal with them by making them absurd, to distance himself from them by boyish comic-book humour. Might it not be that the very narrating voice of all the books is not the author's but Harry's?

(*Order* 3).

Manlove cites the changing operation of humour across the sequence, from the comic-strip crudity of the first novel to the seriousness of the last, from which "comedy [is] largely absent" (4), in support of this reading of the sequence. And there is much to be said for this interpretation. Once he gets onto platform 9 3/4, the reader is drawn into Harry's adventures in the same way that Harry is drawn into the magical world: it is modelled for him, and for us, following the logic of portal fantasy outlined by Mendlesohn (*Rhetorics* Chapter 1).

Indeed, events across the sequence are generally, if not entirely, located from Harry's point of view: Karin E. Westman has persuasively argued that, in imitation of Austen, Rowling's sequence provides "*one character's* experience of the 'real' world, offering a 'portrait' of that individual mind and a record of its moral development" (146). The perspective of the early novel is that of the bewildered child focused on his own immediate interests and needs, and thus understandably incurious about, for example, the source of the food that magically appears on the Hogwarts dining table, let alone the financial considerations surrounding his own upbringing by the Dursleys. Rowling's elision, in the incident of the potions puzzle, of any description of the size and order of the bottles on which the riddle depends demonstrates this focalisation: the reader, although provided with the riddle, is therefore unable to solve the puzzle and must wait with Harry while Hermione does so. Thus, as elsewhere, the reader is aligned with Harry, rather than with the more brilliant Hermione. Relevant, too, is Harry's reflection as he taunts Dudley in the early pages of *Order of the Phoenix*: "He felt as if he were siphoning off his own frustration into his cousin, the only outlet he had" (Rowling, 20). This sentence makes explicit what the ridicule of the opening chapters of *Philosopher's Stone* has in fact been doing. It provides a psychological "outlet" for the reader's sympathies, siphoning off any resistance to Harry himself into rejection of his loutish family, even as they provide us with a vision of the Dursleys as Harry sees them—embodying all the frustration with his surroundings that a young child might feel.

I want, nonetheless, to argue for the importance of the narrative's construction of an implied reader, not only of Harry's own feelings, in accounting for the sequence's narrative projection of emotion. While the sophistication of the above quotation from *Order of the Phoenix* clearly reflects Harry's own maturing understanding of his psychological relationships to those around him, it also demonstrates a shift in the linguistic patterns of the sequence with which Harry's own thoughts and utterances do not usually cohere. Harry is not highly articulate at any stage of the sequence; his comments are banal and his ideas straightforward to the point of naïveté. It is of *Order of the Phoenix* that A.S. Byatt has remarked "Harry's first date with a female wizard is unbelievably limp." I disagree not with her judgement of the date as limp but with the statement that it is unbelievable. Harry would not be the first teenager to regress to "an eight-year-old's conversational maneuvers" (Byatt) in a socially stressful situation, and he is not highly articulate at any stage of the sequence, achieving rhetorical force only briefly, and belatedly, on two occasions in *Deathly Hallows*. Rowling's representation of Harry in the later novels is a portrait of largely unreflective adolescence that develops from the unreflective childhood of the earlier ones. The language of some of the narration in *Order of the Phoenix*, and still more the epigraphs to *Deathly Hallows*, suggests an intellectual sophistication and vocabulary beyond anything we see of Harry.[10]

A noteworthy example is this sentence from *Order of the Phoenix* describing Harry's fear of discovering news of the return of Voldemort: "Every day this summer had been the same: the tension, the expectation, the temporary relief, and the mounting tension again [. . .] and always, growing more insistent all the time, the question of *why* nothing had happened yet" (Rowling, 9–10). Here the appeal to the reader's understanding is expressed through the repeated deictic "the" that assumes a shared awareness of both what Harry's tension feels like and why it exists. Unlike the opening of *Philosopher's Stone*, we are projected directly into Harry's consciousness, a move characteristic of the later novels. At the same time, the rhythms of the first half of the sentence place the tension as indeed familiar in the adolescent experience—not the familiarity of anxious listening to the news, in which Harry is as usual unusual, but the familiarity of more or less constant sexual arousal. Despite our access to Harry's thoughts, however, there is no indication that he is aware of sexual feeling at this moment, as would be expected if the narration were simply adopting his perception. This is, again, a far more subtle appeal to reader empathy than the impersonal recounting of fact that dominates the early pages of *Philosopher's Stone*. Although the point of view is Harry's, the narrator of *Order of the Phoenix* is quite clearly distinguished from Harry, more sophisticated and more observant, and it is that narrator who puts Harry's feelings into sexualised language.

That the language of *Philosopher's Stone*, especially in the opening pages, seems simple to the point of banality suggests that Manlove's diagnosis of the novels as developing in direct correlation with Harry himself, though insightful, is not quite adequate. The evolving vision he describes seems consistent within each novel even where the narrative is not focalised through

Harry. The early sentences of *Philosopher's Stone* describe a day when Harry is only fifteen months old, and their structure suggests neither the perception of an infant nor quite that of an eleven-year-old:

> Mr and Mrs Dursley, of number four, Privet Drive, were proud to say that they were perfectly normal, thank you very much. They were the last people you'd expect to be involved in anything strange or mysterious, because they just didn't hold with such nonsense.
>
> Mr Dursley was the director of a firm called Grunnings, which made drills. He was a big, beefy man with hardly any neck, although he did have a very large moustache. Mrs Dursley was thin and blonde and had nearly twice the usual amount of neck.
>
> (Rowling, 7)

This is the cosy, slightly condescending voice of an adult reading to a child. The first eight sentences of the novel all begin with a noun or pronoun referring directly to one or both of the Dursleys, ensuring a readily accessible continuity of meaning appropriate to a quite young child, and the punctuation consists exclusively of full stops and commas. The vocabulary at this stage is deceptively simple. Bloom points out that in Rowling's first book

> Her prose style, heavy on cliché, makes no demands of her readers. In an arbitrarily chosen single page—page 4—of the [Scholastic edition of the] first Harry Potter book, I count no fewer than seven clichés, all of the 'stretch his legs' variety.

What Bloom does not observe is that many of Rowling's clichés occur in association with characters we are encouraged to see as conventional-minded. It is Uncle Vernon, for instance, who "thought he'd stretch his legs" at lunch-time (Rowling, *Philosopher's* 10), an image as appropriate to his stereotypically suburban vision of the world as the ventriloquism of the opening sentence's "thank you very much" (7).

As with the fairy-tale opening of the sequence, then, Rowling is drawing in readers whom this language posits as quite young. Rowling's strategy, including frequent adverbs and specific *inquit* tags, seems to be in line with what John Stephens calls "a restriction on reader inferencing" (*Language* 34), although it could also be described as providing an interpretive pathway to development of the imagination. Indeed, Rowling's portrait of the giant Grawp, in *Order of the Phoenix*, suggests a belief in the capacity of all children to learn and a commitment to helping them do so. Although even the determinedly unprejudiced and sympathetic Hermione is convinced that Hagrid's project of civilising his half-brother and teaching him to speak is an impossible one, Grawp does eventually demonstrate his capacity to recognise other people and his connection with his brother, through inarticulate but effective speech. The apparently ineducable child can be brought to language as well as to understanding.

It is noteworthy that Bloomsbury's first paperback edition of the second novel included fan letters from children as young as seven who had read *Philosopher's Stone*, rather than from eleven-year-olds. *Philosopher's Stone*, although successful with readers ranging widely in age as well as in personality, seems to have drawn a youthful audience. That Rowling gradually complicates the language as well as the emotional and socio-political vision of the sequence points to an interest both in retaining her original readership as they age and in educating those readers. A late sentence from *Philosopher's Stone*, though still accessible, is very differently structured from the opening ones:

> Neville's toad was found lurking in a corner of the toilets; notes were handed out to all students, warning them not to use magic over the holidays ("I always hope they'll forget to give us these," said Fred Weasley sadly); Hagrid was there to take them down to the fleet of boats that sailed across the lake; they were boarding the Hogwarts Express; talking and laughing as the country-side became greener and tidier; eating Bertie Bott's Every-Flavour Beans as they sped past Muggle towns; pulling off their wizard robes and putting on jackets and coats; pulling into platform nine and three-quarters at King's Cross Station.
>
> (Rowling, 330)

The list of details joined by semicolons evokes the rapidity with which the day of departure passes even as it moves from observation to activity and from the contrast between the children "pulling off their wizard robes" and the train "pulling into platform nine and three-quarters," in an unstated shift of subject far removed from the careful enunciation of the novel's opening sentences.

The sentences immediately following the first eight, which include a focus on Harry Potter and his parents, are grammatically slightly more complex than the first. The child reader is thus implicitly invited to associate sympathetic characters with sophisticated sentence structure, encouraging development of reading skills and preparing for the comparative complexity of that late sentence. In evoking the possibility of an alternative vision to that of the "perfectly normal," moreover, the narrator opposes the personified reader to the Dursleys: "They were the last people *you'd* expect to be involved in anything strange or mysterious" (Rowling, *Philosopher's* 7; my emphasis). Rowling's narration manipulates readers not only to induce sympathy for Harry but to develop a positive attitude to the unusual and the imaginative.

The reader of *The Wee Free Men* is invited to scrutinise Tiffany with the same sharpness of eye and freshness of vision with which she observes her world and herself: "Sometimes Tiffany feels she is nothing more than a way of moving boots around" (Pratchett, *Wee* 14). Although Pratchett often recalls cliché, he rarely writes it directly. Even though his sentences in his children's fiction tend to be grammatically simple, the narrational activity compels a re-evaluation of cliché as of fairy-tale convention.

> "Good. Now . . . if you trust in yourself . . ."
> "Yes?"
> ". . . and believe in your dreams . . ."
> "Yes?"
> ". . . and follow your star . . ." Miss Tick went on.
> "Yes?"
> ". . . you'll still get beaten by people who spent their time working hard and learning things and weren't so lazy. Goodbye."
>
> (51)

Miss Tick's conclusion to her statement, delivered as a nineteen-word unpunctuated rush that contrasts abruptly with the hypnotic parallel rhythms of the preceding conjunctive phrases, shocks the reader and Tiffany out of the comfort of fairy-tale expectations of the world as well as of the conventional language through which such expectations are expressed. It is thus clear from very early in the novel, and the sequence, that the reader is expected to engage as critically as Tiffany with the givens of reading as well as of living. Pratchett's main message to his readers is both accessible and visible from the start. The world of the Tiffany Aching sequence gradually expands from an isolation in *The Wee Free Men* that reflects Tiffany's "picture of the world as a landscape with [her] in the middle of it" (276), as the Queen says, to the dynamics of village life and eventually to the feudal structure of a castle and the complexity of a city. The obstacles and enemies she faces also develop in moral and psychological complexity. Nevertheless, Pratchett engages the critical reader from the beginning of the sequence with a level of sophistication that constantly resists the safety of convention. As Tiffany is challenged repeatedly to defend and rethink her own values, we as readers are never allowed the luxury of Roland's unreflective "of course."

By contrast, the reader of *Philosopher's Stone* is more subtly engaged in an apparently simplistic narration that moves gradually from within cliché—Uncle Vernon's lack of neck, suggesting a simian brainlessness, implicitly compensated for by Aunt Petunia's useful excess of it—to a gentle critique of the conventional vision that never moves entirely beyond that vision. Within the Harry Potter sequence, the moral crudity of Harry's Cinderella situation and of most of the early action gives way slowly to a more complex understanding of human behaviour at both the social and the individual levels. We shall see in Chapter 2 the extent to which this education focuses on literary expectation itself and on critique of the idea of the hero postulated especially within conventional heroic fantasy, with which the later volumes, with their "Chosen One" framework, appear to engage. *Philosopher's Stone* leaves the fairy tale intact, but the reader of the sequence as a whole is invited to develop a more complex understanding of conventional structures and their associated morality.

CONCLUSION

Comparison of *The Wee Free Men* with *Harry Potter and the Philosopher's Stone* highlights the very different ways in which Pratchett and Rowling deploy fairy-tale plots, with implications for the agency of the protagonist and, ultimately, for the trajectory of development proposed within each sequence. Pratchett's debt to traditional fairy tale is precise and extensive. His protagonist quickly emerges as an unusually strong and capable child whose critical intelligence and sense of agency reflects that of traditional characters such as Kate Crackernuts. The reader posited by *The Wee Free Men* is one who admires and wishes to emulate Tiffany's independence and her analytical capacity. By contrast, Rowling's "Cinderella" narrative, focalised through the largely naïve Harry, invites a range of responses for her initially passive hero, potentially broadening her readership; the implied reader of *Philosopher's Stone* is the consumer of fairy tale who identifies with the ordinary boy discovered to be special. Moreover, Tiffany's situation as proto-adult in a working world compels our attention to the extent to which Harry is the schooled child, framed throughout by the expectations of those around him.

Consideration of Rowling's superficially uncritical deployment of the "Cinderella" plot to frame Harry's childhood highlights Pratchett's subversion of the fairy tale he himself deploys. Tiffany's entire experience in *The Wee Free Men* can be described as a fairy tale, but within it she is not only an active protagonist but a literary critic who is suspicious of fairy-tale stereotypes and at one point actually seeks to take control of the narrative: perceiving the Queen's use of the dream-spinning dromes, she encourages the drome to construct a dream with a pre-existing plot, essentially becoming for the moment the writer rather than the consumer or even the agent of fairy tale. Pratchett encourages his implied reader both to enjoy stories and to be wary of the conventional vision they frequently promote. We are encouraged to remember that "[t]he stories *weren't real*. But Mrs Snapperly had died because of stories" (Pratchett, *Wee* 63).

Comparison with Tiffany's, and Pratchett's, metatextual critique of the fairy tale foregrounds Rowling's deployment of the clichés and conventions of the children's story, but also highlights the extent to which that language is modified. Although Rowling could have sustained her sequence entirely in terms of the schoolchild, as the repetitive structures of the first three novels suggested, shifts in language as well as developments in the depiction of Harry's society and his understanding of it underline the fact that Rowling's model is evolutionary. While Tiffany does learn from the situations she confronts across the sequence, as we shall see more fully in Chapter 4, she is already mature in her readiness to look beyond the surface to what is really there and to critique the conventions Roland takes for granted. Pratchett's fiction is educative, but from the start that education is occurring at a sophisticated level; in the developmental universe of the Tiffany Aching sequence, autonomy and analytic capacity precede maturity of social engagement. Rowling's first novel posits a younger and more unreflective reader, but the narrative language as well as the increasing complexity of Harry's experience promotes the reader's skills in reading and in analysis through nuanced representation of the social world itself.

Both writers therefore are strategic in their engagement of readers, but their strategies take very different form. Rowling appeals to a wide range of possible readers and attracts them with the appeal of a fairy-tale situation; only gradually, almost imperceptibly, do changes in Harry's behaviour and in the narrative language imply and persuade to growth. Where *The Wee Free Men* demands that its readers recognise the force of Tiffany's critique of fairy tales even as they take pleasure in her story itself, *Philosopher's Stone* allows a more naïve response that may prepare for a more subtly educative reading experience. *Philosopher's Stone* does not appear to question Harry's fairy-tale situation, but subsequent novels in the sequence develop a sustained critique of heroic fantasy conventions, as we shall see in the following chapter—a critique that emerges from a consistent moral vision to which the reader only gains full access in the final stages of the sequence. Pratchett and Rowling depict child agency in their characters very differently, but both develop a nuanced and complex picture of development and maturity, and both display a profound literary sophistication.

NOTES

1. Lurie appears here to be using "Cinderlad" as the male form of "Cinderella," since she goes on to say that he is "a poor, lonely orphan, despised and abused" (114). The Norwegian folktale hero Espen Cinderlad is a despised child who sits in the ashes, but has a father as well as brothers in at least one of the tales about him.
2. Ximena Gallardo-C. and C. Jason Smith have pointed to the relationship of Harry's story to the Grimms' version of "Cinderella," "Aschenputtel," highlighting such elements as "A bird in Aschenputtel's tree [that] warns of deceit just as Harry's scar warns of the proximity of Voldemort" (195). As they note, however, " 'Aschenputtel' is one of few fairy tales that features a protagonist who actually casts spells herself" (195): although this nicely points to Harry's future activities, it downplays the extent to which, as I indicate, he is passive in the "Cinderella" chapters prior to his arrival at Hogwarts. Uncle Vernon's manoeuvrings ensure that the reader's attention focuses on Hagrid's arrival in the role of fairy godmother.
3. Even the sheep farm in which Tiffany grows up, which provides the context for her grandmother's shepherding code—a code central to Tiffany's system of

values—may recall the sheep's head placed on Kate Crackernuts's naïve but beautiful sister at the start of that story.

4. In the fairy tale this is a somewhat puzzling injunction, as those whom Childe Rowland meets and accosts are quite friendly and even helpful.

5. Tiffany's comments suggest that her book is similar to Andrew Lang's 1889 *Blue Fairy Book*; Lieberman observes that in this influential collection "Beautiful girls [. . .] are chosen for reward" (385).

6. Elisabeth Rose Gruner has argued that "Tiffany's critical engagement with story is central to her education in all [the first] three novels" (228); although I would agree broadly with this statement, it does not sufficiently acknowledge the extent to which she begins the sequence as a conscious critic of fairy tale.

7. Amusingly, as Gruner has observed, Tiffany anticipates attending just such a school when she learns of the "school for witches": "There would be lessons in broomstick riding and how to sharpen your hat to a point, and magical meals, and lots of new friends" (Pratchett, *Wee* 59). It is important to Pratchett's idea of witchcraft, and wisdom, that the witches' school turns out to be a school without walls. Like many a proud self-made man, Tiffany becomes a graduate of the university of life.

8. See for example the punishment of Beauty's sisters in Beaumont's popular "Beauty and the Beast" (136).

9. Gruner has remarked that Tiffany, like Harry, is eleven here and that eleven is the customary age for moving to secondary education in England (225).

10. Harry is not, after all, the kind of child who, like Tiffany, reads the dictionary from beginning to end and meditates on words like "susurrus"; while Rowling clearly takes pleasure in providing etymologically appropriate names for her characters and constructing spells from basic Latin, Harry does not notice the fact that Lupin's name reflects his wolfish nature, and does not ponder the likely meaning of the unknown spell "*Sectumsempra*" (*Half-Blood* 419).

2 The Case of Heroic Fantasy

As indicated in the Introduction, fantasy literature in general has frequently been stigmatised as escapist—just by definition, because its operation is displaced to an imaginary setting or involves events impossible in the mundane. It is heroic fantasy, however, that has received the most opprobrium; indeed, for many non-readers of fantasy, the heroic fantasy, especially the heroic quest-fantasy, has become synonymous with fantasy itself. Casey Fredericks's 1982 chapter "In Defense of Heroic Fantasy" pointed out the already enormously various and frequently sophisticated ways in which American writers such as Poul Anderson had approached the heroic. The genre is indeed protean and has developed a major presence in film and television; in the following discussion I will refer briefly to the films of the Harry Potter novels because the later ones, especially, seem to take an approach to the genre significantly at variance with Rowling's. While contemporary film has recently revived and exploited the popular desire for the heroic figure as Herculean in strength and physical skill (*John Carter*; 2012), even a superhero who must deal with non-human powers and foes (*Man of Steel*; 2013), in written fantasy the heroic has taken a variety of other forms. In much heroic fantasy fiction the "hero" begins as a youth, even a child, who must discover his identity and his powers as a hero, whether these be extraordinary (Frank Herbert's Paul Atreides), or a derivative of destiny (David Eddings's Garion), or simply a set of inherited kingly skills (Tad Williams's Simon).

The quasi-*Bildungsroman* style of heroic fantasy has become so dominant in the popular imagination that it has provoked satiric responses. Diana Wynne Jones's *Tough Guide to Fantasyland* (1996) is a superb example of these. Jones casts the stereotypical fantasy novel, so often presented as a trilogy, as a set of tour brochures, and proceeds to provide an alphabetical encyclopaedia-style listing of the various elements that are inevitably to be found in these "tours." Jones's analysis highlights not only the stereotypical central characters of such stories, such as the Talented Girl or the sagacious Mentor, but also the vividly unrealistic conventions in which Fantasyland abounds. Thus she points to stereotypic groups such as what she terms the Anglo-Saxon Cossacks, who live in the saddle but never develop bandy legs, or the characteristic emptiness of Fantasyland ecologies, with their lack of most insects and of visible meat animals—apart, that is, from horses. Jones's approach in the *Tough Guide* is intriguingly reflected in her novels of the 1990s, as we shall see.

That heroic fantasy has become so conventionalised as to be a target for satire, of course, points to the considerable appeal of its basic operation. Joseph Campbell's famous 1949 analysis of myth in *The Hero with a Thousand Faces*—itself the source for such well-known fantasies as the first *Star Wars* film (1977)—points to the significance of this narrative in the human imagination. In particular, the novel of growth, the story of the apparently ordinary or neglected child acquiring a sense of identity and confidence in his or her abilities, has a powerful psychological appeal. An early stage of this fantasy can be seen in the "Cinderella" narrative that, as I have demonstrated in Chapter 1, underlies the opening of the Harry Potter sequence. In its codified form, however, the heroic quest-fantasy can easily become the kind of consolatory escapism of which its critics accuse the genre. The stereotypical figures and groups identified by Jones become cliché, while the journey itself takes a predictable form that mirrors the psychological short cuts it provides to the reader. The slaying of a dragon can be shorthand for overcoming fear, for instance, but its representation of internal psychological struggles through physical symbols encourages a focus on the symbols, and the physicality of the battles, rather than on the mental and moral struggle. C.S. Lewis noted of the original, fourth-century *Psychomachia* of Prudentius that the allegories do not fit neatly when we see personified Mercy or Humility destroying their foes and triumphing in their victory (69). The quest-struggle, when it becomes a focus of attention in itself, can similarly generate contradictory effects.

The risk of writing heroic fantasy—that it will collapse into conventions and appeal to the desire to escape rather than providing a psychological path to growth—has not been overlooked by recent writers of fantasy. A striking attempt to overcome and indeed depict this risk is Michael Ende's children's fantasy *The Neverending Story* (1979), whose protagonist gradually learns that his own imagination is needed to sustain a world, but who then disappears into that world and almost loses his own identity completely in the enchantment of creating fictions. It is telling that the original film of the novel elided this point completely, first downplaying the importance of the creative role of the protagonist, Bastian, in sustaining Fantasia (Fantastica in the English translation of the novel) and finally depicting him as returning from Fantasia to the ordinary world and enlisting his heroic Fantasian friends to help him beat up the bullies from whom he had fled.[1] Something similar, though not identical, occurs with the later films of J.K. Rowling's Harry Potter sequence, for Rowling too is both evoking and contesting the paradigm of heroic fantasy. In this chapter I demonstrate how she engages with heroic fantasy, which she cleverly merges with the conventions of the school story, in ways that simultaneously allow her readers to enjoy the pleasures of the form and encourage them to move beyond it. Jones, on the other hand, evokes elements of the heroic fantasy and quest fantasy in a wide range of her novels in ways that variously but consistently reject many aspects of its traditional operation. We shall see how this rejection emerges in her novels from the Dalemark quartet (1975–93) and in *Hexwood* (1993) as well as in her apparently parodic treatment of the genre in *The Dark Lord of Derk-holm* (1998), a companion-piece to *The Tough Guide to Fantasyland*.

HARRY THE HERO

Although early reviewers, and young readers, did not seem aware of this, the dominant genre structuring the early Harry Potter novels was that of the school story. There has since been considerable discussion of the extent to which the Harry Potter books conform to the model of the school story as established in Thomas Hughes's *Tom Brown's School Days* (1857) and elaborated in a range of subsequent narratives, particularly by David Steege and Karen Manners Smith. There is no doubt that the first three novels of the sequence in particular can be located very thoroughly within the school story tradition. In the most common versions of the school story, the hero makes friends with the first people he meets and turns out to be a sporting star, the nasty rival is foiled, the godlike Headmaster recognises the hero's true worth and rewards it, the hero and his House eventually win the day.[2] All these elements and more are provided in the early novels of the Harry Potter sequence, shaping the expectations even of a young reader unfamiliar with the boarding school story about how action will unfold and how characters will behave not only in *Harry Potter and the Philosopher's Stone* (1997) but in the subsequent novels. Characterisation, as well as much of the action of *Philosopher's Stone* especially, seems most dependent on the school story genre: in addition to the hero and his accomplice, we encounter the swot (Hermione), the bumbling fat boy (Neville), the tough-but-fair teacher (McGonagall), and the malicious housemaster from another house (Snape), as well as the benevolent and omniscient headmaster (Dumbledore).

What has been less discussed is the ways in which the novels deviate from and complicate this pattern. Initially these deviations appeared almost as decoration; as I have remarked elsewhere, "the early novels follow the school story model, though with added magic" (Webb, "Pottered"). In both *Harry Potter and the Philosopher's Stone* and *Harry Potter and the Chamber of Secrets* (1998), Harry's adventures are thoroughly contained within the school setting and the villains are, at least on one level, members of the school: the stammering teacher of Defence Against the Dark Arts, Professor Quirrell, and the handsome senior boy, Tom Riddle. The unlikeliness of these figures as villains—the apparently innocuous Quirrell and the apparently admirable Riddle—is appropriate to the operation of the early novels as detective stories, a recognisable sub-class of the traditional school story. Even Harry's descent into the bowels of the school in *Chamber of Secrets* has its antecedents: see for example Hylton Cleaver's *The Forbidden Study* (1961)—admittedly not a conventional school story—in which an adventurous schoolboy breaches a school taboo and is led into the darkness beneath the school by mysterious denizens, or Elsie J. Oxenham's *The Girls of the Abbey School* (1921), whose characters discover a lost bell beneath the abbey adjacent to their temporary school. And, as we saw in Chapter 1, the bravery and skill of the central characters in these situations of magical peril are contained within the school story framework, as their activities at the climax of both novels are awarded House points. "[D]aring, nerve, and chivalry" (Rowling, *Philosopher's* 130), the qualities that distinguish Gryffindors, characterise the heroes of the school story as readily as they do those of heroic fantasy.

What is less usual in the school story is the magical element in both the adventures and their villains. Quirrell has been possessed by a fragment of the demonic Lord Voldemort, while the ghostly Tom Riddle turns out to be a memory of Voldemort's younger self—or, as we later learn, his earliest Horcrux. Within these two novels, however, the magical on the whole seems associated with the school itself: Harry's entry into the magical world, a transition common in fantasy fiction, takes the form of admission and travel to Hogwarts. Chris Columbus's films of both novels (2001–02), which were widely loved, captured the extent to which Harry's experiences feel magical in large part because of his pleasure in finding himself in a new environment. Harry's escape from the Dursleys and his relocation in the warmth, comfort, and community of Gryffindor Tower and the Hogwarts dining hall is psychologically gratifying; the magic of these spaces at first merely underscores their emotional effect on him.

Certain elements do mark these novels not only as fantasy but as heroic fantasy, most significantly the identification of Lord Voldemort as a possibly superhuman force of evil and the scar that marks Harry as the Boy Who Lived. Frequent references to dragon's eggs and the deaths of unicorns underscore the fantasy setting, but more importantly the adventures at the climax of *Philosopher's Stone*—the outwitting of a magical monster, the struggle with sentient plants, even the magical chess game[3]—provide links with the heroic fantasy tradition. Harry's and Ron's encounter with Aragog and his descendants in *Chamber of Secrets*, meanwhile, recalls Bilbo's engagement with the spiders of Mirkwood and Sam's with Shelob in Tolkien's *The Hobbit* (1937) and *The Two Towers* (1954) respectively, although it is noteworthy that Harry and Ron escape by luck rather than the skill displayed by Tolkien's characters.

In subsequent novels the school story model begins to fray, as certain repetitions that had satisfied the demands of younger readers start to disappear and magical elements come to the fore. Rowling gradually sets aside or transforms some of the elements that had consistently appeared within the first novels, and which had been part of what engaged her young readers, such as the yearly problem of Hagrid's dangerous pets or the Quidditch matches and the House Cup. Threats ostensibly come from beyond the school walls, even where the actual agent is located within them; the narrative's focus therefore inevitably grows wider, as Harry and his friends peruse newspapers, at least intermittently, and worry about the threat of Lord Voldemort. *Harry Potter and the Prisoner of Azkaban* (1999) introduces a complexity not visible in the early novels, as the unquestionably admirable Professor Lupin reveals a dark side he cannot always control. This development is extended in *Harry Potter and the Goblet of Fire* (2000), where the apparently worthy, if disturbingly ruthless, Professor Moody is revealed to be the Death Eater Barty Crouch, Junior, disguised by the Polyjuice Potion. Although Colin Manlove has pointed out that in this guise "evil here perfectly simulates a good character" (*Order* 125), several of the actions that have most forcefully located the false Moody as "a good character"—notably his kindness to Neville after demonstrating the curse that killed Neville's parents (Rowling, *Goblet* 240)—are subsequently revealed to be manoeuvres designed to further Harry's path through the Triwizard Tournament and therefore to the graveyard where Voldemort awaits.[4] In the process, Barty Crouch leads the reader too out of the school story and into the heroic fantasy.

Much of *Goblet of Fire* appeals to a young reader's desire for both the heroic and the fantastic while retaining the school story framework. The excitement and novelty of the Quidditch World Cup, in which the pleasure of live presence and the power of remote viewing are magically reconciled by the use of Omnioculars, prepares for the more drawn-out but still dramatic experience of the Triwizard Tournament, in which Harry moves from spectator to participant and thereby unwillingly takes on the role of hero. The challenges Harry faces in the Tournament itself are potentially highly dramatic; Mike Newell's 2005 film of the novel capitalised on this, turning Harry's straightforward and laudably rapid outmanoeuvring of a dragon in the first task to a lengthy and hair-raising pursuit among the battlements of the school. Yet its operation within the school initially places his experience as a game. Ron's comment after the first task that "whoever put your name in that Goblet—I—I reckon they're trying to do you in!" (Rowling, *Goblet* 393) brings about his reconciliation with Harry, but Harry's brilliant performance in the task, outstripping those of the older school champions, reassures the reader that any such plan must be doomed to failure. It is only afterward that we may perceive how the episode of the Quidditch World Cup, with its aftermath of terror created by Death Eaters, prefigures the eventual trajectory of the novel, in which victory in the Triwizard Tournament is followed by a more serious reunion of Death Eaters as they are summoned by the resurrected Voldemort.

The turning point of the sequence comes at the end of the Tournament, when Harry and Cedric take the Triwizard Cup together and are transported to the graveyard. The almost immediate death of Cedric at Voldemort's cold command *"Kill the spare"* (691) radically transforms what would traditionally have been a climactic as well as a triumphant moment. The dialogue between Harry and Cedric in the centre of the maze concerning who should take the Cup and thereby claim victory has perfectly enacted the values of good sportsmanship extolled in the school story. Its appearance at the culmination of the Triwizard Tournament would traditionally be followed—generally briefly—by the novel's conclusion. Instead we enter a different literary space: the space of heroic fantasy. The duel in the graveyard situates the last part of *Goblet of Fire* firmly within conventions of the heroic. Harry is first trapped and forced to watch his own blood being used to resurrect his enemy, then taunted by his foe, now ringed by minions. Voldemort's decision to defer Harry's death by defeating him in battle rather than simply to remove him as he has Cedric, however plausibly presented, is a choice stereotypical of bad guys in adventure stories generally.[5] Further, Rowling's description of the duel recalls Katherine Kurtz's depiction of the climactic duel in the first of her popular sword-and-sorcery Deryni novels, *Deryni Rising* (1970): in both novels, the duelling ground is protected by a magic halo and the current status of the battle can be measured by the progression of a magical interface toward one or other of the duellists.

The Deryni battle concludes with the hero—who at barely fourteen is just a few months younger than Harry—managing to defeat his powerful and experienced challenger and take his rightful place on the throne. Rowling, however, does not end her novel with even the temporary triumph Kurtz allows King Kelson in the first book of her series. Instead Harry returns in great distress to the grounds of Hogwarts with the dead body of Cedric, and is then abducted by the false Moody. As in *Prisoner of Azkaban*, where the unmasking of Peter Pettigrew was followed first by a flight from a werewolf and escape from Dementors and then by the confrontation with disbelief that resulted in Harry's journey back in time to save Buckbeak and Sirius, victory in the Tournament is followed first by what seems a climactic battle and then by a subtler and even more sinister threat. Voldemort's evil nature and intentions are never in doubt; the false Moody has posed as a protector. Moreover, as in *Prisoner of Azkaban* the truth about the reality of evil—here, the fact of Voldemort's return—is denied by the spokesman for the wizarding world, the Minister for Magic, suggesting a problem not readily amenable to heroic confrontation that will indeed become central to *Harry Potter and the Order of the Phoenix*. Although a lighter note is introduced by Hermione's capture of Rita Skeeter and by Harry's handing over his Tournament winnings to Fred and George Weasley, both acts that might seem at home within the school story, on the whole the last hundred pages of *Goblet of Fire* project the reader out of these conventions and into what now seems a complex but unmistakable heroic fantasy. The evil of Lord Voldemort—a flat character—ensures that, once resurrected, he will attempt once again to conquer the wizarding world; Harry, who has revalidated his status as the Boy Who Lived, will inevitably be called on to act as its champion.

On one level the final three books of the sequence can be described as enacting Harry's preparation to be a hero, and they culminate in a battle at Hogwarts itself in which he confronts and defeats Lord Voldemort. In plot terms, that is, the sequence operates as heroic fantasy. It provides the reader with the stereotypical situation of Harry as orphaned by an evil force; as growing up outside the walls, as it were, of his true kingdom; as learning the identity of his foe and seeing that foe rise again to threaten his world; and finally as devoting his life to the defeat of evil and achieving that defeat. Along the way Harry is mentored by Dumbledore—who fits Jones's tongue-in-cheek account of the Mentor all too well[6]—and seeks out magical objects. Above all, his position as hero is affirmed by his identification as the Chosen One, whose fate is inextricably bound to that of his enemy by prophecy; I shall discuss the implications of Rowling's treatment of prophecy and of choice in Chapter 5.

Yet Rowling does not choose simply to satisfy the demands of the heroic fantasy situation she has constructed. Like Harry himself, the reader of *Order of the Phoenix* (2003) will expect prompt and spectacular action. But that expectation is frustrated across most of its eight hundred pages. Manlove has described *Goblet of Fire* as "a long, lazy book" (*Order* 160), but Rowling's readers will not experience it that way if they are reading sympathetically to Harry. For much of *Goblet of Fire*, Harry is dreading the approach of tasks he believes he cannot perform—fighting with a dragon, working out the clue of the egg, going underwater, asking a girl to the Yule Ball. His tendency to procrastination influences the mood of the book; we are given the sense that time is moving more rapidly than Harry, at least, might wish. By contrast, the mood of *Order of the Phoenix* is impatience. From the start Harry is waiting for something to happen. Unlike most heroes of the *Bildungsroman*-type fantasy, he is aware not only of his situation but of his importance within it, and he expects the drama and respect appropriate to that situation.

The later novels of the Harry Potter sequence in fact rebuke both Harry's and the reader's desire for heroic fantasy. One of the delights of the Harry Potter sequence has been that it is full of action and energy, even though the action may be directly school-related, but that energy is gradually drained away in the last part of the sequence—just where we might expect that it would be heightened by its movement into heroic fantasy. In *Order of the Phoenix* Harry is frustrated for hundreds of pages by his exclusion from the activities of the Order, and the action remains slow; Harry does not even reach Hogwarts, his and the reader's magical refuge in the preceding novels, for more than two hundred pages. The suppression and indeed torture he suffers from Dolores Umbridge mirrors his larger experience as an adolescent who believes he is ready to act as an adult—but who has a narrow understanding of what that action means. It could be argued that Harry's frustration for so much of *Order of the Phoenix* recapitulates the reader's sense of what it is to be a vicarious enjoyer of heroic fantasy. The reader is normally in the situation of reading about people doing heroic things, which is pleasurable as long as the reader can be satisfied with investing energy in the text, but may be frustrating to a reader who starts to desire that excitement in his or her own life, a common adolescent phenomenon.[7]

When Harry does finally act in heroic style, at the climax of the novel, the consequences are disastrous. As Hermione has warned him, he has "a *saving-people thing*" (Rowling, *Order* 806) of which Voldemort has become aware; the phrase itself denigrates the heroic value of chivalry Harry might have been proud to claim. The very qualities that have made Harry a hero in the early novels—his determination to brave danger and his willingness to put himself at risk for others—are here easily exploited by Voldemort. Thus Harry's reckless attempt to save his godfather Sirius Black results more or less directly in the death of Sirius, who has to go to Harry's own aid in the Department of Mysteries and is killed in battle there. Although Dumbledore, who appears to have been avoiding Harry across the novel, finally breaks his silence and explains to Harry the nature of the prophecy that Voldemort was seeking—a prophecy that appears to bind Harry and Voldemort together—Harry is overwhelmed by grief over Sirius: "More to stave off the moment when he would have to think of Sirius again, Harry asked [about the prophecy], without caring much about the answer" (927). Whatever the reader may feel at this confirmation of Harry's status of Chosen One, Harry himself feels only "a deep well of despair" (927) at his loss of Sirius. So, earlier, faced with the photograph of the original Order of the Phoenix, he felt not as though he had been given "a bit of a treat" (196) as Mad-Eye assumes, but depression at the doom most of its members had met shortly after: "He felt older than he had ever felt in his life and it seemed extraordinary to him that an hour ago he had been worried about a joke shop and who had got a prefect's badge" (200). That moment of recognition highlighted the extent to which Harry was outgrowing the school story; the novel's ending, with Harry's bleak misery, suggests the inadequacy of heroic fantasy to his experience.

As a result, *Harry Potter and the Half-Blood Prince* (2005) is comparatively sober in tone. Here too the expectation of high fantasy is thwarted, ironically because of the initial absence of conflict with the wizardly authorities. Harry is no longer at odds with the Ministry, which has been forced to admit that he was telling the truth about Voldemort's return; Dumbledore has returned as Headmaster of Hogwarts, freeing the students from Umbridge's oppression—but also from the need for secrecy that generated one of the few pleasurable activities of *Order of the Phoenix*, Harry's training of Dumbledore's Army. Instead Harry is explicitly given a version of the authority he craved in *Order of the Phoenix*. Although he was not made a prefect, he is now Quidditch captain for Gryffindor, which as Ron points out gives him equal status with prefects. The school story resumes, but at a point where its gratifications seem belated and childish; Harry even contemplates missing a Quidditch match in order to pursue his self-assigned mission of detection, a thought unimaginable in previous novels. It seems ironic that one of his major obsessions in the novel for the first time involves a distinctively school-related object, his second-hand Potions textbook.

Despite his failure in *Order of the Phoenix*, in *Half-Blood Prince* Harry is still seeking to engage in heroic activity at a different level from what his circumstances require. He is at last singled out by Dumbledore for special lessons and told that he will have tasks that will further his preparation as Chosen One, but these activities turn out to involve thinking and planning and talking, which are not Harry's strengths and not stereotypically important in heroic fantasy. First, Harry's "lessons" require inactivity: he has to watch and listen and think about the memories that Dumbledore has shown him about Voldemort's early life. His major assignment is not to go on quest or battle a dragon, but to obtain a true memory from his new Potions teacher, Professor Slughorn. This task involves diplomacy, never one of Harry's strengths and not typically required of the fantasy hero—although it may be performed by one of the hero's companions. The best Harry can do is to imitate the Tom Riddle of the occluded memory, an obvious stratagem that Slughorn detects and that makes him avoid Harry. Ignorant of how to proceed, and still seeking some form of action, Harry neglects his assignment and instead focuses on Draco Malfoy, who he is convinced is doing something dangerous and must be found out. His repeated attempts to track down Malfoy are attempts to be a hero in his own school life, trying despite his friends' warnings to take an initiative that Dumbledore has not sanctioned. Although he is in fact right about Malfoy, we eventually recognise that he is also wrong to be disobeying Dumbledore's commands, because the two are intimately connected. What Harry does not know is that Dumbledore is aware of Malfoy's activities and that they form part of his own larger plan.

Harry's situation in both the fifth and sixth books of the sequence is therefore that of a boy who wants to take personal heroic action but is frustrated from doing so; it is significant that one of the reasons Harry is repeatedly punished in *Order of the Phoenix* is that he is unwilling, or unable, to keep his mouth shut. Harry is trying to practise the heroic virtues in a situation where these are increasingly less possible, even impractical and dangerous. As Professor McGonagall points out with increasing irritation, they are not what is most needed at the time. Daring, nerve, and chivalry, although admirable, are not the qualities most important in negotiating most ordinary situations, nor even most situations involving the defeat of evil.

In *Half-Blood Prince*, Harry's desire for action is finally gratified by the journey to seek out a Horcrux of Voldemort, but he is throughout Dumbledore's accomplice, doing little himself, and on their return to Hogwarts he is immobilised and silenced during Dumbledore's confrontation with the treacherous Malfoy and the Death Eaters, just as he was on the arrival of the Hogwarts Express earlier in the novel. Despite his age, and the stage of the sequence, Harry is less active than ever before. Although he pursues and challenges Professor Snape, who has killed Dumbledore, Harry fails to kill Snape because, according to Snape, he has not put the effort he should into learning skills required of adult wizards: "Blocked again, and again, and again until you learn to keep your mouth shut and your mind closed, Potter!" (Rowling, *Half-Blood* 562). Heroes, of course, are expected to speak out against oppression—as Harry did to Umbridge. The final straw is Snape's revelation that he himself was the Half-Blood Prince, the source of the clever spells Harry has tried to use as weapons. Harry has unknowingly chosen as a model someone whom he despises and who at this point appears to be a traitor to everything Harry values.

It should not be surprising, therefore, that *Harry Potter and the Deathly Hallows* (2007) is depressing. Here it is Ron who enacts the reader's frustration that the story does not seem to be progressing, that the characters, and the reader with them, are just running and hiding. This is the reality of quest that most fantasies elide: the tedium of travelling for days and weeks and months is frequently evaded by its condensation to a page or even a paragraph. But Rowling refuses her readers and her characters such shortcuts. She insists on the difficulty that a well-fed boy like Ron would actually find in going short of food and living on stewed mushrooms—a fantasy staple—and on the stir-craziness induced by being confined to a tent. The dramatic slaughter of a faithful companion common in heroic fantasy is replaced, more realistically, by Ron's angry departure due to his impatience, misery, and jealousy, all feelings appropriate to his situation, especially as he is recovering from a serious injury. The psychological effects of this are generally ignored in fantasy fiction, where a wounded character, especially the hero or his companion, frequently experiences healing miraculously quickly due either to inborn defences or to the application of magic. At most the reader expects that he will look interestingly pale and perhaps be more silent than usual to conceal his pain. Ron's irritated complaints, and even his abandonment of the quest, are far more plausible in his circumstances. Again Rowling's focus is on the physical and emotional reality of experience rather than its glamorised or fantasised version.

Moreover, where Tolkien's Frodo went on a quest to destroy a single magical object of power, Rowling, apparently more conventionally, builds her quest around the attainment of magical objects, but makes its goal the destruction of those objects, the Horcruxes. For a brief period Harry dreams of acquiring more typical objects of power, the Deathly Hallows, but he eventually recognises that this is a false dream. Voldemort's evil is hubris, the belief that he can be master even over natural forces, over life and death. If Harry wielded objects that gave him corresponding power he would only be replacing Voldemort, not defeating him. As he recognises, Voldemort must instead be stripped of power. With this recognition Harry abandons the desire for heroic fantasy; it seems ironic that his decision is followed by such adventurous acts as robbing a bank and escaping on a dragon.

Although Harry and his companions have left school to take up the traditional heroic quest, therefore, the reader is largely disappointed of a typically heroic adventure. The last stages of the novel, including the foray into Gringotts and the battle of Hogwarts, seem intended perfunctorily to placate a desire largely thwarted by the novel as a whole. In *Deathly Hallows* the heroic activity is literally happening elsewhere. Ironically, it is happening back at Hogwarts, where Neville Longbottom leads Dumbledore's Army in resistance to the Death Eaters now running the school, and the students defy torture to assist each other. When Rowling turns her back most fully on the school story she appears after all to be turning her back at least in part on heroic fantasy as well. It is therefore appropriate that in the final battle the passage that most reads like something out of a heroic fantasy describes not Harry but Neville:

> In one swift, fluid motion, Neville broke free of the Body-Bind Curse upon him; the flaming hat fell off him and he drew from its depths something silver, with a glittering, rubied handle—
>
> The slash of the silver blade could not be heard over the roar of the oncoming crowd or the sounds of the clashing giants or of the stampeding centaurs, and yet it seemed to draw every eye. With a single stroke Neville sliced off the great snake's head, which spun high into the air, gleaming in the light flooding from the entrance hall
>
> (Rowling, *Deathly* 587).

That phrase "in one swift, fluid motion" is almost as clichéd as anything Jones satirises in *The Tough Guide to Fantasyland*. This is the traditionally heroic moment, when the hero flings aside the curse and destroys the monster—a much more glamorous version of the event than Harry's removal of the Cloak and emergence to battle with Voldemort—but it is not Harry's, and it is narratively subordinate to Harry's rather different struggle.

Rowling here appears to be playing a double game with her reader. On the one hand she gratifies the expectation of a heroic fantasy conclusion that the early novels have created, as Harry and his companions flee imprisonment with the aid of the faithful Dobby, rob Gringotts amid magical showers of burning gold and escape on dragon-back, and enter Hogwarts via a magic portrait. On the other, and overwhelmingly, she depicts the reality of a tiring and apparently pointless quest, and shows her characters maturing to the point where even Ron can comment sardonically on Peeves's victory doggerel "Really gives a feeling for the scope and tragedy of the thing, doesn't it?" (Rowling, *Deathly* 598).

This is nowhere more evident than in Harry's own behaviour. The twelve-year-old Harry drew the sword of Gryffindor from the Sorting Hat and stabbed the diary in *Chamber of Secrets*, but in *Deathly Hallows* it is Ron who retrieves the sword—and Harry—from the frozen pool and stabs the locket, and it is Neville, the alternative Harry as we learned in *Order of the Phoenix*, who draws it again from the Sorting Hat and slays the snake. By contrast, Harry's heroic gesture is made alone, when he walks into the circle of Death Eaters in the Forbidden Forest, and as Voldemort sees, it is a gesture of weakness; when Harry returns from death to face Voldemort again it is logic, and a wand with a mind of its own, that destroys Voldemort. Harry enacts a very different kind of heroism.

By the end of the novel, Harry has bypassed the dangerous attraction of the Hallows and—contrary to the film version, *Harry Potter and the Deathly Hallows Part 2* (2011)—he tacitly refuses to engage in aggression against Voldemort. Significantly, Harry's final spell is a defensive spell, not an attacking one. In *Order of the Phoenix* the first spell he taught to Dumbledore's Army was the Disarming spell "*Expelliarmus*," learned from Snape three books earlier (Rowling, *Order* 433); the usefulness of this spell was questioned by Zacharias Smith, who was rebuked by Harry's response that "I've used it against [Voldemort . . .] It saved my life in June" (433). Harry's use of *Expelliarmus* was again challenged in the opening chapters of *Deathly Hallows*, when his refusal to attack the Imperiused Stan Shunpike enabled the Death Eaters to identify that he was "the real one" among six Polyjuiced impostors (Rowling, *Deathly* 55) and drew Lupin's reprimand: "the Death Eaters—frankly, most people!—would have expected you to attack back!" (64). "Most people" surely includes the readers of conventional heroic fantasy. But even at this stage Harry has learned that there are things more important than attacking back. Facing the Dark Lord at the end of the novel, therefore, he shouts "*Expelliarmus!*" (595), his characteristic and defensive spell, so that Voldemort is killed not by Harry but by his own rebounding curse.

As in Harry's submission to death at Voldemort's hands, there is an implicit echo here of a Christian message, in this case the pronouncement, "all they that take the sword shall perish with the sword" (Matthew 26:52).[8] The message here is both moral and literary. Harry destroys Voldemort not by killing him with sword or wand but by allowing his enemy to fulfil his own destiny. This is a commonplace idea of heroic fantasy, but rarely represented so literally as it is in the fall of the wand onto Voldemort. As hero, Harry has moved away from the active urgency of the teenager depicted in the previous two novels and demonstrates that he has finally learned the importance of patience and restraint. It is unsurprising that the epilogue to *Deathly Hallows* disappointed many readers, as it represents the ordinariness of Harry's subsequent life and supplies its final messages—tolerance for the previously despised Draco Malfoy and his son, respect for the courage of the previously loathed Severus Snape—in the prosaic terms of railway platforms and casual family conversations. The final novel of Rowling's sequence encourages her readers to abandon heroic fantasy as they have abandoned the school story, and to learn more complex and difficult challenges than can be defeated even by Gryffindor's sword.

Rowling's approach to her reader across the Harry Potter sequence remains educative. In *Philosopher's Stone*, as we saw in Chapter 1, she focused on engaging naïve readers and drawing them into sympathy with the plight of an ordinary yet extraordinary boy, gradually complicating her own narrative language as she did so. As the sequence develops, she moves away from the comforting repetition of her school-story-with-magic formula first to engage her reader with the drama of heroic fantasy, but subsequently to demonstrate the inadequacy of stereotypical heroic fantasy to the challenges of human experience. She exploits the reader's desire for the heroic, but depicts through Harry the difficulties resulting from facing complex problems with a simple active response. Harry learns finally that the way to defeat his enemy is with a patience and thoroughness foreign to the swashbuckling of the conventional hero; he not only surrenders his life to Voldemort, but surrenders the joy of battle and the satisfaction of slaying his enemy to what he recognises as a larger purpose. Rowling manipulates her growing readers' youthful desire for the school story and for the heroic fantasy to the end that they too may recognise the limitations of formulaic responses.

THE SUBVERSION OF QUEST FANTASY IN THE DALEMARK QUARTET AND *HEXWOOD*

Novelist Diana Wynne Jones experimented with a variety of forms over her long and very productive literary career. Her treatment of these forms has throughout been thoughtful and complex; like Rowling, she frequently implicitly critiques genre tropes. She early experimented with heroic fantasy in the three Dalemark novels of the 1970s. Farah Mendlesohn has demonstrated how Jones complicates narrative strategies to make the reader's gaining of knowledge about the fantasy realm untypically plausible and realistic in *Cart and Cwidder* (1975), *Drowned Ammet* (1977), and *The Spellcoats* (1979) (*Diana* chapter 5). Mendlesohn has also observed how Jones disillusions the reader, as well as the characters, about the genuinely escapist elements in some fantasy, observing the fact that the lines on Mitt's face, in *Drowned Ammet*, unmistakably identify him as a poor boy and therefore "the idea of an unknown king growing fit and strong in poverty is rubbished" (Mendlesohn, *Diana* 122). Similarly,

> Moril's realization [in *Cart and Cwidder*] that "legendary deeds always take place in a world of rain and anxiety and irritation [. . .]", is an element of the reader's discovery that adventure in the fully immersed world, in a world that seeks to counterfeit mimesis, is something had, looked back on from the past; hence Moril's disgust when he learns that Kialan is the Adon [. . .] They have been living the adventure he so desired, and it was not the least bit fun or romantic.
>
> (112)

This recognition is similar to Harry Potter's remark, in *Deathly Hallows*, that "[s]tuff like that [Ron's rescue of Harry and destruction of the locket Horcrux] always sounds cooler than it really was" (Rowling, 308). Jones, even more forcefully than Rowling, demythologises the heroic; even though the Dalemark novels are set in an imagined medieval country, where wandering singers, cruel earls, and oppressed peoples abound, they do not give the reader the satisfaction of swordfights, daring adventures, and the culminating overthrow of a tyrannical ruler. Moril's father Clennen has indeed been operating as a spy in South Dalemark, but although his children have accompanied him almost all their lives they do not realise this. Moril's confrontation with the Justice who is imprisoning his brother Dagner is therefore made in innocence, rather than being a heroic deception, and he realises that if he had in fact known, "He certainly could not have acted the surprise he felt when they told him what Dagner had been arrested for" (Jones, *Cart* 124). Later, his sister Brid consciously attempts to deceive the suspicious, and very unpleasant, Earl Tholian and fails, with the result that their Northern companion Kialan, who has been hiding nearby to protect them instead of fleeing, is captured. Moril muses sadly that "[t]hat was the trouble with people who thought too well of themselves" (163). As in the later Harry Potter novels, heroic virtues—Brid's daring, Kialan's chivalry—are seen as problematic in practice.

Cart and Cwidder ends with Moril's destruction of Tholian's army with the aid of his magical cwidder (a stringed instrument), but it is clear that this is a temporary victory that simply enables Moril's and Brid's escape to the north with Kialan and his father Earl Keril, rather than a victory that will change the ruler or social structure of the country. In *Drowned Ammet*, indeed, a novel whose longer timespan includes the timespan of *Cart and Cwidder* in just a few pages,[9] Mitt and his fishermen friends dream of revolution, but they make the mistake widely prevalent in heroic fantasy of believing that the death of a single oppressive individual, in this case Earl Hadd, will instantly lead to an uprising. Instead, Mitt, who has placed a homemade bomb in front of Hadd only to see it kicked away by the earl's youngest son, is forced to flee from the soldiers who unsurprisingly maintain their feudal allegiance. Mitt's journey to the north is accompanied by omens he does not recognise, in a gesture to the convention of the unknowing Missing Heir of fantasy; however, more attention is paid to the relationships around him, including his discovery that his lost father, far from being a dead hero, is a living and entirely callous murderer who makes a living out of betraying people. Mitt is compelled to recognise not his own potentially heroic qualities, as in formula fantasy, but his capacity to behave as badly as his father, or worse. Similarly, Earl Hadd's granddaughter Hildy, the novel's other focal figure, on whose yacht Mitt had hidden himself, is forced to recognise that her own emotional rebellion against her family, in which she has taken pride, has only been made possible by the conditions of privilege in which she has grown up. As the reader sees, too, Hildy's behaviour is inevitably limited in its expression, tightly constrained by the conditions of the Earl's household, and her position of privilege is accompanied by an emotional likeness to the Earl and his elder sons that is also natural in ways often unacknowledged in formula fantasy.

The Spellcoats is a complex and fascinating novel that in many ways seems so unlike conventional heroic fantasy that I do not propose to discuss it here. Its publication marked the apparent end of Jones's interest in the Dalemark world; she did not return to it for over a decade, during which she published a range of other novels—including much of the Chrestomanci series (1977–2006)—that engage with heroic convention only tangentially. In the 1990s, however, she returned to the heroic, though in very different ways.

Several of Jones's 1990s novels play with, invert, and subvert elements of heroic fantasy. Notable among these is *Hexwood* (1993). *Hexwood* is a complex novel that is highly confusing to the reader because of its shifts not only in time—several events appear to be revisited, with different results—but even in character identity. Its apparently twelve-year-old protagonist from our own world, Ann Stavely, eventually recognises that she is in fact a twenty-year-old woman named Vierran from the political centre of a galactic business based far away from Earth; importantly, the reader comes to this recognition only when Vierran/Ann does. The novel includes quite a number of features characteristic of heroic quest fantasy, including the quest itself—but this is presented multiply, and can primarily be seen in the consecutive journeys, in ones and twos, of the villainous Reigners from their world to our own—and the growth of a boy who desires to be a knight and slay dragons. Hume is, however, neither a real boy nor, as Ann believes, a magician's creation, but Martellian, an ancient imprisoned ruler. The customarily symbolic effect of the confrontation between hero and dragon is modified here, as the dragon/Reigner Orm is slain not only by Hume/Martellian's sword but by another dragon, Mordion, who has accepted his own transformation into a dragon in despair at what the Reigners have made him become. Hume is not a heroic youth, but has been set up to learn a slightly different message from the encounter—to "kill your own dragons" as he has avoided doing in the past (Jones, *Hexwood* 369).

The denouement of the novel reveals its story to involve identification of virtuous missing heirs to an empire currently ruled by evil, as is commonly the case in heroic quest fantasy. However, in *Hexwood* that identification has been managed by the Bannus, an enormously powerful artificial intelligence, as a process of testing and construction of a number of possible candidates, rather than by its manifesting unmistakably within a single individual, and includes bringing some individuals literally from the past to resume rule—a move Jones was to repeat in *Deep Secret*—rather than suggesting, as in much heroic fantasy, that the world is so static that a modern hero has exactly the qualities of his distant ancestor. And more important than the straightforward struggle of good against evil is Mordion's discovery that although he has been shaped by the Reigners into being the Servant who executes not only their commands but their enemies, he is nevertheless a valuable person who protects children and who is worthy of love, as well as worthy of taking the role of First Reigner. *Hexwood*'s games with heroic fantasy appear to shuffle its elements, much as the reader's and Ann's experience of the wood itself appears shuffled—a moment when Ann enters the wood and passes an empty chip packet is repeated a number of times, with varying outcomes—and in so doing undoes many of its assumptions.

Somewhat surprisingly, *The Crown of Dalemark* (1993) picks up the threads of the earlier Dalemark sequence, beginning a few months after the separate arrivals of Moril (*Cart and Cwidder*) and Mitt (*Drowned Ammet*) in what Mitt is learning bitterly to call "the free north" of Dalemark (Jones, *Crown* 97). Moril is no longer a focal character, though he remains prominent in the narrative; instead, a second perspective is brought by Maewen, a girl from a period two hundred years later, when Dalemark has become what readers will perceive as effectively a version of contemporary Westernised society. Unlike nearly everything else Jones has written, especially its contemporary *Hexwood*, *The Crown of Dalemark* seems very visibly to follow the pattern of heroic fantasy. It includes a quest for magical objects that is explicitly intended to achieve the restoration of a ruler after an extensive period without kings, and culminates in the crowning of a new king—although the novel does not conclude there. Mitt, the protagonist from the poverty-stricken South, does indeed turn out to be a lost heir to the throne, which he eventually claims. The inclusion of Maewen even gestures to the convention prominent in portal-quest fantasy that change cannot be achieved without intervention of a visiting protagonist.

However, reading *The Crown of Dalemark* in conjunction with *Hexwood*, published in the same year, highlights the fact that *The Crown of Dalemark*, like the Harry Potter sequence, consistently resists the very tropes it exploits. The reader early discovers that although the society of Dalemark has appeared to be medieval, the husband of the Countess of Aberath is not only not Earl—this is a country where women can at least sometimes rule in their own right—but is an inventor experimenting with engines, known as "Alk's Irons" (Jones, *Crown* 12), that suggest the potential for industrial development. Later, we learn that the questing band remains a small company not because it must travel in secret, but, as Maewen discovers, because the people of the north are too busy with their own local problems to want to go off and form an army (96), no matter how well liked its apparent leader, Noreth of Kredindale, may be. Maewen herself has joined the group as a substitute for Noreth, the original claimant of the throne, who has mysteriously disappeared; her own engagement with the place in which she finds herself is complicated by her need to disguise her own identity and by her very superficial knowledge, as a modern thirteen-year-old, of the actual history and operation of Dalemark at this period. That knowledge is nonetheless one of the elements that destabilises the fantasy convention: Maewen brings from the future her awareness that the throne was restored by a man, Amil the Great, who reunited North and South Dalemark and encouraged industry. Unlike in much quest fantasy, where the action is structured by prophecies from the far past, the characters of *The Crown of Dalemark* must eventually act on the basis of knowledge from the future. The prophecies on which Noreth was in fact acting turn out to be false predictions by the evil Kankredin, a magician last seen being scattered into fragments in *The Spellcoats*, which is set in the far past of the other novels. Noreth, though encountered by the reader at the start of *The Crown of Dalemark* as an engaging youth calling herself Rith, turns out to have been killed very soon afterward, although neither the characters nor the reader discover this for certain until after the conclusion of the quest proper (Jones, *Crown* 255). Maewen's substitution for her was arranged by one of the "Undying" (200), the god-figures of the world, now known as Wend. But Wend, though apparently immortal, turns out to be both fallible, biased by his love for Noreth's mother and for Noreth herself, and ignorant, having failed to learn the truth behind Noreth's disappearance at the time—Mitt complains, "Of all the idiots! [. . .] There were several hundred people you could have *asked*!" (319). Maewen's reliance on him to guide her is also mistaken because she believes that the Wend of two hundred years ago must have travelled in time from her present and is therefore fully aware of her own identity. Prophecies and guides alike fail in this fantasy.

It is appropriate, then, that what seems the most magical moment for the reader is also undermined in its operation in relation to fantasy conventions. Moril's cwidder has previously transformed the landscape, at least temporarily, plunging himself and Mitt into an ancient River that no longer exists; at the novel's climax, he uses it to expand a waystone to the size Maewen remembers from her own past—which is of course the novel's future. Moril, Maewen, and Mitt, now in possession of the other magical items of the quest, step through the enlarged waystone to locate the hidden crown of Dalemark, the last object needed by a claimant to the throne, in a space that is both real and unreal: "Will you hush! Moril made this out of *sounds*, don't you understand!" Mitt warns Maewen (Jones, *Crown* 270). But there are oddities here. The lead characters have been joined by two seemingly minor ones, Kialan (from *Cart and Cwidder*) and Ynen (Hildy's brother from *Drowned Ammet*), who have not been part of the questing company, although Moril and Mitt, respectively, recognise them as the best and most promising claimants to the throne. And when they discover the ghost of King Hern, the first king of united Dalemark whom we know from *The Spellcoats*, he declares that "[a]ll but one of you have a perfect right" to the crown (*Crown* 275). The idea of the missing heir is nonsensical in human societies where an individual may have hundreds of descendants over hundreds of years; the questers see elements of King Hern in each other's features.

The gaining of the crown becomes, as seen by Maewen, the outsider, a sort of competition in which King Hern makes comments and asks questions that the boys have to interpret. In this contest Ynen is disabled by emotion, as he is filled with pity for Hern's ghostly imprisonment, and Moril, significantly, by his reliance on past knowledge: "Moril would be disqualifying himself, Maewen thought, if he just went on sticking to what Singers knew" (Jones, *Crown* 278). Mitt wins the contest not because he is, in Gryffindor terms, chivalrous—this better describes both Ynen and Kialan—but because he is shrewd. His years first of poverty and then of service to others have after all taught him how to pay attention to what is not said as well as to what is said; these are survival skills, unlike the often frightening innocence and ignorance typically manifested by the youthful missing heirs of heroic fantasy, and they are also the skills needed to run a country. Ruling does not, after all, consist of sitting on a throne and manipulating a magic orb or sword. Once Mitt has been crowned, he is immediately plunged into further situations requiring wit and diplomacy. Maewen, meanwhile, is returned to Mitt's future as soon as the mystery of Noreth has been solved. She has no place in the past. It is Mitt, himself a descendant of the Undying, who survives into her present— but he is now a grown man with several lifetimes behind him, and although the novel ends with Maewen's vow to seek him out immediately, the reader remains uneasily aware that the romance between a thirteen-year-old and a fifteen-year-old must take a very different shape in the new circumstances. Like *Hexwood* and like the Harry Potter sequence, *The Crown of Dalemark* shatters the expectations of heroic fantasy. It highlights how far those expectations fall short of the complexity of the real world.

PARODY AND THE PROBLEM OF DEHUMANISATION

The apparently typical quest form of *The Crown of Dalemark* made it seem unremarkable in the 1990s as heroic fantasy became very widely popular. But the 1990s were also an era when parody gained prominence in popular culture. In 1990, Martin Rowson's graphic novel *The Waste Land* presented T.S. Eliot's poem from the point of view of a Chandleresque gumshoe protagonist called Chris Marlowe. Amy Heckerling's film *Clueless* (1995) not only relocated Jane Austen's *Emma* into a contemporary setting—another popular cultural fashion of the late 1990s—but gently satirised its own heroine and her milieu. And Terry Pratchett's Discworld novels, with their complex play on tropes from a range of genres including heroic fantasy, rose up the UK best-seller lists. Diana Wynne Jones caught the tone of the period in her *Tough Guide to Fantasyland*, an alphabetically arranged guide to fantasy novels according to the formula common in the previous twenty years or so, in which the terrain of fantasy and the reading of a fantasy novel—or "brochure" (9)—is represented in terms of tourism, with the reader as tourist of an existing land, Fantasyland, containing an assortment of characters and races, and in which the tour will inevitably include a set of well-described incidents. *The Tough Guide*, like most of Pratchett's Discworld fiction, is not strictly a work for children, and therefore lies outside the scope of this book. It is nevertheless worth noting here that Jones brings to bear on the genre of popular heroic fantasy not only a sharp eye for stereotype, but a scepticism that interrogates both details such as the peculiarly soundproof nature of Fantasyland tents and broader issues such as the nature of the Fantasyland ecology. As in some guidebooks, she also adopts a colloquial style that inverts the artificial high style found in some fantasy novels, courtesy of Tolkien, and that highlights her deflation of fantasy givens.

The Tough Guide to Fantasyland provides an important backdrop to understanding of Jones's next novel, *The Dark Lord of Derkholm*. Although initially published in the UK by Gollancz's Millennium imprint, which is not a children's book imprint, *Dark Lord* was published in the US by Greenwillow as a children's book, and subsequently won the 1999 Mythopoeic Fantasy Award for Children's Literature; it has been republished by HarperCollins as a children's book. Like much of Terry Pratchett's fiction, *Dark Lord* can be enjoyed by children or by adults—Gollancz presumably felt that its explicit knowingness about the clichés of late twentieth-century heroic fantasy made it more suitable for an adult readership. *Dark Lord*'s claim to be a children's book rests primarily on the prominence of teenage characters, especially one of the two major focal characters, fourteen-year-old Blade. Blade's age renders him a perfect candidate for protagonist in a heroic quest fantasy, and his adventures include some elements of such fantasy, notably growth, the eventual discovery of an appropriate instructor in magic, and of course the overcoming of evil. But none of these is conventionally represented, and much of the novel's energy is directed at critique of heroic fantasy expectations. The part played in the novel by Blade's six siblings, who range in age from ten to seventeen, lends weight to its categorisation as children's fiction, but somewhat conflicts with its operation as conventional heroic fantasy—as does the characterisation of his father, Derk, the other major focal figure. Jones's practice in this novel is in fact to complicate the conventions of fantasy even as she acknowledges them.

Dark Lord takes as its premise a suggestion from *The Tough Guide to Fantasyland*, in which Jones speculates over the puzzling nature of the economy of Fantasyland in general and specifically that of the Vestigial Empire:

> Here we have a large civilized area in the centre of the land-mass, with a vigorous Economy, large building programs, faultless engineering, and full employment. But no Industry. How is this managed? One has to suppose that regular paying Tours from other worlds secretly support the whole tottering edifice.
>
> (Jones, *Tough* 87–88)

The Dark Lord of Derkholm imagines a fantasy world precisely dependent on such tours—but with the difference that the requirements of tourism have become so onerous that the previously stable economy of the country, which is unnamed, is at risk of collapse. The tour management's contract demands that the tours be led by wizard guides, that they experience many of the encounters Jones outlined in *The Tough Guide*—attacks by bandits and by leathery-winged avians, bewitchment by an enchantress, capture by pirates—and collect clues to the weakness of a Dark Lord, who is appointed from among the world's wizards each year. At first glance, then, *Dark Lord* is a joke novel the purpose of which is simply to invert and mock the expectations of heroic fantasy.

But the joke is effectively both made and surpassed in the first chapter, in which Jones portrays the residents of the fantasy world as resenting the exploitation of their resources—agriculture, labour, magic—by the demands of the tours. Charles Butler remarks,

> The disorientation the reader may feel in trying to distinguish the force of the fiction from the possible point of the satire [. . .] certainly make[s] the book more complex as a novel, but the clear lines of the *Tough Guide*'s parody become blurred in the process.
>
> (*Four* 240)

Another way to put it is that Jones is moving on from the simplicity of parody. By representing the inhabitants of the reluctantly theme-parked world as having their own perspective on the tours, Jones engages with ethical concerns around exploitation of the exotic. Thus for much of the novel, the story provides us not with adventures from the genre but with commentary on it. We see Derk's children struggling to manufacture "leathery-winged avians" from pre-fabricated animated kites (Jones, *Dark* 142), and hear the complaints of the rulers whose lands are ploughed up by battles, or the Horsewoman who points out that her horses are being destroyed "by stupid *fools* who think they're some kind of walking *chairs*" (189)—an observation Jones also makes in *The Tough Guide*, where she notes that Fantasyland horses "are capable of galloping full-tilt all day without a rest [. . .] Horses can be used just like bicycles, and usually are" (*Tough* 127–28). If the horses of Fantasyland are, as Jones suggests in *The Tough Guide*, unhorse-like creatures who may even breed by pollination, their serviceability may be accepted. If the horses are perceived as real, of course, such treatment amounts to abuse. *The Tough Guide* points out that the crude world-creation of formula fantasy is ridiculous; *Dark Lord* points out that the assumptions it generates may be dangerous.

The cliché conflict in heroic fantasy is the battle of Good against Evil. In *Dark Lord* Jones re-examines the nature of these ethical opposites. The primary experience of the unnamed world is the experience of exploitation; the novel demonstrates and critiques the exploitative mentality as the major form of evil, one that requires a different viewpoint, rather than a more powerful sword, to combat. The plot of *Dark Lord* therefore operates differently from stereotypical heroic fantasy, although it deploys some of its tropes. For instance, it opens with a council seeking to stop a world-shattering evil, and that council even appoints high-ranking representatives to seek answers to their problem; however, their journey is quickly achieved—they translocate directly to their objective, an obvious move for characters with magic powers—and results in their appointment of yet other characters, the wizard Derk and his son Blade, to take key roles in the current tour season. From this point forward it is Derk and his family who become the focal figures.

Derk's appointment to the role of Dark Lord furthers Jones's mockery of heroic conventions, as he is a nature-loving wizard who enjoys nothing better than the design of new and wonderful creatures very different from the monsters characteristically produced by wizards' breeding programs as described in *The Tough Guide*. Derk and his household are a rich invention. The grounds of Derkholm swarm with cheerful creatures including "Friendly Cows," carnivorous sheep, intelligent and sardonic geese, invisible cats, and flying pigs. The latter provide a humorous version of prophecy, as the elf Talithan scoffingly announces that his lost brother will return "when pigs do fly"—a hyperbolic expression of the impossible from our ordinary experience—and rejoices to see them doing so (Jones, *Dark* 135). More significantly, Derk's children include not only two teenage humans, Blade and his elder sister Shona, but also five griffins aged between ten and fifteen that Derk has bred using the cells of various animals as well as cells from himself and his wife. The result is that much of the novel consists of family interactions, an element noticeably absent from stereotypic heroic fantasy. It is perhaps coincidental that Derk's family, humans and griffins together, total nine in all, recalling the Nine Walkers who oppose the Nine Riders in Tolkien's *Lord of the Rings* (1954–55); in any case, their relationships are inevitably very different from those between those conventional in quest fantasy. They have a history together, including shared memories, habits, and rivalries.

This is made very clear when Blade seeks out his mother and finds her in the kitchen with his sister:

> Lydda was the only one of the griffins who really liked cooked food. And she not only liked it, she was passionate about it. She was always inventing new dishes. Blade found it very hard to understand. In Lydda's place he would have felt like Cinderella, but it was clear that Lydda felt nothing of the kind. She said, turning her yellow beak and one large bright eye towards Blade, "Do you *have* to come and get under my feet in here?"
>
> Mara looked up at Blade's face. 'Yes,' she said. 'He does.'
>
> (Jones, *Dark* 22)

This passage vividly depicts a set of family relationships. Blade is aware of his sister's different interests, but recognises that he cannot share or even understand them, while Lydda's question indicates that she has taken the kitchen as her territory and its tone suggests a habitual impatience. While Blade here speculates about Lydda's feelings, Lydda, absorbed in her cooking, is comparatively unobservant; it is their mother, Mara, who is able to discern Blade's neediness at this point. The reference to Lydda's beak is made casually, within a participial clause, making clear that her griffin nature is something taken for granted. Within this family, outward shape is unimportant, again countering the conventional coding by appearance, whether species or race or even colour of eyes, that Jones had observed in *The Tough Guide*.

Jones's critique of the exploitative mentality in fact focuses on the kind of automatic discrimination that separates human from other, those who matter from those who do not. Mr Chesney, whom the dwarfs correctly identify as the real Dark Lord, is the most obvious example of this. He eventually explains to his tourist daughter Sukey that her new fiancé, head of the Guild of Thieves in Derk's world, is "not real life. None of them are. They're all just the way they are because I turned their world into a theme park. If they didn't happen to be under contract to me they'd be nothing" (Jones, *Dark* 321–22). This is the tourist mentality writ large: Mr Chesney genuinely cannot conceive of the people of Derk's world as humans deserving of respect, or people with whom one could form a relationship. Jones makes clear, however, that this blindness is not to be understood or forgiven. It extends not only to Mr Chesney's destruction of the dragons, to whom he is denying the gold they need for survival on the basis that "[t]here's no suffering involved. I had an expert assess the exact amount they needed" (322), but also to his treatment of his own stepson, whom he has marked down as "expendable" so that Geoffrey will not claim any of Sukey's inheritance (320–21). Rather than being dramatically destroyed, however, Mr Chesney is punished by being forced to live forty years trapped in a paperweight, as he has previously forced a demon to do.

But Mr Chesney is only the most extreme example of a tendency Jones represents in various figures across the novel. As in the Harry Potter sequence, in which Professor Snape is genuinely jealous, malicious, and unfair despite his equally genuine and well-concealed labours against Voldemort, not all characters on the "right" side are automatically good. Querida, the wizard chancellor who sets in motion the actions that will lead to Mr Chesney's come-uppance, also sees people as potential possessions. She dislikes Derk and attempts to separate him from his wife not only physically, by appointing Mara as Glamorous Enchantress, but by enchanting Mara to believe that she no longer has feelings for her husband. Querida eventually confesses that "I used to be married to Mara's father, you know, and I've never felt that Derk was good enough for the daughter of a man like that," but her "miscalculation" (Jones, *Dark* 309) is represented as typical rather than exceptional. Earlier she had "longed, yearned, lusted for ownership of Callette" (169), another of Derk's griffin daughters, and the discovery that Callette is a speaking and thinking creature does not deter Querida from attempting to acquire her. Only Mara's awareness of Querida's acquisitive trait, and Callette's intelligent framing of the conditions of their encounter, keep Callette safe from becoming an object.

Another version of this tendency is represented in Blade's older griffin brother, Kit. Kit does not seek to own other people, but he causes damage nonetheless. When Derk is injured by a dragon, his children take over running the tours; this experience, rather than the customary quest, provides the basis for their growth toward adulthood. Kit likes to plan and manage, and he loves holding meetings; he takes great pleasure in organising the battles required to entertain each Pilgrim Party. His younger brothers Blade and Don both find the experience of the battles tormenting because of their "double feelings" (Jones, *Dark* 211): Blade "hated the heavy brangling din of the battle, and yet it still excited him enormously" (210). Jones makes clear that part of what Blade hates is meeting "increasing numbers of people who died just as he met them" (210), and whom he can see suffering. Kit, on the other hand, perhaps because he flies above the battles as fake Dark Lord, seems simply to enjoy the excitement of the battles as well as the fun of planning them, ignoring the real pain and real death he is producing. Kit represents the teenage boy playing *Dungeons & Dragons*—a common consumer of heroic fantasy for whom violence is only a marker of victory. He is also the teenage boy learning his own skills: he and Blade both feel resentful and "babyish" when their father returns to take over (179), rather as Harry Potter feels irritated at his exclusion from the action in *Order of the Phoenix*. Nevertheless, like Mr Chesney, Kit is punished by the gods. Told by the god Anscher that he "really had to learn that killing people wasn't a game" (Jones, *Dark* 304), he is captured by hunters seeking fighters for their gladiatorial arena, and forced to kill his opponents in order to survive until he and his brother are freed—ironically by the intervention of a dragon, stereotypically the enemy in most heroic fantasy novels and games.

The importance of remembering the reality of other people's existence is perhaps most succinctly summarised in an exchange between Derk's youngest daughter, Elda, and her mother. Irritated by Elda's persistent reminders of Derk's illness, the enchanted Mara exclaims, "I'm saving the world single-handed and I don't have *time* to think about Derk. Understand?" Elda replies, "I understand [. . .] Baths and sheets and wine are more important than people!" (Jones, *Dark* 176). Mara's reference to "saving the world" claims the justification for unethical behaviour common in many heroic fantasies: the end is more important than the means. Elda's response is deflatory, as she accurately observes the local implications of Mara's behaviour. In so doing she also implicitly comments on the hierarchy of values common in many heroic fantasies, in which the acquisition of objects such as swords and rings becomes a major narrative goal, and the description not only of these objects but of the imagined landscape becomes the writing goal. The complexity of human interaction gives way to a diagrammatic view of characters performing necessary roles.

As Mendlesohn has pointed out, quest fantasies are frequently structured as portal fantasies, in which the reader is introduced to the changing scenery of an unfamiliar world; the scenery, including its imagined creatures and races, becomes the centre of attention. Mendlesohn comments that "the hero *moves through* the action and the world stage, embedding an assumption of unchangingness on the part of the indigenes. This kind of fantasy is essentially imperialist: only the hero is capable of change; fantasyland is orientalised into the 'unchanging past'" (*Rhetorics* 9). While Mendlesohn emphasises the effect of this approach on perceptions especially of history, Jones focuses in *Dark Lord* on the implications of that imperialism for the characters' treatment of each other and for the reader's perception of them as real human beings. She deplores the tendency to exploit other people for one's own pleasure, even if that pleasure is cast as obligation or duty, and to deny the reality of their suffering for the sake of any cause from crass indifference to noble sacrifice. It is noteworthy that the tourists in the Pilgrim Parties express distress at the exploitation of the world and refuse to destroy the Dark Lord even though they have joined the tours in order to do so. Jones shows how personal satisfaction need not stand in the way of recognition of a shared humanity.

At the same time as she both mocks and critiques the conventions of heroic fantasy, Jones does, like Rowling, incorporate some of its tropes within her novel. Belatedly, Blade joins his Pilgrim Party as their wizard guide, thereby taking him on a journey; in the course of that journey Sukey is abducted by the malevolent soldiers, and Blade and her fiancé, the thief Reville, go to find her. Jones therefore provides a miniature quest that turns out to have larger significance in the narrative. Blade, Reville, and Sukey discover that someone is mining earth and exporting it to Mr Chesney's world, and realise that this is in fact removing magic from Blade's own world, in an apt image that recalls Michael Ende's portrayal of Fantastica. Moreover, Blade is then captured and sent off to fight in the arena as an "expendable" (Jones, *Dark* 298), thus enacting an episode identified by Jones as conventional in *The Tough Guide*, as the wizard Barnabas turns out to be the traitor again so often found in stereotypical fantasy fiction. "Cargo, thought Blade. That's me. It was not good to know that someone who had been like an uncle to you all your life could talk of you as cargo. And mean it" (*Dark* 294). Barnabas too ignores the humanity of others to pursue his own ends, in this case service of his alcoholism—a disease rarely represented in heroic fantasy, which tends to represent the drinking of alcohol as natural and masculine. During his imprisonment of Blade, the boy discovers that he is growing; this is a physical growth, in which Blade wonders if he will burst the bars open (294), that at once literalises and stands for the emotional growth at the heart of the *Bildungsroman* fantasy.

The novel ends with the inevitable confrontation with the Dark Lord. However, confrontation with the appointed Dark Lord, Derk, involves for Querida recognition of the enormous grief for which she is partly responsible in her enchantment of Mara. Confrontation with the "real" Dark Lord, Mr Chesney, involves not magical or physical battle, but legal and financial accusations. Three of the tourists in Blade's Pilgrim Party reveal themselves respectively to be agents from the Police Bureau of Missing Persons, Inland Revenue, and the Monopolies Commission from Mr Chesney's home world, all of whom have taken the tour to investigate Mr Chesney's activities and indict him of crimes, in another of Jones's indications of the exploitative implications of much stereotypical fantasy. Mr Chesney is defied by his daughter and stepson, and almost trampled by a stampede of Derk's animals. But it takes intervention by the gods actually to deal with Mr Chesney, who is impervious alike to legal, to emotional, and to physical charges—and Anscher points out that

> [t]he gods have been forced to wait too [. . .] until the people of this world asked to be able to rule their own affairs. [. . .] And for forty years the people of this world found it easier to do what Roland Chesney said than to ask for this world for themselves.
>
> (Jones, *Dark* 325)

Fantasyland has become clichéd over decades of formulaic repetition, as emblematically represented in *Dark Lord* by the exhaustion of its valleys during perpetual battles.

Jones implicitly accuses the consumers as well as the writers of heroic fantasy of accepting both clichéd writing and a dehumanised vision. Like Rowling, though to very different effect, she deploys tropes from the tradition of heroic fantasy while establishing a critique of its values. For Rowling, the danger of heroic fantasy is that it encourages a focus on adventure for the sake of adventure, at the cost of engagement with the intricate realities of ordinary life. For Jones, the danger is that it promotes a dehumanising mindset that reduces other people to possessions or to "cargo." The "tourists" of Fantasyland, Jones argues, are engaging in a view of the world as available for their consumption, a world in which the morality of ordinary life gives way to the pleasures afforded by heroic adventure and defeat of a cardboard Dark Lord.

CONCLUSION

Both Rowling and Jones appeal to their readers' desire for the satisfactions of heroic fantasy: drama, adventure, magical creatures, vivid displays of courage, the discoveries made through quest. Rowling's strategy is subtle. After wooing her young readers with the delights of the school story, she

gradually departs from the conventions and values of that genre and emphasises the apparently fundamental conflict of good and evil around which
so many heroic fantasies have been constructed. The later novels of the
Harry Potter sequence achieve a sobriety of tone that contrasts with the
dramatic pleasures and pains of Harry's earlier, less complex adventures.
The reader, like Harry, is constantly being frustrated in the later novels of
the sequence: Harry's status as Chosen One is known, his struggle with
Voldemort constantly anticipated, but Rowling provides moments of high
drama and heroism comparatively rarely. Instead, the energies of the novels
lead in the opposite direction, as Harry is required to learn patience and
diplomacy. At the end of the sequence he demonstrates the extent to which
his experiences have educated him morally. He refrains from direct violence,
allowing Voldemort to kill himself with his own rebounding curse and relying instead, as he had unwittingly as a baby, on the power of love—in this
case his own love for the people who have come to support him against the
Death Eaters, and his own self-sacrifice for them, replicating and expand-
ing the more individual love and self-sacrifice his mother had demonstrated
seventeen years before.

Rowling continues to engage her readers with elements of heroic fantasy—
Neville's triumphant destruction of Nagini, Harry's own confrontation with
Voldemort in the Forest—but she modifies these. The bodies of the dead in
Hogwarts, many of them individuals known personally to Harry and the
reader rather than being what Alexei Panshin's Mia calls the "spear carri-
ers" of traditional heroic adventure (222), are an unmistakable testament to
the possible cost in human lives of the battle against evil. The reading experience of *Harry Potter and the Deathly Hallows*, however, has presented a
more subtle version of the cost of that battle: it involves constant struggle
against such unheroic issues as tedium, exhaustion, and despair, and the
reader is drawn to share at least some of these feelings. Rowling implicitly
rejects the idea that violence is a solution to real problems. The end of the
sequence urges the reader toward a broader understanding of the complexity of the real.

As we have seen, Jones's strategies in combating the stereotype of heroic
fantasy are multiple. In the Dalemark quartet she offers the pleasure of oth-
erworldly adventure in a feudal landscape that appears to replicate the typical setting of such fantasy, but like Rowling points out the extent to which
the conventional heroic values fail their practitioners. In *Hexwood*, she plays
narrative games with elements of heroic fantasy, confusing the reader as
well as her characters with tricks of time and viewpoint and thereby resist-
ing the format customary in the genre. *The Dark Lord of Derkholm* clarifies
the purpose of such resistance. In this novel, Jones's ethical concern with the
practices of the genre in their cliché form becomes most visible. *Dark Lord*
depends on the reader's familiarity with conventional heroic fantasy, but
in this case Jones initially invites laughter, as that very familiarity becomes
the ground for satire in the form of a theme-park world, and subsequently

74 *Fantasy and the Real World*

encourages us to query the values underlying formula fantasy. Heroic fantasy, Jones suggests, despite its grandiose depiction of conflicts between Good and Evil, may project a vision of the world that is exploitative rather than altruistic. At worst, its readers operate as consumers, encouraged in an appropriative mindset. Jones points out that the reader who chooses fantasies that simply locate these qualities in a swashbuckling protagonist may potentially be adopting an exploitative attitude to the imagined landscapes of what they read—an attitude severely at odds with the heroic values themselves. The plot and characterisation of *Dark Lord* strenuously resist that mindset, demonstrating the dangers of a vision that reduces people—and horses—to mere devices of gratification.

Jones offers images of family as a corrective to the isolating rhetoric surrounding the idea of a Chosen One or a missing heir on quest, and depicts the damage produced by an exploitative attitude to the world. As in *Hexwood*, she deploys recognisable elements from literary fantasy—fabulous monsters, quests, conflicts with dark forces—in new ways, so that her novel acts not only as critique and satire but also as a model for a new kind of heroic fantasy. The conventional heroic fantasy in *The Dark Lord of Derkholm*, as in the Harry Potter sequence, is represented as a stage to be outgrown.

NOTES

1. The first sequel to this film, *The Neverending Story II: The Next Chapter*, did draw on the second half of the novel, but changed it in ways that considerably altered its message.
2. Steege notes also the tradition of moral development highlighted by Edward C. Mack (155).
3. Characters find that they are pieces in chess or similar games in, for instance, Edgar Rice Burroughs's *The Chessmen of Mars* (1922), Sheri Tepper's *True Game* trilogy (1983–84), and Susan Cooper's *Seaward* (1983). Jones's *The Homeward Bounders* (1981) also deals with such a situation.
4. Manlove has pointed out that the fake Moody's actions in rigging the Triwizard Tournament seem unnecessarily elaborate: he could have turned an object in his study into a Portkey and sent Harry to Voldemort (*Order* 162). We can only presume that Voldemort's and Wormtail's preparations require the extended delay, although this does not explain why, in plot terms, Harry must reach the graveyard only by winning the Tournament.
5. Dorothy L. Sayers's *Murder Must Advertise* (1933) suggests that the villain's deferral of direct murderous attack on the hero was a recognised cliché in the Sexton Blake stories, which date back to 1893 (95).
6. "He will be several hundred years old and will probably have a long white beard; this will give him the right to be bossy, smug, tiresomely philosophical, and infuriatingly secretive about all-important facts. You will be glad to see the back of the old idiot. Unfortunately, you won't have. He will reappear, smugger and bossier than ever, near the end of the Tour, just when you thought you were doing rather well on your own" (Jones, *Tough* 167).

7. It is perhaps unsurprising, if disappointing, that the 2007 film of this longest of the Harry Potter novels was the shortest of the eight films made of the sequence, favouring the visually dramatic and spectacular elements that appear sparsely within the narrative.
8. Emily Griesinger identified the Christian associations of much of Rowling's imagery prior to the end of the sequence, which makes these very visible.
9. The prisoners from Hannart, including Kialan's brother, are executed on page 80 of *Drowned Ammet*, and the blocking of Flennpass is mentioned on page 83; these events frame the action of *Cart and Cwidder*. The escape of Kialan, politically significant because of his status as Earl Keril's younger son, is appropriately not mentioned in *Drowned Ammet*—it is not, after all, an occurrence that the Southern Earls would let become known, as it would lead to loss of face.

3   Ontologies of the Wainscot

Heroic fantasy is associated with matters of high adventure and importance—with noble heroes fighting monstrous enemies, with powerful men wielding great swords, with battles of Good versus Evil on which hang the fate of kingdoms and even of worlds. But, as we have already seen, there are many other forms of fantasy. At the opposite end of the spectrum from the heroic are the many tales and legends told of societies of animals, typically rats or mice, or of little people such as brownies or leprechauns, living unknown to us within the real world. Terry Pratchett's *The Amazing Maurice and His Educated Rodents* (2001), discussed in the Introduction, provides an example of such a concealed society. John Clute has called such peoples in fantasy fiction "wainscot societies," referring to the panelling in old houses behind which such societies of creatures were long believed to live (991), and his account suggests that tales of such societies can be taken as forming a subgenre of fantasy. As Kerrie Anne Le Lievre has observed, the Harry Potter sequence deals with the clandestine society living within ours but concealing its activities—Clute's second type of wainscot society. In this chapter I examine works featuring Clute's first type of wainscot society, in which the central characters are differentiated from humans by size and live hidden and unsuspected in the ordinary world (991). I compare Pratchett's Nome Trilogy, or Bromeliad (1989–90), with its predecessor Mary Norton's Borrowers series (1952–82) and with Jones's very different *Power of Three* (1976). All three deal with societies of little people; distinctively, all three are explicitly framed as stories in ways that highlight their contrasting concerns. As we shall see, the Bromeliad and *Power of Three* use the concept of the wainscot to develop accounts of how the perspectives of ordinary human societies, and individuals, may be constrained by unthinking assumptions.

Although Clute provides some comment on the thematic deployment of the wainscot societies, he does not discuss the ontological justifications by which writers seek to sustain the fantasy of the wainscot society as existing within the known world. Yet this is an important consideration for the reader of such a fantasy. Brian Attebery has pointed out not only that mimesis in fiction involves fantasy, but also that "[f]antasy without mimesis would be a purely artificial invention, without recognizable objects or actions" (3). Attebery's observation highlights the extent to which any writer of fiction constructs a world to which his or her readers can relate; the reader's suspension of disbelief is maintained by the coherence of the world portrayed, whether that world be a representation of our own or a purely fantastic projection. In most fantasy literature, the onus falls on the writer to generate a coherent and plausible world—hence, among other things, the popularity among writers of fantasy of the prefatory map of the fantasy domain, satirised by Diana Wynne Jones in her *Tough Guide to Fantasyland* (1996). Wainscot fantasy, like intrusion fantasy, requires the reader to accept both that the story is set in the ordinary world we know and that it contains elements unknown to us; it thus problematises the reader's acceptance of the story's setting to an extent that normally requires some form of justification for how the wainscot societies can exist unknown within the ordinary world. One task of a wainscot story is therefore to overcome the reader's doubt, either by providing a satisfactory explanation for the anomaly or, as is the case in some children's literature, including J.K. Rowling's Harry Potter sequence (1997–2007), to generate sufficient enthusiasm for the wainscot world that its problematic connection to the everyday can be ignored. In the case of *The Amazing Maurice*, the location of the rat community within Pratchett's magical Discworld voids the problem: the opening pages, which reveal that the rats are in commercial alliance with a cat as well as a human, make clear that the novel is set in a world that is not our own.

Although their depictions of wainscot societies seem very similar, Norton and Pratchett appeal to very different ontological positions to validate the reader's acceptance of their existence, with consequently very different thematic implications. Jones's *Power of Three*, meanwhile, deals with the problem in yet another way: it obscures and then obtrudes its own operation as wainscot fantasy. This narrative legerdemain also has important thematic effect. We shall see how both Pratchett and Jones deploy wainscot fantasy to comment on the human capacity for self-deception and to encourage intellectual and emotional openness. Their treatments of the wainscot concept make manifest the ethical concerns that energise their work.

PRATCHETT'S NOMES AND NORTON'S BORROWERS

In 1989–90 Terry Pratchett published a fantasy trilogy variously known as the Nome Trilogy or the Bromeliad (its original title), consisting of *Truckers* (1989), *Diggers* (1990), and *Wings* (1990). These novels all feature a race of little people who live, unknown to ordinary human beings, within the world we know. Like Mary Norton's borrowers, in her popular sequence of novels, Pratchett's nomes operate largely parasitically in relation to the human world, and their experiences, especially in *Truckers* and *Diggers*, like those of the borrowers, involve disruptions to their existence that impel them to journey into different spaces in and attempt different accommodations with that world.

Pratchett has been asked whether he was influenced by the Borrowers series in his Bromeliad. He responded,

> I know about the *Borrowers*, and read one of the books in my teens, but I disliked them; they seemed unreal, with no historical background, and it seemed odd that they lived this cosy family life more or less without any supporting "civilisation". The nomes are communal, and have to think in terms of nomekind. No.
>
> (Breebart)

Despite Pratchett's disclaimer, his Bromeliad shares noteworthy similarities with Norton's Borrowers novels—perhaps unsurprisingly, given the premise. Both feature groups of little people who contemplate their own relationship to humans, and who move between inside and outside worlds, under pressure from conditions largely imposed by humans, and deal with the physical difficulties produced by their own small size in each case. In any case, comparison between Norton's Borrowers sequence and Pratchett's Bromeliad is instructive: through assessment of these works, separated chronologically by nearly forty years, we can observe similarities that belie Pratchett's rejection of Norton's work, but also can identify the key concerns that distinguish them. The ontological issues raised by positing the existence of the little people in each case are presented radically differently, with interesting implications.

Pratchett's suggestion that the borrowers seem "unreal, with no historical background" sheds light on his own concerns in the Bromeliad, in which the nomes discover their own very surprising origins. But in justice to Mary Norton it should be pointed out that she makes very clear in *The Borrowers* (1952) that the little Clock family, living "their cosy family life [. . .] without any supporting 'civilisation,'" as Pratchett puts it, are aware of their unnatural isolation. Homily, mother of the child protagonist Arrietty, reminisces more than once about the rich social life that used to exist in the wainscot world of the manor:

> We had a whole suite of walnut furniture out of the doll's house [. . .] and the cousins would come, and we'd have parties. Do you remember, Pod? Everybody came—except those Overmantels from the morning-room. And we'd dance and dance and the young people would sit up by the grating.
>
> (Norton, *The Borrowers* 36)

Homily describes a house replete with families of different subcultures, making evident that the life of the borrowers is, or was, socially complex, as she muses on the comparative age of the Clock and Harpsichord families and deprecates her sister-in-law's pretensions. But the point for Arrietty, as well as for Pratchett, is that those days are over.

> Oh, I know papa is a wonderful borrower. I know we've managed to stay when all the others have gone. But what has it done for us, in the end? I don't think it's so clever to live on and on, for ever and ever, in a great big half-empty house; under the floor, with no one to talk to, no one to play with.
>
> (46)

Following her encounter with the Boy, in which she is forced to recognise that there are "thousands and millions and billions and trillions of great, big, enormous people" (75), Arrietty is even inspired to talk of the need to "save the race" by communicating with her cousins (101). Although it is clear that their social structure, like everything else in their lives, is "borrowed" from the human world, the precarious status of the borrowers' unsupported "cosy family life" (Breebart) is indeed central to the action of the sequence. The implication that Arrietty's own family are the last remaining borrowers, meanwhile, casts a shadow over *The Borrowers*. The Clocks, as their name hints, have remained alive by sticking to a rigid mechanical routine, but that very rigidity may cause their "race" to die out—if they stay in the house, Arrietty will have no one to marry.

Whatever Pratchett may have felt about Norton's books, his Nome Trilogy in fact presents a substantially similar vision of a wainscot society, at least in the early chapters. Like those of the borrowers, on which Norton's narrator comments, the names of nomes in both the major groups we meet—Masklin, Granny Morkie, Angalo—sound like echoes of human ones. Also like the borrowers, in the manner of *Robinson Crusoe* (1719), they have to work out practical solutions to physical problems. In *Truckers*, the nomes eventually work out how to drive a truck—very badly—with the aid of sets of strings attached to levers, in a manner evocative of the borrowers' efforts with their balloon in *The Borrowers Aloft* (1961). When *Truckers* opens, too, we are faced with a remnant group, "[t]here had been plenty of them [. . .] Masklin could remember at least forty" (Pratchett, *Truckers* 16), of whom there are now only ten, "and eight of those were too old to get about much" (17). Like the borrowers, Masklin's group of nomes is forced to emigrate, and in so doing they discover the huge social world of life in the Store (with its god "Arnold Bros (est. 1905)" [39]). Much as Arrietty believes that "Human beans are *for* Borrowers, like bread's for butter" (Norton, *The Borrowers* 75), the Store nomes believe that Arnold Bros (est. 1905) created the Store and the human beings that run it for *them*, and even doubt the existence of a world Outside the Store. For Pratchett, it is this doubt that is important. Arrietty's mistake is amusing to the reader, but it is her adventures that matter in *The Borrowers*. The insularity of the Store nomes underlies their culture—which retains the complexity Norton's

Homily remembers from her youth, here in the form of a rigid and feudal society. The arrival of Masklin and the Outside nomes disrupts the assumptions of both groups, and that disruption generates Pratchett's narrative.

Pratchett's interest in how societies function is made manifest in his depiction of the Store nomes, as well as the Outside nomes, coming to terms with realities beyond the frame of their vision. In public the Store nomes' Abbot shrieks "Intolerable! There is nothing Outside, and no one to live in it!" (Pratchett, *Truckers* 71), forcing one of his monks to "cross [his] eyes frantically with the effort of not seeing" the Outside nome Granny Morkie (72), but in private the Abbot can talk calmly with Masklin:

> Ten minutes ago it was official. Goodness me, I can't go around letting people believe that I've been wrong all along, can I? The Abbots have been denying there is anything Outside for generations. [. . .] The important thing about being a leader is not being right or wrong, but being *certain*.
>
> (78)

Societies are complex, and it is not always rational behaviour that succeeds—although excessively irrational behaviour can also be catastrophic, as shown in the fate of the evangelical Nisodemus in *Diggers*. In this sense Pratchett's vision, as the Abbot indicates, is political—certainly going far beyond the awkwardness of Homily and Lupy trying to share living quarters in *The Borrowers Afloat* (1959).

Where Pratchett insists on the importance of the social, Mary Norton's interest in describing the life of the borrowers appears to be primarily practical, even physical. She explains in a 1966 letter published as a preface to the omnibus edition of *The Complete Borrowers* (2002) that

> the idea seems to be part of an early fantasy in the life of a very short-sighted child, before it was known that she needed glasses. [. . .] What would it be like, this child wondered, [. . .] to live among such creatures [as a small toad]—human oneself to all intents and purposes, but as small and vulnerable as they? What would one live on? Where make one's home? Which [creatures] would be one's enemies and which one's friends?
>
> (Norton, Introduction 3).

The narrative of all five Borrowers novels emphasises realistic details of the borrowers' lives: at times the novels become a manual to coping in the human world if one is only a few inches tall, much as Arthur Ransome's *Swallows and Amazons* (1930) becomes in places an instruction book for camping and sailing. In *The Borrowers*, Arrietty watches her father climb a chair and curtain with a pin and name tape in order to "borrow" blotting paper that can be rolled down into the tunnels to make a carpet (Norton,

85–86); in *The Borrowers Afield* (1955) Homily realises that a bulrush would have been "[j]ust the thing for cleaning out the flues" (71), while Pod works out how to sew shut an old boot to make a house; in *The Borrowers Aloft*, most elaborately, when the borrowers are imprisoned in Mr and Mrs Platter's attic, Pod constructs a gas-filled balloon—aided by the fortuitous presence in the attic of rubber balloons as well as an old magazine containing the necessary diagrams.

These details, richly imagined as they are, underline the reality of the borrowers for the reader. We are invited to share Arrietty's perspective on the world, to empathise with her desire to experience for herself the adventure of "borrowing" and her yearning to explore the natural world outside the walls and floors beneath which she spends her confined life.[1] Yet that vivid rendering, and our response to it, may be seen as a betrayal of the borrowers. As it turns out, the borrowers' major preoccupation is a worry about being "seen," or rather being believed in, by human beings. Although the otherwise paranoid Pod talks quite happily with Great Aunt Sophy, who according to Arrietty "thinks he comes out of the decanter" from which she drinks her evening Madeira (Norton, *The Borrowers* 70), when the Boy sees him Homily observes in horror that "[n]o one [. . .] hasn't never been 'seen' since Uncle Hendreary and he was the first they say for forty-five years" (27). The issue for the borrowers is epistemological: their existence, as they see it, depends upon them being, at most, fictional for human beings.

The novels are structured to reflect this concern. In both the first two novels, *The Borrowers* and *The Borrowers Afield*, the story is framed by the discoveries of a child who does not herself see the borrowers, but who learns of them at least secondhand. In *The Borrowers* the narrating Mrs May explains to the child, Kate, that she herself has been told the story by her young brother, who was the only visitor at the great house where the borrowers lived, and was renowned for lying and making up stories. At the end Mrs May confesses that on her own later visit to the house she took things to where, according to her brother's story, the borrowers should now be, and found the book called *Memoranda* in which Arrietty kept her diary:

> "Then that proves it," [Kate] said finally, "underground chamber and all."
> "Not quite," said Mrs May.
> "Why not?" asked Kate.
> "Arrietty used to make her "e's" like little half-moons with a stroke in the middle—"
> "Well?" said Kate.
> Mrs May laughed [. . .] "My brother did, too," she said.
>
> (Norton, *The Borrowers* 153)

The novel ends there, giving the last word to Mrs May's implied doubt that Arrietty and her family were other than a fiction—though a very elaborate one—created by Mrs May's brother. The first novel thus remains ontologically poised. On the one hand, readers are provided with immense detail about the day-to-day lives of the borrowers—far more, in fact, than Mrs May's brother could have learned through his brief encounters with Arrietty—and these details are, in most editions, endorsed by illustrations, evoking the borrowers as real and validating the plausibility of their hidden existence. On the other hand, the novel's elaborate framing implicitly distances the reader from Arrietty's story and renders it dubious: a tale recalled by one adult as told to her when she was a child with whom she cannot identify herself,[2] by an old woman who was herself told the tale as a child by a young brother noted for fabulation. However, the ontological ambiguity may be "mastered" by the reader if we consider the importance Norton's characters place on that very uncertainty. It is as though Norton is providing a safety net for the borrowers: her own fictional surface becomes one of the many devices that protect the borrowers from being seen, and believed.

Subsequent novels repeat the pattern of doubt; the final novel, however, expands the field of ontological interrogation. Miss Menzies and the thieving Platters believe in the borrowers' existence, though the policeman to whom Miss Menzies reports the theft of the borrowers from Mr Potter's village does not; however, the borrowers themselves meet ontological challenges in their new home. The Hendrearys, their in-laws, have now set up in a vestry, and Homily is confused at Lupy's references to "the Lord" (Norton, *The Borrowers Avenged* 636), as the Clock family is completely ignorant of Christianity. Further, their new acquaintance Peregrine Overmantel, last of the cultured and snobbish Overmantel family recalled in *The Borrowers*, tells Arrietty that the Rectory in which the Clock family are establishing themselves is haunted. Arrietty hears and sees the ghosts, but is told to ignore them. " '[I]t was just [. . .] a photograph on air.' He thought a moment. 'Or on Time, if you prefer' " (631). Meanwhile, in the human world, Mrs Platter seeks to track down the borrowers with the aid of a medium, providing her with a handkerchief that the medium promptly returns to its owner, Miss Menzies—who thereby realises that the Platters had kidnapped the borrowers. Several levels of reality are therefore established: the humans, who are real, and in whom everyone believes; the borrowers, who may be real, but whose existence is kept so hidden that humans can find little or dubious evidence for it; the medium, who is a real person with supernatural capacities affirmed in the text; the ghosts, who are for Pod at once "nothing" and "often there" (630); and "the Lord," who remains at the level of allusion, but whose significance is underlined by the action of *The Borrowers Avenged* (1982), in which the wicked Platters trap themselves and are caught stealing from the church. ("Vengeance is mine [. . .] saith the Lord" [Romans 12:19]). If the sequence begins by layering doubt around the vivid world of the borrowers, its final message, as implied by the coda novel *The Borrowers Avenged*, is that although, like Mrs May, we may have plenty of reason to doubt, we must accept that the world is full of "things visible and invisible" (Colossians 1:16).

In the Borrowers novels, then, the reader learns that the world is richer than we imagine, filled with little people who may be unseen but who operate as effectively as any other creatures to occupy the world. Norton is perhaps responding, at least initially, to the austerity of the post-war England in which she began the sequence, implicitly replenishing a country depleted of people and things by war even as she replicates that depletion in the isolated and make-shift lives of her borrowers. However, the epistemological issues raised in the novels' frames, the fact that we may never be able to prove that the borrowers exist, because they and their creator have arranged for them to be effectively hidden, adds a further dimension to her narrative. At this level the message of Norton's Borrowers novels, as implied in *The Borrowers Avenged*, is also a message about the possible and practical existence of the supernatural—ghosts—and the superhuman—God—as well as of the little people. Norton appears to point to the numinous in her account of human doubt about the borrowers: we are invited to see them as continuous with psychic phenomena, and even, perhaps, to connect our desire to believe in the reality of the borrowers to belief in the reality of God. In the 1982 world in which she completed the sequence, late in her writing life, Norton perhaps felt the need to encourage a spiritual openness going beyond the hard-headed materialism of Thatcherite England.

Whereas Norton's framing in each of the five Borrowers novels locates the story initially in relation to an often doubting human observer, emphasising the ontological problem of the borrowers' hypothetical existence within the world we know, Pratchett's Bromeliad pays comparatively little attention to the human perspective. Even when, in *Diggers*, the nomes imitate Swift's Lilliputians and tie up a human security guard in order to present their own claim for territory, the perspective remains firmly with the nomes, and not with the guard. Nevertheless, Pratchett does pay some heed to the presumed perspective of his own readers. In a move with which readers of his Discworld novels would become familiar, he frames his fiction by offering an external viewpoint. *Truckers*, the first of the trilogy, is in fact framed three times over, which is unusual even in Pratchett's oeuvre. The first page, "Concerning Nomes and Time," explains the nomes' short lives and fast experience of time: "Nomes are small. On the whole, small creatures don't live for a long time. But perhaps they live *fast*. Let me explain" (Pratchett, *Truckers* [7][3]). Pratchett's comparison is quasi-scientific, as he discusses the short-lived mayflies and very long-lived bristlecone pines, though less so when he imagines how these creatures might perceive time: "Perhaps old mayflies sit around complaining about how life this minute isn't a patch on the good old minutes of long ago" ([7]). Pratchett's move is in fact to humanise the nomes, like Norton, even as he seems to distance them by assimilating them to mayflies, and commenting "To a nome, a year lasts as long as ten years does to a human. Remember it. Don't let it concern you. They don't. They don't even know" ([7]). Pratchett thus invites his readers to take a distant, even scientific, perspective on the nomes—but quite definitely a believing one. Where Norton's Kate is led to speculate on the possibility of the borrowers' existence "[b]ecause of all the things that disappear. Safety-pins, for instance [. . .] Where do they go to?" (*The Borrowers* 9), Pratchett's nomes are asserted as existing from the very first sentence.

The second page of *Truckers* is different again: it establishes a pattern of epigraphs that goes right through *Truckers* and *Diggers*. These epigraphs appear to be taken from a Bible-like text called *The Book of Nome*. They are divided into chapters and verses, and the language is frequently archaic, quasi-King-James-Bible, though amusingly framing more contemporary, and mundane, positions:

> In the beginning . . .
>
>   I. There was the Site.
>   II. And Arnold Bros (est. 1905) Moved upon the face of the Site, and saw that it had Potential.
> III. For it was In the High Street.
>   IV. Yea, it was also Handy for the Buses.
>
> (Pratchett, *Truckers* [9])

The mixture of, in our terms, high style and low style, seventeenth-century framing and twentieth-century diction, validates the prefatory comment on how the nomes' relationship to time is different from ours. Perhaps more importantly, the comedy of the disjunction prepares both for the generally upbeat tone of the novel, implicitly promising a happy ending, and for the dominant concern of the trilogy, the nomes' human-like behaviour in all its human inconsistency—of which the Abbot's apparent change of heart, cited earlier, is a good example.

Even when we turn at last to the action of *Truckers*, Pratchett holds us off for most of another page from the nome perspective, offering statements that locate the reader outside the main action: "This is the story of the Going Home. This is the story of the Critical Path" (11). The definite article used about the story, and the capital letters, imply a pre-existing story with which the narrator, if not the reader, is already familiar—a move in fact epistemologically opposite to the layers of doubt provided in *The Borrowers*. However, the following paragraph does situate what turns out to be the climax of the novel in human terms:

> This is the story of the lorry roaring through the city [. . .] smashing street lamps [. . .] and rolling to a halt when the police chased it. And when the baffled men went back to their car to report *Listen, will you listen? There isn't anyone driving it!* it became the story of the lorry that started up again, rolled away, and vanished into the night.
>   But the story didn't end there.
>   It didn't start there, either.
>
> (11)

Although "the story" appears briefly to be the story told by the police, "the story of the lorry that started up again [. . .] and vanished into the night," the subsequent comments make clear that this is not in fact their story. Pratchett's narrator provides a god's-eye view very different from Norton's curious humans piecing together a world from glimpses and stories and conjecture and possible lies. The novel in fact makes a further concession to the human perspective of its readers: it invites us to "Look at [Masklin]. Wet. Cold. Extremely worried. And four inches high" (11). Unlike in the Borrowers sequence, where the reader is invited to infer that we reach the direct narrative of the Clock family's adventures as Kate does, through layers of narration and recollection, we as readers of *Truckers* can look directly at Masklin. What we see implicitly locates him as himself human—"Wet. Cold. Extremely worried"—but the single truncated sentence "And four inches high" also implicitly distances him from us, punctuating the sentence with a familiar human measure that is arrestingly unfamiliar in its collocation with an apparent description of a person.

Thus far, the movement of *Truckers* appears more or less consistent with that of many fantasy novels. The preface "Concerning Nomes and Time" seems a deliberate evocation of Tolkien, whose Prologue to *The Lord of the Rings* (1954–55) begins "Concerning Hobbits" (Tolkien, *Fellowship* 10); the material from *The Book of Nome* parodies not only the Bible but many high-style historicising epigraphs by which writers seek to give a Tolkienian depth to their fantasy worlds. As I have suggested, however, Pratchett also evokes a scientific atmosphere, and it is here that his sequence differs most importantly from Norton's. As noted above, Pratchett complains that the borrowers lacked historical background; while *The Book of Nome* provides a local history to the Store nomes, the events of *Truckers* supply a far grander background for nomekind. The Thing, a small black box that the Outside nomes have been carrying in effect as a talisman—old Torrit explains that "[w]hen old Voozel passed it on to me he said that it *used* to [tell the leader what to do], but he said that hundreds and hundreds of years ago it just stopped" (Pratchett, *Truckers* 46)—turns out to be a very powerful miniature artificial intelligence that can charge itself on ambient electricity. The Thing tells the nomes that fifteen thousand years have passed since they landed from their spaceship: the nomes are, in fact, an alien race. What has seemed to be another fantasy of little people, in the line of the borrowers, the Hobbits, and tales of leprechauns and fairies from many cultures, turns out not just to be wainscot fantasy but also to belong to a quite different genre: the lost colony. In this sub-genre of science fiction, probably best known now via Anne McCaffrey's Dragonriders novels (1967–present), a group of people living on a planet is discovered, or discovers, itself to be descendants of a colony deliberately or accidentally landed there many years before.

The history of the nomes, then, is not just the history of how they came to live in the Store, but of a space-faring race that has, as generally in this sub-genre, lost touch with its origins and its own technological development.

And the direction of the Nome Trilogy is shaped by this. The outside nomes, like the borrowers, just want to "go home and be safe" (Pratchett, *Truckers* 50), but where the borrowers spend most of the five books fleeing from one temporary refuge to another, the Thing gives the nomes direction: "Going Home" is after all going back to their home planet, which means going back to their ship, which means getting to Florida to send a signal via a human space shuttle so that the nome ship will come out of stasis to fetch them. The nomes have a recognisable goal.

Pratchett thus appeals to a very different truth validation than Norton. Her validation of the borrowers' existence depends, paradoxically, on our ignorance about them and the doubt in which Mrs May and others are kept, a doubt which speaks to the borrowers' paranoia about being "seen" and believed in. The reader's, like Kate's, initial ignorance of the borrowers and subsequent doubt about their existence points to the borrowers' success in maintaining what they see as a necessary condition for that existence. They thus remain firmly in the realm of fairy tale, evanescent as leprechauns despite the practical details Norton supplies about their lives. By contrast, Pratchett's history appeals to the late twentieth-century speculation that aliens exist, that there is life on other planets, and that these things can be discovered and communicated through technology—even if this has not yet happened. This appeal depends on a belief that the universe is larger than we have yet discovered, and implies that we should be open to such discovery.

The trilogy's original sub-title, the Bromeliad, points to this concept. While it comically if appropriately evokes national epics such as Homer's *Iliad* or Virgil's *Aeneid*, the word is the name of a type of flower. Early in *Diggers*, the intelligent Grimma confuses Masklin with a story she has read about a kind of frog that lives inside such flowers: "these little frogs live their whole lives in the flowers right at the top of the trees and don't even know about the ground" (Pratchett, 47). In *Wings*, Pratchett extends this image to contemplate the intellectual experience of a frog that discovers that there are other flowers beyond its own, and even that there are trees holding them up. The image, like that of Plato's Cave, is one of the confinement of ignorance that can be expanded and transformed—a characteristic trope in "lost colony" fiction, but also a concept central to Pratchett's ethical as well as his intellectual message. The journey of the nomes in *Truckers* and *Diggers*, as well as *Wings*, in which three of the nomes undertake the trip to Florida, reflects this theme: the Outside and Store nomes, first separately and then together, must expand their horizons to recognise the vast and complex nature of the world they actually inhabit. Although both the first two novels appear like the Borrowers novels to be about flights from danger, much of the social focus is in fact on that process not of local but of intellectual discovery—and on the forces that impede it, like sceptics such as the Duke de Haberdasheri and (briefly) the Abbot in *Truckers*, and the more dangerously fanatical Nisodemus, who in *Diggers* seeks to outface the human threat by reactionary behaviour and narrow belief in Arnold Bros (est. 1905).

Pratchett, unlike Norton, treats religious belief as a social need and political mechanism. He points rather to the universe itself as a validation for the existence of the nomes. The message of the Bromeliad, to the reader as well as to Masklin and Gurder, is that the universe is not just a richer place, as in the Borrowers sequence, but a far bigger place than we imagine; that there are horizons beyond our own physical and mental ones; and that belief in a personal God tells us about human need rather than about the nature of the universe. Near the end of the trilogy, Masklin realises from listening to "Grandson Richard, 39," the heir of the Arnold Brothers, that, as he tells the priest Gurder, "You know you believed in Arnold Bros (est. 1905.)? [. . .] Well, he believed in you, too!" (Pratchett, *Wings* 200). The founder of the Store and its tiny inhabitants were both real, but each perceived the other as supernatural beings because only in this way could they make sense of their experiences within the limitations of their assumptions about the world.

But the world is bigger than the Store or England or even planet Earth. The nome Dorcas realises at the end of *Diggers*,

> Of course there were a lot of questions, but right now the answers didn't matter; it was enough just to enjoy the questions, and know that the world was full of astonishing things, and that he wasn't a frog.
>
> Or at least he was the kind of frog who was interested in how flowers grew and whether you could get to other flowers if you jumped hard enough.
>
> And just when you'd got out of the flower, and were feeling really proud of yourself, you'd look at the new, big, wide endless world around you.
>
> And eventually you'd notice that it had petals around the horizon.
>
> (Pratchett, 173)

Pratchett implies that we too may be constrained by our own cultural stories as we confront the physical and moral universe. His appeal to science and science fictional tropes, though appropriate to the late twentieth century, is thus primarily an appeal to intellectual openness. It is also a very conscious appeal: the Thing tells Masklin that *"Humans find it a lot easier to really believe in little people from the sky than little people from the Earth. They would prefer to believe in little green men than leprechauns"* (Pratchett, *Wings* 166–67), highlighting both the nomes' affinity (like the borrowers') with leprechauns and this trilogy's somewhat sardonic evocation of the scientific to engage the contemporary reader. After all, science too can act as blinkers for the imagination: the replacement of the Bible-like *Book of Nome* by *A Scientific Encyclopaedia for the Enquiring Young Nome*, by Angalo de Haberdasheri, as source of the epigraphs in *Wings* does not make those epigraphs any more authoritative or less comical than those in the first two novels.

> GRAVITY: *This is not properly understood, but it is what makes small things, like nomes, stick to big things, like planets. Because of SCIENCE, this happens whether you know about gravity or not. Which goes to show that Science is happening all the time.*
>
> (Pratchett, *Wings* 182)

Angalo's phrasing is comic in its informality, which contrasts with the abstract assertions of traditional science textbooks. That informality points to the fact that science is itself a human construction, a story through which people try to explain their world. But, as Angalo reminds us, reality exists *"whether you know about [it] or not."*

At the end of *Wings*, Gurder decides that he should stay on Earth to gather and teach the thousands of other nomes of whom he has learned, each with their own cultural backgrounds and legends, about their true history as space-faring people, and to prepare them too to return to the stars. Norton's sequence ends with the borrowers finding what they hope may be a permanent refuge, in a slightly larger society—including at least two possible partners for Arrietty—and safeguarded by at least one sympathetic human. Their journey remains framed within the human world and its customs. The doubts raised about the borrowers' existence seem laid by the attempts of various individual humans to seize or save them; instead the reader is invited to contemplate the existence of an unknowable spirit world that must be taken on faith. Pratchett's Gurder, by contrast, has had to move beyond faith: he, Masklin, and Angalo have discovered the existence not just of a few Outside nomes but of thousands, and indeed of an Outside far greater even than the sky to which Masklin is accustomed. Gurder's own experience teaches him, and the reader, that this expansion of belief is both difficult and vital, and he chooses to act as a guide to open understanding where before he has acted as a priest to curtail it. His decision appears to mirror that of his author. The Bromeliad teaches the dangers of cultural constraint visible in so many cultures and subcultures, including western ones, that even in 1990 preferred to retain the rigidities of fundamentalist theories, or theologies. Pratchett deploys the wainscot fantasy to encourage openness to a full engagement with the wonders of the real world.

JONES'S *POWER OF THREE*

Diana Wynne Jones's early novel *Power of Three* takes a very different approach to the relationship between the ordinary world and the wainscot society. Although, like *The Borrowers* and the Bromeliad, *Power of Three* belongs to Clute's first group of wainscot societies, where little people are imagined living interstitially, the reader does not at first realise that this is the case. Where *The Borrowers* is framed to draw our attention to the unknown but not unsuspected existence of the little people, and *Truckers* insists on the strangeness of the nomes as requiring explanation, *Power of Three* is initially presented as what Farah Mendlesohn terms an immersive fantasy, that is, a narrative wholly located in an imaginary world "built so that it functions at all levels as a complete world" (*Rhetorics* 59). In the opening sentence, "This is the story of the children of Adara—of Ayna and Ceri, who both had Gifts, and of Gair, who thought he was ordinary" (Jones, *Power* 7), the reader is introduced to characters with names that, as often in fantasy fiction, conform to English phonemic rules—and associations, such as the -a ending for feminine names—without seeming either actual English or, like the names of the borrowers and the nomes, misheard English. The reference to "Gifts," with the capital G, also distances the story from ordinary life, implicitly locating it in another and separate space.

But the novel's opening sentence is doing more than this. As in both *Truckers* and *The Borrowers*, *Power of Three* calls attention to itself as story. In this case, the phrase "the story of Adara's children" points to a sense of history, which is developed when the first chapter turns out to focus on Adara as a child rather than on Adara's children. The reader is being asked to take a long view—though not quite as long as Pratchett's ancient bristlecone pines in his preface "Concerning Nomes and Time." The comment on Gair "who thought he was ordinary" then indicates that Gair is not ordinary, locating him as special. Since the bulk of the narrative turns out to feature Gair as focaliser, this comment is significant in its warning that we should not rely too thoroughly on Gair's interpretations of events and situations. But it also warns us not to rely too much on our own understanding. As it turns out, what we think is "ordinary" immersive fantasy will turn out to be something quite different.

The story of *Power of Three* is complex, as is usual in Jones's narratives. Adara and her family are part of a people who live in mounds on a Moor (the capital is Jones's); their world, as is again common in immersive fantasy, contains enemies of other species, the frightening shapeshifter Dorig, who live beneath the water, and the intimidating Giants, who appear largely to ignore the people of the mounds. But there are conflicts within the apparently human focal group as well. The first chapter describes an episode in which the child Adara's brother Orban confronts and bullies a Dorig child, eventually killing it in order to gain its precious and very elaborate gold collar. In this incident it is Orban, not the Dorig, who is both arrogant and destructive:

> Orban shuddered, thinking of the way the Dorig skulked out their lives under stinking marsh-water. And they were cold-blooded too, so of course they would have to sun any gold they stole. Ugh! "Where did you get that collar?" he asked sternly.
>
> The Dorig seemed surprised that he should ask. "From my father, of course! Didn't your father give you yours?"
>
> [. . .] The Giants interrupted with another distant thump and rumble, but Orban's mind took that in no more than what the Dorig had just

said. If it was true, it meant that this wretched, skinny, scaly creature was more important than he was. And he knew that must be nonsense.

(Jones, *Power* 13)

Whereas the Dorig responds "politely" to Orban (13), Orban is blinded by his own prejudice against Dorig and determination to impress his little sister Adara—who in fact is shocked by Orban's aggression and sympathises with the Dorig. Already the reader can see that hostility and destructive behaviour are not universal characteristics of the enemy Dorig but may be lacking in the polite and reasonable Dorig child and instead manifested in the apparently human Orban. Orban himself, however, is constrained by his own assumptions, especially the assumption that he is important. Any challenge to his value therefore "must be nonsense."

When he kills the Dorig, Orban is able to explain away the fact that its blood "was bright red and steamed a little. [. . .] H]e remembered that fish sometimes come netted with blood quite as red, and that things on a muck-heap steam as they decay" (Jones, *Power* 13). Jones's narration is operating doubly here: on the one hand it provides us with facts—the Dorig's blood was red, and steamed—and on the other with Orban's assumptions and rationalisations. Already, however, because these are *Orban's* assumptions and rationalisations, the reader should be challenging them; thus, already we are being prepared to interpret the Dorig as quite different not only from what Orban thinks, but even from what the people of the mounds think.

But there are layers within layers in Jones's storytelling. The reader is encouraged through this scene to suspect that the Dorig may not be hostile reptiles to be destroyed but sentient mammals, almost like human beings. Where the brutal Orban thinks "what business had the Dorig to imitate the customs of men?" (Jones, *Power* 14), the reader should notice that whereas Adara's people have lost the skill of making elaborate collars, the Dorig's father had its very fine collar made for it, suggesting not only an alternative but a superior civilisation. What the reader is less likely to question, however, is Orban's use of the term "men." Buried within not only Orban's assumptions but our own is the idea that Orban's people are "men," that Adara and her children are, allowing for the displacement of the fantasy world, just like us: human beings. This turns out not to be the case.

Power of Three in fact turns out to focus on the problem of cross-cultural, and even intracultural and individual, conflict, and especially misinterpretation. As Adara's children grow up, her elder son and middle child, Gair, feels inadequate to what he believes are his father Gest's expectations of him, and broods on this constantly. Where his sister Ayna and young brother Ceri have magical Gifts that can assist the tribe in certain circumstances, Gair thinks he is just ordinary. His life is made more miserable when the people of Otmound, now led by the despotic Orban, move in with the people of Garholt, where Gest is chief; not only Orban but his shrewish wife Kasta and bullying son Ondo make life unpleasant for the people of Garholt and especially for Gair. He wanders away and, with his brother and sister, discovers a Giant's house. It is at this point that the reader's interpretation of the novel's location and characters changes dramatically. The Giant's house, unlike the mound dwellings of the Moor, looks like an English house; the Giantess nearby is clutching what the narrator, focalised through the children, describes as a magic box making noises "and it was clear that she took it for music"; a Giant yells at the Giantess "I told you to get out, Fatso!", using an ordinary slangy insult, and she replies, "That was last Easter" (Jones, *Power* 91), displacing the earlier references to Powers of the Sun and Moon with reference to a Christian holiday—or, from context, school vacation. It does not take the Giant's addressing of the Giantess as Brenda to make us realise that the Giants are in fact ordinary human beings living in the ordinary world.

Unlike either *The Borrowers* or *Truckers*, therefore, the reader of *Power of Three* discovers only belatedly that it deals with a wainscot society— two, in fact, as both the "people" (whom the Dorig know as Lymen) and the Dorig are unknown to the Giant/human world. We have been led, as in an immersive fantasy, to empathise fully with the tender-hearted Adara and later with the thoughtful Gair without feeling any constraint of separation, still less the somewhat condescending humour that Pratchett evokes for his nomes. The reader thus looks on the "Giant" Gerald with a double vision: on the one hand he is a human being of similar age and habits to Jones's own contemporary readers; on the other he is the alien creature whose peculiar ways are mysterious to Ayna and Ceri especially. A subsequent distanced description of the house's interior from the point of view of our focal characters supports this: "Everything possible was square. Giants seemed to want things square as naturally as people wanted them rounded. Gerald led them to a square hard-white room, full of silver things, where they took off their sopping clothes and dried themselves with vast white towels" (Jones, *Power* 148). The description invites the reader to challenge his or her own preconceptions about what rooms should look like, to wonder why English people do make things square rather than rounded, and to feel surprised pleasure when the word "towels" reshapes the mysterious room into a familiar bathroom.

This doubled vision of the familiar as estranged and the alien, for the duration of the novel so far, as "normal" is key to Jones's concerns in *Power of Three* and turns out to be crucial to the novel's resolution. A central conversation highlights both the reader's confusion and the characters' problem:

> "Shut up, Brenda!" growled the heartily embarrassed Gerald. "They're *not* fairies. They've told you."
> "They must be," Brenda insisted. "They can't be people, because *we* are."
> "No. You aren't people," Ceri explained. "You're Giants."

"Well!" said Brenda, very pink. "Big I may be, but Giant I am *not*! Giants are huge, big as houses. Anyway, I thought you were called Lymen."

"That's what the Dorig say. We say people," Ayna said. "We haven't any other name but people."

(Jones, *Power* 156)

Each group of course believes itself to be "people," as no doubt do Jones's readers. Jones, like Pratchett, is arguing for open-mindedness, but in her case the concern is both racial and personal. Gloomy and lonely, the reflective Gair has already observed that Gerald behaves and looks as though he too is gloomy and lonely; he further perceives that "To look at the Giant Gerald, you would have thought his fortunes followed gloomy Saturn's, if anyone's did. He suspected his own did too" (114), thereby questioning his people's beliefs that the three species are each influenced by different astronomical features and that Saturn and the Moon belong to the Dorig. Gair's empathetic perception of similarity undercuts the traditional cross-species prejudices that have structured their relationships both locally and theoretically.

Empathy turns out in fact to be crucial to the resolution of the novel, in which the three groups confront each other over two problems. The first is the threatened flooding of the Moor to turn it into a Giant/human reservoir, which would destroy both Gair's home and Gerald's but be of benefit to the Dorig—a political problem. The second is a personal and religious problem: the Dorig King Hathil's vow to avenge his brother—the child Orban murdered at the novel's opening—by sacrificing both Gair and Gerald, who have gone to him as ambassadors to discuss the water problem. The Dorig King is subjected to the pacifying ritual speech of Gest's friend the Chanter Banot; the clarification of Gest, who explains that Gair is his own son and not the son of the hated Orban, and who also points out that he and the King have exchanged collars, from context in the novel a significant act of brotherhood; the discovery that the King's son has become a voluntary hostage to the people/Lymen; and the arguments of the clever Mr Claybury (a human/Giant), who points out alternative ways in which the Giants and the Dorig may be able to get water. Stimulated by Banot's comments on how the three peoples behave as groups, with his own people as hunters, Gair "had a sudden vision of Hathil as a stag, hunted this way, pushed that, running in bewilderment to the one place from which he could not escape" (Jones, *Power* 289). This vision arouses Gair's sympathy and remorse. He offers himself as sacrifice to appease the curse Hathil's brother has placed on the collar that Orban stole from him, explaining to Hathil that " 'My people are hunters [. . .] and I was sorry.' He could see that Hathil understood" (297). Hathil in turn is freed by his understanding of Gair's sympathy to recognise the absurdity of the situation that would force him to sacrifice Gair. He declares, "The Powers can do what they like, but I'm not going to touch either of you!" (297)—a gesture of life-giving that appeases the

New Power, the Power of life, and dissolves the curse.[4] Gair's capacity to perceive the underlying truth in a situation, and still more his empathetic concern for the plight of another, turns out to be more important to all the people of the Moor even than his siblings' Gifts or his own lately revealed Gift of Sight Unasked. His more human insight enables him to reconcile the enemy peoples and thus both dissolve the curse and further the solution of the water problem.

Jones's endorsement of empathy and similarity is underlined by her depiction of the three peoples in the text.

> Then a sudden perception came to [Gair]. Ayna, Brenda and [the Dorig] Halla were all glaring [. . .] Each had her head tilted in identical angry haughtiness. [. . .] "Have you noticed," Gair said loudly, "that we're all people really?"
>
> (*Power* 225)

Although Brenda adduces as support for her claim that Gair and the others are fairies the fact that they are "so little and sort of delicate, and so pretty" (156), they recognise that there is in fact little difference between the Giants/humans and the people/Lymen and that they can be mistaken for each other. Gerald's Aunt Mary is able to accept the children as human, if perhaps from Malaysia, affirming the novel's implied comment on racism (174). Mr Claybury recalls how he and Gerald's father met, when drunk, a little man—or at least although "George and he were much the same size [. . .] Titch *seemed* smaller" (189)—whom the children, and the reader, realise must have been their father Gest. The Dorig, though indeed shape-shifters, are discovered to be scaly not because they are fish-like but because they wear armour over bodies much like those of the other peoples. The focus of this wainscot fantasy, despite its initial introduction of an apparently imaginary society, is not on what is unknown in the world but on what may be known and misunderstood.

The justification Jones provides for positing the hidden existence of other peoples within ordinary English life is therefore very different from either Norton's or Pratchett's. While both those writers depict their characters as little people who can hide in the wainscots and crevices of the ordinary world, Jones represents her characters as near-human in size and appearance, but having extraordinary abilities of concealment. The Dorig live in underwater halls well beneath customary human diggings; more significantly, they have the power to change shape. Jones thus invites her readers to speculate that fish, crows, or sheep may in fact be transformed Dorig. Her depiction of the Lymen, her central characters, is more subtle, but depends ultimately on the same capacity: the Lymen can pass as human and are also extremely skilled at hiding themselves. Thus the Lymen can be readily overlooked or mistaken. A Lyman may be seen, like Gest, simply as a "little man," a "Titch," or, like the children, as Malaysian; a child Lyman may be mistaken, in fact, for a human child, as Gest warns Gair early in the novel that the Giants "steal children. [. . .] They stole a little girl from Islaw. [. . .] They seem to think they can bring children up better" (Jones, *Power* 49). Gest's comment highlights what we belatedly recognise to be the human tendency to assume that we know how the world works and what should happen—and also points to the human imperialist tendency to believe that our own society's practices are best for everyone. As in the Bromeliad, the reader is invited to consider the limitations of our assumptions, and to recognise that even actual differences—the Dorig really can shift shape, the Lymen can speak words that have magic effects—do not prevent the groups from being "all people really." Jones's deeper message warns against racism.

Any scepticism the reader may feel following the discovery that the characters are posited living in our own world is allayed by Jones's appeal to our own human capacity to misinterpret what we see: if the Dorig might exist unknown to us by disguising themselves as familiar creatures, the Lymen might exist unknown to us by being mistaken for human beings. Further, the suggestion that peoples could exist in the known world without our being aware of them because of our own capacity for misperception is narratively endorsed by the novel's deferred revelation that it is wainscot fantasy. Just as Orban affirms that the Dorig are cold-blooded creatures deserving death and Brenda can only accept the Lymen by identifying them as fairies, so the reader misidentifies the world of the novel as an alien fantasy world until compelled to recognise that it is our own. Gair becomes a model for the reader as he looks past the prejudices of his people to recognise the similarities between himself and Gerald and, even more astutely, to recognise the pressure placed on Hathil as that of hunters trapping a deer.

From its opening, Jones's narrative teaches its readers to read beyond the obvious. The double messages of this novel are, first, that things may be other than what they seem—an admired elder brother may be an arrogant bully, a scaly Dorig may be a warm-blooded person, an immersive fantasy may be contained within a wainscot—and, second, that the ability to see past our prejudices involves the expansion of our empathetic capacities. Both these messages are conveyed not only through the action of *Power of Three* but through its narrative production as wainscot fantasy and the ontological grounding Jones supplies for the unknown existence of the wainscot societies. Jones's narrative emphasises cross-cultural communication and the breaking down of prejudice by heightening perceptions to discover the reality beneath the illusion. Like Pratchett's, it encourages an open mind.

CONCLUSION

Jones and Pratchett both use the fantasy concept of the wainscot society, traditionally charming readers with its opportunities to re-imagine the physical world, as a starting point for complex consideration of how humans in ordinary life remain within mental barriers generated by social forces such as religious dogma or racial prejudice. They provide different answers to the ontological question implicitly raised in their fiction of how their wainscot societies can exist unknown within the ordinary world, but their narratives generate similar moral messages. Each very differently grounds the posited existence of their wainscot society, Pratchett through a somewhat tongue-in-cheek appeal to contemporary flirtations with scientific possibility and Jones not only through her depiction in the novel's action of how easy it is to misunderstand what we see, but by demonstrating the deceptions through which narrative itself can operate to conceal truths.

Pratchett's speculations, like Norton's, open up the known world, but where she emphasises its physical richness, he draws attention to the complexity and rigidity of many human social structures, which may blind us to more complex realities. By displacing human narrowness onto the nomes, especially in *Truckers* and *Diggers*, he provides the reader with the capacity to reflect on that narrowness and move beyond it, so that by the time the reader comes to *Wings* the limitations of the scientists anticipating the arrival of little green men can be recognised as just another form of preconception. Jones's *Power of Three* underlines especially the importance of intellectual and emotional openness in transcending the conventional modes of thinking that give rise to racism. The lesson here emerges not only thematically but as an effect of narrative structure: the narrator's deception of the reader, the belated revelation that Gair's people are a wainscot society within the ordinary human world, compels a reappraisal of the familiar, as we briefly perceive ourselves as Giants, and invites a broader vision of what being "people" is all about.

Both writers highlight the nature of their narratives as story. In the Bromeliad this emerges as a layering of narrative that emphasises the socially constructed nature of cultural assumptions. This parodic movement manifests Pratchett's literary project of raising readers' awareness of the authorities on which they so often rely, whether these be non-fiction or fictional texts, or simply the set of assumptions taken for granted within a culture. The Bromeliad demonstrates the necessity of intellectual openness to the survival of a community: if the Outside nomes had retained their traditional practices they would have died out, while if the Store nomes had refused to believe in the Outside they would have been destroyed when the Arnold Bros. building was demolished. The image of the frogs in the bromeliad provided in *Diggers* and elaborated in *Wings* underscores the importance of metaphorisation to this process of recognition—the nomes, and the reader, learn from images and stories how to reimagine their world.

In *Power of Three* Jones signals the extent to which narrative itself may be deceptive. The fact that it is a story with a teller actually matters to our experience of this narrative. We think we are reading immersive fantasy, but the narrator, focalising through Orban and Adara and Gair, is deceiving us rather in the way that Tom Riddle deceived Harry: she is not telling us the whole truth about the world she describes. The world is not as simple as the story says it is. Jones's transformation of the everyday into the fantastic points to the importance of reading as an interpretive strategy. As we shall see in the next chapter, Pratchett's and Jones's treatments of the figure of the witch/crone in their respective later novels also invite their readers to interrogate widespread cultural stereotypes both intellectually and emotionally. Jones and Pratchett deploy fantasy to stimulate readers to engage more effectively with their own realities.

NOTES

1. In the first novel this yearning is in tension with the borrowers' determination to remain unseen; in the next two Arrietty's desire and her parents' anxiety mainly work together, as the need for flight provides Arrietty with the adventure of exploration.
2. The novel begins with a peculiarly doubled, or negated, identification of the narrator:

   > It was Mrs May who first told me about them. No, not me. How could it have been me—a wild, untidy, self-willed little girl who stared with angry eyes and was said to crunch her teeth? Kate, she must have been called. [. . .] Not that the name matters much either way: she barely comes into the story.
   >
   > (Norton, The Borrowers 7)

   This shift from the identity posited in the first sentence disconcerts the reader and prepares for a shift in our understanding of what makes up the world.
3. The framing pages of *Truckers* do not carry numbers; the first numbered page is 11.
4. Mendlesohn points out that the novel takes a "radical turn" as "[t]he King rejects the prophecy. His resistance, not destiny, is what brings him to agency" (*Diana* 48), highlighting how, as we will see in *The Lives of Christopher Chant* (1988), Jones works to disable prophecy structures traditional in heroic fantasy.

4   Representing the Witch

Fairy tales, heroic fantasy, and to a lesser extent wainscot fantasies rely on the reader's acceptance of stereotypes: the princess in need of a rescuer, the sword-girt hero who must confront evil, the little person negotiating a world too big for them surrounded by monstrous enemies. Many of these stereotypes function as psychological archetypes, but their characteristic traits and attributes emerge from particular cultural contexts. It is therefore especially interesting when such archetypal figures retain features, and indeed whole behaviours, apparently long obsolete within the contemporary culture. One such figure is the witch, who gained prominence as an object of fear in the European Middle Ages, when the populace believed in the capacity of individuals to harm others magically, but who survives as a recognisable and indeed frequently visible icon. Moreover, the witch persists in contemporary cultural mythology specifically in her crone form, despite the fact that the woman beyond childbearing has ceased to be irrelevant to her community in an era that has expanded ideas of productivity beyond physical fertility. This chapter examines the representations of the witch in Jones's *Howl's Moving Castle* (1986) and Pratchett's Tiffany Aching sequence (2003–10), which directly respond to earlier stereotypes particularly of the crone-witch, and not only revise them but radically revalue them. In these novels Jones and Pratchett pursue the project visible in their wainscot fantasies of breaking down limiting assumptions. Both authors also depict characters coming to terms with their own identities and capacities and developing confidence in their personal agency. In the process, Jones and Pratchett also represent their characters dealing with confining fictions while themselves exploiting fictional possibilities to provide ever more complex models for their readers of reading and of living.

Cultural anxieties surrounding the figure of the witch have been modified, but not erased, since the Enlightenment. Intriguingly, the figure of the witch has become a primarily visual icon in popular culture, although her well-known features—the pointed hat, the broomstick—are intrinsic neither to her bodily nature nor to her activities. During the eras of witch persecutions young women and even a small number of men were targeted along with the crones we now associate with the tradition of the wicked witch, often as family groups (Sanders 181), but subsequent representations have focused on the witch as a hook-nosed, malicious old woman in a black cloak. Roy Porter notes that

> Witch personae [. . .] could blossom as comic grotesques at the very time when real witches were disappearing from the daily fears of the edu-cated. [. . .] Meanwhile the shawl-clad crone [. . .] lived on in Romantic fairy-tales, children's fiction, and, in the twentieth-century, Disney.
>
> (246–47)

Although there have been some attempts to rehabilitate the witch in chil-dren's literature and elsewhere—notably through the revival of Wicca—until recently most of these have been superficial. Diane Purkiss remarks that "despite the subtleties of radical feminists, historians and modern witches, the dominant image of the witch is still of a shrieking hag on a broomstick" (276). In various picture books of the past half century or so, witches feature as central characters, but the stories generally play, usually to comic effect as in Don Freeman's *Tilly Witch* (1969), on associations of the witch with mischief and ill-temper. Even where the witch is positively represented, her goodness is frequently contrasted with more traditionally malign witches, as in Otfried Preussler's *The Little Witch* (1961) and James Stevenson's similar though more light-hearted *Yuck!* (1985). Jill Murphy's *The Worst Witch* (1970) and its sequels feature a child witch attending a witch school and learning how to ride a broomstick with a cat perched on it; even here, how-ever, Murphy's Mildred compensates for her ineptness in the eyes of the authorities by accidentally discovering a plot by an evil coven to take over the school.

Elizabeth George Speare's *The Witch of Blackbird Pond* (1958) provides an early example of a more serious investigation of the witch stereotype and its cultural implications. In this novel, to be a witch is to be an outsider in a society itself seen by the outsider-protagonist, Kit, as rigid and repressive. The "witch" Hannah represents generosity, tolerance, and appreciation for beauty in a society (Puritan Connecticut Colony) that appears to permit none of these things. In *The Witch of Blackbird Pond*, the gentle tolerance of Hannah is set in sharp contrast with the rigid morality of Kit's Uncle Mat-thew and the jealous hostility of Goodwife Cruff. The eventual accusation that impulsive, generous Kit is herself a witch who curses children makes clear to the reader both the absurdity of the label and the personal spite frequently responsible for its application. However, *The Witch of Blackbird Pond* is concerned with the underlying problem of communal scapegoating for which the witch label is a device, rather than with any attempt to imag-ine the witch in genuinely positive terms. Hannah is revealed to be simply an old woman demonised because of her Quaker faith, and the job of the protagonist and the novel is to demonstrate this. The underlying story of the novel is Kit's discovery of a society and a way of life that can fit her personality. The attempt by some members of this society to label Kit a witch is in effect an alternative categorisation of her position as outsider—a categorisation neither she nor the reader accepts. Speare's novel reads as a powerful defence of those who have been wrongly identified as witches.

E.L. Konigsburg's *Jennifer, Hecate, Macbeth, and Me* (1967; originally published as *Jennifer, Hecate, Macbeth, William McKinley, and Me, Elizabeth*) provides a different account of the possible cultural usefulness of the witch stereotype. In *Jennifer, Hecate* the role of the witch is deliberately played by the child Jennifer and learned by Elizabeth, the narrator, who is "hungry for company" (Konigsburg 10). The witch identity here is a way for two friendless children to gain power, initially over one another, but also over others. Here too, however, the witch label is revealed as a convenient device to serve other goals. In this case, the children discard the roles of master and apprentice witch when Elizabeth discovers Jennifer's secret. Elizabeth and Jennifer then shed the power relationship that has governed them and even play with other girls: "Neither of us is lonely any more. [. . .] Neither of us pretends to be a witch any more. Now we mostly enjoy being what we really are" (Konigsburg 96). The goal of the novel has been for Elizabeth to overcome her temporary situation as outcast; the witch role is merely a means to that end. Like *The Witch of Blackbird Pond*, in other words, *Jennifer, Hecate* is more about fitting into a society than about rejecting or reimagining its assumptions.

More recently, J.K. Rowling's Harry Potter sequence (1997–2007) has renamed the witch as the female version of a wizard rather than, as is traditional, of a warlock, so that witchcraft there is assimilated to its historically more intellectually impressive and less stigmatised counterpart, wizardry.[1] In both *The Worst Witch* series (1974–present) and, more powerfully, the Harry Potter sequence, the trappings of the witch, including black robes and broomstick, become part of the glamour with which the authors endow their characters to establish them as figures of fantasy and, especially in the case of Murphy's characters, of humour. Meanwhile, John Stephens has observed the consciously revisory stance of some young-adult novels of the past few decades, which substitute for the crone-witch a conception of the witch as wise woman ("Witch-Figures"). Such portrayals draw on the arguments by some feminists that the medieval crone was treated with suspicion by authorities because she represented an alternative source of knowledge to that provided by the Church. As Stephens notes, these revisory fictions provide social critique ("Witch-Figures" 201). In many cases, however, notably Monica Furlong's *Wise Child* (1987), the wise witch is still portrayed as rejected by her society, underlining her role as outsider and emphasising that she remains a problematic figure.

The image of the witch has, however, been radically reconsidered by two of the novelists I am discussing here, Terry Pratchett and Diana Wynne Jones, both of whom use the figure of the witch, particularly the crone-witch, to represent their concerns with literary and social convention. Their representations of the witch can be read as positively re-valuing the nature and potential of this figure: indeed, their representations become not just depiction but advocacy. As indicated in Chapter 1, Pratchett's Tiffany Aching sequence focuses on the education and maturation of a child witch; as I demonstrate here, it includes extensive consideration both of the cultural significance of the crone-witch image and the potential social power of the witch as agent. Across the sequence, Pratchett develops an increasingly complex discussion of the witch as stereotype. He not only explores the attraction and fear displayed in attitudes to the witch, but also examines the strategies, both social and literary, that contemplation of those feelings makes possible. Diana Wynne Jones focuses specifically on the image of the crone in her novel *Howl's Moving Castle*, the protagonist of which is early transformed from a young woman to a crone and discovers agency only in her new role. Not only Sophie's crone appearance, however, but her magic capabilities are central to the plot of the novel, which features a number of characters who are described as witches. Like Pratchett, Jones critiques cultural conventions and assumptions through her protagonist's experiences, constructing images both of the crone and of the witch that acknowledge and subvert traditional representations and clichéd behaviours. At the same time, her narrative's complex intertextual operation insists on the literary heritage that informs contemporary attitudes not only to the figure of the witch but to our expectations of life generally. Both writers act as advocates for the witch in quite different ways from their predecessors, as we shall see. They revisit the witch/crone image in order above all to underline the illusory nature of appearances and the extent to which stereotypes must be recognised and overcome as their respective protagonists gain agency.

THE ENCHANTMENT OF LITERATURE

Howl's Moving Castle centres on a young girl named Sophie who believes herself doomed to failure—or at best a dull life—because this is what happens to eldest daughters in fairy tales, which routinely privilege the youngest of three. The setting of this novel is established from the beginning as a magical one, and specifically one governed by story:

> In the land of Ingary, where such things as seven-league boots and cloaks of invisibility really exist, it is quite a misfortune to be born the eldest of three. Everyone knows you are the one who will fail first, and worst, if the three of you set out to seek your fortunes.
>
> Sophie Hatter was the eldest of three sisters. She was not even the child of a poor woodcutter [. . .] True, her own mother died [. . .] and their father married his youngest shop assistant [. . .] Fanny shortly gave birth to the third sister, Martha. This ought to have made Sophie and Lettie into Ugly Sisters, but in fact all three girls grew up very pretty

indeed. [. . .] Fanny treated all three girls with the same kindness, and did not favour Martha in the least.

(Jones, *Howl's* 9–10)

Right from the start, we are told both that "[e]veryone knows" that fairy-tale patterns are true, and yet that this is not always the case. Sophie and Lettie are not "Ugly" despite being Martha's stepsisters, and Fanny is not the Wicked Stepmother who is cruel to her stepchildren. This gives us two hints: first, that Sophie is wrong in her assumptions; second, that what "[e]veryone knows" is not necessarily true. The first point informs the plot as it relates to Sophie, telling us that her view of her life is unnecessarily gloomy, and the second the plot as it relates to the wizard Howl, of whom we and Sophie learn things that "everyone knows" in the next few pages. Again, what "everyone knows" will turn out to be wrong. As Sophie eventually realises, Howl is "heartless" (12) only because he has given his heart to Calcifer, a fire demon, in order to keep him alive. The plot in fact turns on the contract between Howl and Calcifer, which Calcifer recognises is bad for both of them, and on the parallel contract between the malevolent Witch of the Waste and the equally malevolent fire demon first known to the reader as a schoolteacher from our own world named Miss Angorian. Both contracts must be broken in order to save the lives of Howl and Calcifer, and to protect the realm of Ingary from Miss Angorian, working through the Witch.

Like Pratchett's Tiffany, Sophie perceives the roles assigned by stories to be confining, although unlike Tiffany she is initially resigned to her role. She believes that the potential heroine must be born into the position, mentally observing that "Lettie, as the second daughter, was never likely to come to much [. . .] Martha[, the youngest, . . .] was bound to strike out and make her fortune" (Jones, *Howl's* 13). When her stepmother Fanny tells Sophie, not to Sophie's surprise, that she will inherit the family hat shop, Sophie grows increasingly passive and despairing. Her understanding of life, shaped by fairy-tale stories of destiny, leaves no room for agency. Thus Sophie is shocked when she discovers that Lettie and Martha have swapped places, evading Fanny's plans for them, because Lettie is ambitious and Martha wants only to marry young and have ten children. Sophie's own increasing frustration with her lonely life making hats only finds expression, however, through her habit of talking to the hats—telling them things that, as the reader realises but Sophie does not, have magical effects—and eventually talking back to exigent customers.

One of these customers turns out to be the Witch of the Waste, who transforms Sophie into a crone because she is "meddl[ing] with things that belong to" the Witch (Jones, *Howl's* 32)—presumably by casting spells and thereby usurping the Witch's authority.[2] At this point, interestingly, Sophie does not react either like the passive spinster she has appeared or like a traditional fairy-tale heroine waiting to be rescued. Instead, she tells her image in the mirror "Don't worry old thing [. . .] this is much more like you really are" (33), and leaves to seek her fortune. Thus, Sophie finds room for agency outside the conventionally accepted roles for young girls. Despite her aches and pains, she is both more active and more optimistic as a crone than she ever was as a girl. She invades the dreaded moving castle, owned by Howl, in search of a comfortable armchair, confident that "Wizard Howl is not likely to want *my* soul for his collection. He takes only young girls" (38). To be a young girl is experienced by Sophie as confining; to be a crone, outside the limits of maiden, wife, or mother, is to be liberated. Later, she muses "It was odd. As a girl, Sophie would have shrivelled with embarrassment at the way she was behaving. As an old woman she did not mind what she did or said. She found that a great relief" (66). In some children's fiction, going back to F. Anstey's 1882 novel *Vice Versa*, a child magically becomes an adult who is seen as a figure of free power, and has to learn about constraints on that role; by contrast, Sophie gains from losing her girlhood. In taking on the physical constraints of the crone, Sophie feels herself free to be personally expressive and so gains her own agency. Her inhabiting of the crone role recalls Elizabeth's and Jennifer's taking on the witch role, as all three extend their social capacities through the role play; but Sophie's experience is in all ways less superficial.

Jones's depiction of Sophie might appear to distinguish the possibly neutral crone from the wicked witch, but the situation is not as simple as this. One of Sophie's first encounters with people as an old woman is with a farmer who automatically assumes that, being a crone, she must be a witch, and fears her as a result: " '[. . .] I wish you good luck, Mother, provided your fortune don't have nothing to do with charming folks' cattle.' And he took off down the road in great strides, almost running, but not quite" (Jones, *Howl's* 37). As the novel's opening paragraph suggests, Sophie is not alone in Ingary in believing in fairy-tale stereotypes, and the depiction of the Witch of the Waste appears to confirm their accuracy. Yet other elements complicate this picture. After all, Sophie's stepmother Fanny had planned for her own daughter Martha to be apprenticed to a witch, her own old schoolfriend Mrs Fairfax:

> "You mean the one who talks such a lot," said Martha. "Isn't she a witch?"
>
> "Yes, with a lovely house and clients all over the Folding Valley," Fanny said eagerly. "She's a good woman, Martha. [. . .] You'll be all set up in life when she's done with you."
>
> "She's a nice lady," Martha conceded. "All right."
>
> (13)

Despite what might be taken as an objection—"Isn't she a witch?"—Martha is quite ready to acknowledge that Mrs Fairfax is a nice lady and that she herself might do well to learn her trade.[3] Although Martha subsequently runs away to take her sister Lettie's place as a baker's apprentice, her decision has to do with their joint ambitions in life rather than any fear of the witch herself or her trade—Martha actually makes use of one of Mrs Fairfax's spells to make the exchange—and Lettie appears to have no qualms in taking Martha's place. Later, Sophie is compelled to visit Howl's old teacher, the witch Mrs Penstemmon, and discovers her to be a very formidable, and formal, old woman, but by no means an evil one. Again, the fairy-tale stereotypes in which Ingary is purported to abound are shown to be far from universal.

Although Sophie is made indignant by the farmer's assumptions, she later accepts the label of witch assigned to her by the citizens of Porthaven and Kingsbury, to both of which the door of the magic castle leads, and so prepares herself unknowingly for the discovery that she can in fact work magic. She eventually regains her own body through the conscious use of magical power. When the Witch of the Waste's fire demon steals Howl's heart, with Calcifer attached, Sophie realises that she herself must act. Following Calcifer's endorsement of her growing recognition that she can "talk life into things" (Jones, *Howl's* 297), she gives Calcifer himself more life as she removes the heart, saving both Calcifer and Howl from the enemy. In so doing she breaks the contract that binds Calcifer to Howl and so ensures that Calcifer in turn will fulfil his promise and break the spell placed on her by the Witch of the Waste. Sophie thus reveals herself as indeed a witch, and, more significantly, as the heroine of her own story. As her sisters have believed all along, their destinies are not determined by fairy tale conventions but by their own decisions and desires. Only when Sophie accepts her own success, as woman and witch, can she return to her youthful self and acknowledge its beauty. As crone and witch, Sophie has learned her own value. Jones thus provides a double revisiting of the witch stereotype, depicting the witch's stereotypical crone form as a way for the timid Sophie to explore alternative aspects of her identity, and her underlying witch powers not as embodying the destructiveness implied by the farmer's fears and the resonant title of the Witch of the Waste, but as a source of life.

Although Sophie, like Konigsburg's Elizabeth and Jennifer, clearly profits from wearing the witch label, *Howl's Moving Castle* presents the role of witch/crone in a very different light from Konigsburg's novel.[4] It is true that Sophie returns to her younger incarnation at the end of the novel, but she does not lose the power that she has gained, and it is clear that she has accepted the status of witch. Although it is arguable that Sophie's experience as a crone is like Elizabeth's in serving as a stepping stone—in this case to Sophie's discovery of agency—it is significant that she retains and indeed claims the power of a witch in her extension of Calcifer's life and restoration of Howl's heart to his body. Sophie's constraint as young woman has been due to her own belief in the controlling power of story, a belief not shared by others in her community. It is Sophie's acceptance of what "everyone knows" but few apparently believe that has left her feeling isolated and unable to act. As with the fairy tales in *The Wee Free Men* (2003), the conventions of story have proved dangerous; Sophie becomes empowered through taking on the role not only of crone but of witch.

The spell that visibly transforms Sophie is cast by the Witch of the Waste, but there are numerous hints that Sophie herself is also partly responsible for her enchantment. Reading backward, the reader can work out that Sophie has bewitched herself into the belief that she is "[l]ike an old maid" (Jones, *Howl's* 19); her exceptional timidity dates from the moment she tells her reflection this. Howl eventually tells her that "I came to the conclusion that you liked being in disguise" (261). Clearly, Sophie's magic extends beyond the capacity eventually identified by Calcifer when he tells her, "I could tell you could talk life into things" (297). What is interesting is the reason behind Sophie's self-enchantment, which is to say her determination that her life must conform to the patterns found in fairy tales. *Howl's Moving Castle* presents a critique of the conventions of story and, by extension, of the often arbitrary customs that shape social roles. Jones points out how the unreflecting acceptance of convention can be limiting, but conversely demonstrates that the conscious choice of a role, even a stereotyped one, can be liberating. The key is reflection: Sophie learns to recognise what she wants herself to be and how her personal qualities may best be expressed independent of cultural assumptions.

This attention to story itself can be observed especially through Jones's treatment of specific intertextual material. Carolynn E. Wilcox has observed the novel's evocation of Donne's "Song (Goe, and catche a falling starre)," a poem that Sophie first reads with Howl's apprentice Michael, who believes it to be a spell Howl has left him to perform for practice. As a result of this mistake, Michael and Sophie approach the first stanza of the poem as a list of puzzles, despite Sophie's recognition—accurate in real-world terms— that "[i]t looks to me like a set of impossible things to do" (Jones, *Howl's* 128). Their behaviour makes evident the ways in which the novel repeatedly offers both Sophie and the reader sets of puzzles and mysteries. What is the second layer of enchantment that Calcifer detects beneath the Witch's spell on Sophie? What is the nature of Calcifer's contract with Howl? What lies behind the castle door when the knob is turned to black? What has happened to Wizard Suliman and to the king's brother Prince Justin, who went in quest of him? Why does the scarecrow Sophie found in the hedge before she entered the castle start pursuing the castle? Sophie comes to her own conclusions about some of the smaller puzzles she discerns, generally informed by her fairy-tale assumptions, and these are often—but not always—wrong. The novel as a whole, for instance, does have what may be considered a fairy-tale ending, in which Sophie is not only restored to youth but rewarded with a handsome lover, and her sisters find partners as well. However, Howl's looks are cosmetically and magically enhanced, and his character is far from perfect even when his heart is restored:

"[. . .] Would you call your hair ginger?"

"Red gold," Sophie said. [. . .] "Unlike some people's," she said, "it's natural."

"I've never seen why people put such value on things being natural," Howl said, and Sophie knew then that he was scarcely changed at all.

(299–300)

Realism and fairy tale remain intertwined in the novel's conclusion.

This intertwining affects other elements as well. The reader may laugh at Sophie's, and apparently her fellow citizens', literal interpretation of the rumour that Howl "was an utterly cold-blooded and heartless wizard and no young girl was safe from him if he caught her on her own" (Jones, *Howl's* 12); however, Howl does turn out to be literally heartless, having given his heart to Calcifer to keep under the logs on which he burns. Likewise the reader who recognises Donne's "Song" will be amused at Michael's belief that it is a spell with lines that can be carried out, and unsurprised when Howl reveals it to be a piece of his nephew's homework back in Wales. But Wales itself appears through Sophie's eyes as the fantasy space here, and the poem is after all being used by the fire demon Miss Angorian to capture Howl. Sophie recognises that the "impossible things" are being fulfilled: "He's being honest! And this is a wind. The last bit of the curse has come true!" (292). Readers who believe that—unlike Sophie—they have a secure grasp on the difference between story and reality may find their assurance disturbed by the events of the text.

Gili Bar-Hillel has discussed Jones's evocation of L. Frank Baum's *The Wonderful Wizard of Oz* (1900), which is most noticeable to the reader as the echo of the wicked Witch of the West in Jones's villainous Witch of the Waste. As in Baum's novel, the protagonist passes through different zones that are colour-coded; in *Howl's Moving Castle*, however, these zones are not literally coloured, as in *The Wonderful Wizard of Oz*, but are entered by turning a knob on the castle door to a different spot of colour. A reader who notices the parallel may infer that, as in Baum's novel, each zone has its appropriate witch—Mrs Pentstemmon lives in Kingsbury, Mrs Fairfax in the direction of Porthaven, Sophie herself comes from Market Chipping above which the castle roams—and so gain a clue to the fact that the most dangerous figure in the novel may be found in the fourth zone, Wales: the fire demon/school-teacher Miss Angorian. But again this solution is right but wrong. By the time Miss Angorian's demonic identity is revealed, Howl has moved the castle and its entries and recoded the door from the familiar red, blue, and green to yellow, purple, and orange, and only then does one exit lead to the edge of the Waste, home of the Witch. Baum's novel is not a template for Jones's, but a paint pot into which she dips; as Bar-Hillel explains, *Howl's Moving Castle* is "something new created from the pieces of past texts" (391).

Thus the independent child Dorothy seeking to return home follow-ing the tornado becomes in Sophie a figure who must not only attain the agency of which Dorothy is already a mistress, but do so in the person of the witch. Sophie objects to the Witch's "mak[ing] jigsaws out of people" (Jones, *Howl's* 287); it is arguable that the whole of *Howl's Moving Castle* makes a jigsaw out of *The Wonderful Wizard of Oz*. In doing this, however, Jones transforms both characters and concepts from Baum's novel to make something quite different. One of the resulting messages to the reader, as to Sophie, is that we should never rely on literature, or literary convention, as a template for life. Rather, we should recognise the witch who constructs each story as a spell, and should be prepared to talk our own life into the way we want it to be. Sophie starts the novel as a naïve reader, but she ends it as a conscious agent, and her journey becomes a model for Jones's readers.

THE GLAMOUR OF MAGIC

Pratchett too depicts his central character as on a journey that may provide a model for his readers. As we have seen in Chapter 1, *The Wee Free Men*, the first of his four Discworld novels featuring Tiffany Aching, makes clear from the start the problematic portrayal of crones as witches in story even as its protagonist critiques that portrayal. Pratchett has previously demonstrated fairly detailed knowledge of the Lancashire witch trials of the seventeenth century in *Good Omens*, his 1990 collaboration with Neil Gaiman, which draws on names and incidents from that period. The Tiffany Aching sequence displays his engagement with folklore both as a source of knowledge and as a somewhat troubling zone of possibly erroneous beliefs that nevertheless have real force within people's lives. It also examines the ways in which alert individuals can consciously respond to and manipulate those beliefs in order not only to shape their own identities but to revise community expectations.

The action of *The Wee Free Men* frequently hinges on Tiffany's memories of her grandmother, whom she insists may have been a witch. Miss Tick is initially sceptical when Tiffany interprets "cursing" as Granny Aching's habit of "cuss[ing] the sky blue" (Pratchett, *Wee* 41), and Tiffany's own recollection of seeing her grandmother "*bring lambs back to life*" (40) turns out to involve the explanation that the warming oven in which her grandmother placed the lambs was just warm enough to thaw them when they were nearly frozen to death. Tiffany's italicised memory, however, concludes with the comment that "*[i]t didn't stop being magic just because you found out how it was done*" (41). The sequence in fact depends on the developing perception of the relationship between what is seen, what is known, and what is actually happening. Through Tiffany's memories, we see that Granny Aching used her knowledge of the ways of the natural and social world to transform behaviour, as when she teaches a sheep-worrying dog to fear sheep by shutting it up with a ewe and her lamb—and in the process teaches the Baron, the dog's owner, both that her judgement cannot be commanded or bought and that he himself must take responsibility for his desires. Granny Aching's mastery of her community seems magical, but depends on her thorough understanding of the ways of her world and commitment to natural justice. For Pratchett, it is this combination of perception and ethical commitment that defines the witch. Rather than being simply a social reject or a cursing crone, the witch takes responsibility for the well-being of the community—an idea Pratchett had already developed in his adult Discworld novels. Outside the community only in so far as she sees beyond its assumptions, the Discworld witch oversees the life of her society.

In this first novel of the sequence, then, the iconic characteristics of the witch are de-emphasised in favour of a vision of the witch as a potential figure of ethical capacity and authority. The novel's stress on the delusive nature of appearances, underlined by the dream-illusions Tiffany encounters in Fairyland, ensures rejection of the simplistic stereotyping that caused the death of the hapless old woman Mrs Snapperly, who is identified as a witch by her community. It is significant that when Tiffany finally meets the two senior witches of Pratchett's Discworld, Granny Weatherwax and Nanny Ogg, she perceives them not as witches but just as women wearing shabby black dresses, one of them able to stand tall, "which could easily fool you [into thinking her tall] if you weren't paying attention" (Pratchett, *Wee* 300). These details represent Tiffany's own ability to "see what's really there" (140) and refusal to draw easy inferences; the effect for the reader, however, is further to dissociate the identity of the witch from her physical being. Only the pointy hat, by apparent *lack* of which Tiffany first identified the witch Miss Tick, remains, not as stigma but as a private badge of membership. When Mistress Weatherwax acknowledges Tiffany's potential to be a witch, she makes the shape of a hat above her head—a symbolic gesture with magically real effect, as Tiffany discovers that the hat, though invisible, can be very faintly felt by her fingers (308). *The Wee Free Men* appears to reject the visual details of the witch as other than iconic; Tiffany ends by making a butter-stamp featuring a witch on a broomstick and vowing that "[t]hings would be different one day" (318). At this stage of the sequence, the image of the witch is, socially and culturally, under revision.

Tiffany's vow establishes a straightforward resistance to the traditional associations of the witch stereotype. However, Pratchett extends and complicates his reassessment of the meaning of the witch in his subsequent novels about Tiffany. What may be described as the Mrs Snapperly problem, together with the inherently human habit of reading the world symbolically, remains an important concern throughout the Tiffany Aching sequence, and is addressed differently in each novel as Tiffany's development progresses. In *A Hat Full of Sky* (2004), the Mrs Snapperly problem at its simplest—the hatred of the witch—appears to have been solved. When Tiffany returns to her community at the end of the novel, the villagers become quite proud of her. Tiffany is one of them, so if she is a witch that must be an acceptable role. "We got a witch now, and she's better'n anyone else's! No one's throwing Granny Aching's grand-daughter in a pond!" (Pratchett, *A Hat* 348). This is a very different solution to that hatred from that provided in *The Witch of Blackbird Pond*, which required the exculpation of Kit and the removal of Hannah from the hostility of their neighbours. The idea of the witch as outsider or as needing to respond to a social constraint is discarded; Pratchett's focus instead is on the positive value of the witch.

However, *A Hat Full of Sky* has posed a further problem with that valu-ation. As Elisabeth Rose Gruner has observed, much of the action of this novel concerns the education of young witches in the physical and moral demands of ordinary life. The problem here is the obverse of the Mrs Snap-perly problem: the young witches desire the special glamour that has more recently been associated with the witch—the allure of the siren. Anna-gramma, apprenticed to the glamorous Mrs Earwig, sees magic as a mys-tical means to power over other people. Even Tiffany—who as we have seen prides herself on seeing beyond stereotypes—is bored and frustrated by the humdrum nature of her work with Miss Level, to whom she herself is apprenticed. "She'd expected—well, what? Well . . . to be doing serious witch stuff, you know, broomsticks, magic, guarding the world in a noble yet modest way, and then *also* doing good for poor people *because she was a really nice person*" (Pratchett, *A Hat* 149). Tiffany's expectations coincide with those of many readers—and non-readers—of fantasy, and could be taken as a description of Harry Potter ("guarding the world in a noble yet modest way"), but Pratchett makes clear that this is not what witchcraft, or by extension moral action, is centrally about. Later, Tiffany asks the senior witch why she was sent to Miss Level, whom even the villagers do not respect, and is told it was

> "Because she likes people [. . .] Even the stupid, mean, dribbling ones, the mothers with the runny babies and no sense, the feckless and the silly and the fools who treat her like some kind of a servant. Now that's what I call magic—seein' all that, dealin' with all that, and still going on. [. . .] That is the root and heart and soul and centre of witchcraft, that is. The soul and centre!" Mistress Weatherwax smacked her fist into her hand, hammering out her words. "The . . . soul . . . and . . . centre!"
> (249–50)

This passage emphasises the value of a set of behaviours and a moral atti-tude as opposed to a glamorous appearance—although this is somewhat undercut as the passage goes on, as I shall demonstrate below.

When she is possessed by the monstrous hiver, Tiffany grows aggres-sive as well as vain and arrogant. Exploiting her magical powers in one of the few scenes in the sequence where these are displayed, she transforms a young pseudo-wizard into a frog because he is obstructing her in her acquisition of several useless but impressive magical objects—including a tall pointy hat covered in silver stars, a gauze black cloak, and a spangled wand. Importantly, Tiffany later accepts responsibility for her actions while under the influence of the hiver, acknowledging that it was acting on her own desires. "It was me!' wailed Tiffany. 'The hiver *was* me! It wasn't thinking with my brain, it was using my thoughts! It was using what it found in my head!" (Pratchett, *A Hat* 251). However, as Mistress Weatherwax points out, these are desires Tiffany always represses.

> "That . . . nastiness. All it was was me with—"
> "—*without* the bit of you that was locked away," said Mistress Weatherwax sharply. [. . .] "The locked-up bit was the important bit [. . .] Learnin' how not to do things is as hard as learning *how* to do them. Harder, maybe."
>
> (251)

Tiffany's moral education is clear in *A Hat Full of Sky*. Evil is above all something to be confronted within the self; the hiver, like a Renaissance allegorical monster, merely externalises a problem within the whole human being. Good and evil are states of mind, co-existing even within the one person. The hiver itself turns out to be a fundamentally lonely and frightened entity; its evil turns out to be a function of weakness and insecurity. Tiffany recognises that what it wants is safety and closure, and teaches it to die. When Mistress Weatherwax in turn rescues Tiffany from behind Death's door at the Witch Trials—here equivalent to sheepdog trials[5]—both are content to let others show off their witch powers, secure in the actuality of their own achievements. This conclusion underscores the message that real power does not consist in appearances. Annagramma and her mentor are irrelevant to the fight against the hiver and unconsidered during the Witch Trials, and the other apprentice witches recognise this and reject the influence of Annagramma in favour of the reality of Tiffany's achievement.

At the same time as it elevates moral worth as opposed to glamour, however, *A Hat Full of Sky* does cater to the reader's desire, like Tiffany's, for magic. The short paragraph that follows Mistress Weatherwax's endorsement of Miss Level's behaviour as "the soul and centre" of witchcraft underlines the importance of what she is saying, but also undercuts it. "Echoes came back from the trees in the sudden silence. Even the grasshoppers by the side of the track had stopped sizzling" (Pratchett, *A Hat* 250). Paradoxically, Mistress Weatherwax's own passionate conviction that the centre of witchcraft is helping people with daily life and not with magic is expressed with a fervour that seems to have magical effects. The action of the novel also bears out the idea that there is something intrinsically more interesting about dealing with magical beings than about living like a cross between a district nurse and community social worker. The adventure of the novel for the reader lies in Tiffany's dealings with the hiver, and the quest of the Nac Mac Feegle to help free her from it, rather than in her mundane work assisting Miss Level; like Jones, Pratchett acknowledges and indeed exploits the enchantment of fiction itself. This disjunction between the novel's explicit message and implicit operation becomes important as Pratchett expands the discussion of the nature of appearance in the subsequent novels of the sequence.

In *A Hat Full of Sky*, the elements of magical adventure and personal responsibility come together in Tiffany's last visit to Mr Weavall, the old man whose savings she has stolen when under the influence of the hiver. Dreading his discovery of the empty box, Tiffany discovers that the Nac Mac Feegle have replaced the stolen coins with gold, and Mr Weavall decides to get married on the strength of this, dismaying her by thanking her for the theft. Mistress Weatherwax inquires,

> "It would have been better if he'd been buried in some ol' cheap coffin paid for by the village, you think?"
>
> "No!" Tiffany twisted up her fingers. Mistress Weatherwax was sharper than a field of pins. "But . . . all right, it just doesn't seem . . . fair. I mean, I wish the Feegles hadn't done that. I'm sure I could have sorted it out somehow, saved up . . ."
>
> "It's an unfair world, child. Be glad you have friends."
>
> (Pratchett, *A Hat* 266)

As in her "murder" of Miss Level, one of whose two bodies she has killed, the wrong Tiffany has done Mr Weavall has been righted by magic, and she feels guilty about this. But Mistress Weatherwax is a realist—and so is Pratchett. The world is unfair in all sorts of ways, Tiffany's friendship with the Nac Mac Feegle being only one of her advantages, and magic does make things easier, including the provision of education in how the world works to child readers. If she had not been possessed by the hiver, and aided by the Nac Mac Feegle, Tiffany might have spent a lot longer being frustrated by cutting Mr Weavall's toenails, and have been more likely to be swayed by Anna-gramma's dreams of glamour. The pleasure of reading *A Hat Full of Sky*, like the pleasure of reading Harry Potter, starts with its promise of magical adventure; the reader, like Tiffany, learns through those magical adventures as well as through the more prosaic lessons her mentors emphasise. Pratchett's literary strategy makes clear that style, not just substance, does matter.

It is perhaps unsurprising, then, that the issue of the witch's physical appearance and its effect on the viewer takes a new form in *Wintersmith* (2006). Here the adventure and plot of the novel is provided by Tiffany's encounter with the elemental wintersmith who mistakes her for his counterpart the Summer Lady and falls in love with her—to embarrassing and eventually dangerous effect. The Nac Mac Feegle teach Roland, the baron's son from *The Wee Free Men* with whom she has had a not-quite-amorous relationship since, to be a Hero; he penetrates the underworld in true mythic fashion to bring back the true Summer Lady, energised by his own hatred of his domineering and lying aunts. Tiffany, who turns thirteen in the course of this novel, takes lessons not so much in sex education as in the art of flirtation from Nanny Ogg, and when she is taken by the wintersmith to his ice palace she melts him, quite literally, with a kiss, ending the prolonged winter and allowing the Summer Lady to return to her seasonal power.

Despite its dependence on underlying myth, Pratchett's story in *Wintersmith* emphasises the importance of appearances. Tiffany is mistaken for the Summer Lady because she steps in and takes the Summer Lady's place in the mysterious dark Morris dance that, in Pratchett's Discworld, complements the more customary spring dance by summoning winter. But the wintersmith's error also depends on Tiffany's own appearance, "A witch who won't wear black. No, it's blue and green for her, like green grass under a blue sky," as Granny Weatherwax puts it, and that appearance reflects the reality that "[s]he calls to the strength of her hills, all the time. An' they calls to her! [. . .] And this shapes her life" (Pratchett, *Wintersmith* 132). The wintersmith's mistake may look like the villagers' misreading of Mrs Snapperly, but is more subtle in that there is a reality behind Tiffany's appearance, even if the wintersmith misunderstands it. He also further mistakes appearance for reality by trying to make himself a man, again in a classic folktale error, by compounding what he hopes is a human body from the list of elements—though crucially with the essential emotional ones omitted—that he learns from a children's song. The magic of the story in turn depends on the reality of the wintersmith and the Summer Lady as avatars who have drawn life from human uses of their images to symbolise the seasons. It is therefore appropriate that the wintersmith attempts to woo Tiffany by making snowflakes and even icebergs in her image, making the courtship ritual of gifts out of tribute to her appearance.

The story of Tiffany's witch education in *Wintersmith* reflects this focus on the power of appearances. In this novel she encounters what Granny Weatherwax, elsewhere in Pratchett's Discworld novels, calls "headology" (*Witches* 111), and what is here called "Boffo." Tiffany is currently in service to the witch Miss Treason, who claims to be one hundred and thirteen years old, who can see out of the eyes of animals, whose house is festooned with cobwebs and skulls, and of whom "[t]here was a story in the villages that [her] clock was Miss Treason's heart, which she'd used ever since her first heart died. But there were lots of stories about Miss Treason" (Pratchett, *Wintersmith* 39). As Tiffany discovers, not all of these stories are quite true—although Miss Treason can indeed see out of the eyes of animals, as can some of Pratchett's other witches. More significantly here, Tiffany learns that Miss Treason herself spreads and feeds the stories. When Miss Treason berates her for entering the dark Morris, Tiffany responds by shouting "Boffo, Boffo, Boffo!" (83), revealing her knowledge that many of the trappings of witchery in Miss Treason's house are fakes purchased from the Boffo catalogue of joke witch items. Miss Treason affirms, "Boffo, indeed. The art of expectations. Show people what they want to see, show 'em what they think ought to be there. I have a reputation to keep up, after all" (87).

This is a further twist on the concept of stereotype and its power: expectations based on stereotypes can be manipulated. Miss Treason exploits the traditional anxieties about the wicked old witch by playing up to them, and thereby gaining power over the community she both serves and rules. As Tiffany recognises, "Miss Treason had power because they thought she did" (Pratchett, *Wintersmith* 89). Armed with her fake skulls, the currants that look like flies in the machine-made spider webs festooned around her cottage, and the rumours she herself generates, Miss Treason can be more than just "a little half-deaf and blind old lady" (89) and can compel the villagers to obey her. The novel's subplot thus involves the problems that ensue when Annagramma, the apprentice who has not learned what witchcraft is really about, inherits Miss Treason's cottage and attempts to clear it out in the belief that "after that old woman just about anyone would be popular" (146). Annagramma has no understanding of just how the witch's authority works in the community—nor of what to do with it: she believes that "nature should be allowed to take its course" when it comes to delivering a baby, and Mrs Earwig has told her that "the village women know what to do [. . .] She says to trust in their peasant wisdom." As Tiffany points out, "what [one village woman] has got is simple peasant ignorance" (242); as she does not point out, the village women of the Discworld expect peasant wisdom to be vested in the witch, and that is precisely the justification for her role. Tiffany has to assist Annagramma at least to appear to have the wisdom of the witch; Annagramma herself belatedly recognises the importance of appearance, and emerges at a key moment with a green face, clawed hands, and lots of warts, driving off the wintersmith and reducing the villagers to the terrified but grateful obedience to which they had been accustomed under Miss Treason.

In *Wintersmith*, convention and stereotype, even negative stereotype, thus become sources of power that the confident girl, or witch, can manipulate to her own advantage. The disjunction between the message and the surface in *A Hat Full of Sky* appears to have been resolved by Pratchett's explicit engagement with the power of appearances. This is a much more sophisticated account of the witch icon as stereotype than Elizabeth George Speare's, despite Speare's valuable attempt to draw her readers in through empathy for Kit and sympathetic understanding for the frail Hannah and even, to a limited extent, for her troubled persecutors. Through his assessment of the witch icon, Pratchett's fiction both represents and enacts the power to manipulate emotional reactions through adroit deployment of appearances. Tiffany has learned that false images need not be simply defied; they can be engaged with and deployed to create new relationships. This is, after all, what fiction is about.

HATS, LABELS, AND FEARS

The power to exploit stereotypes that rely on fear, however, plays up the reality of that fear. If the first three novels of the Tiffany Aching sequence, with their evocation of fairy tale and myth and magical adventure, might look escapist, this cannot be said of the fourth. *I Shall Wear Midnight* (2010) forcibly confronts the reader with the problem of human evil, and does so in part by revisiting the Mrs Snapperly problem evoked in the early pages of the sequence. It therefore provides a further light on the operation of story and in so doing, like Rowling's Harry Potter sequence, in effect demands that its readers grow beyond the fairy tale.

I Shall Wear Midnight quickly establishes a very different atmosphere from that of the earlier novels. Although it begins apparently cheerfully, with an account of the summer scouring fair—in the course of which we learn that Tiffany no longer has a boyfriend, as Roland is now engaged to someone else—by the second chapter Tiffany is rebuking a man who has just beaten his thirteen-year-old daughter into a miscarriage. At fifteen, Tiffany has learned realities, not just magic, and does not express surprise when her father comments that

> Seth Petty was a decent enough lad when we were young. It was his dad who was a madman. I mean, things were a bit rough and ready in those days and you could expect a clip around the ear if you disobeyed, but Seth's dad had a thick leather belt with two buckles on it, and he would lay into Seth for just looking at him in a funny way.
>
> (Pratchett, *I Shall* 35)

In addition to exposing his young readers to the realities of domestic violence, Pratchett is making a further point. The feudal world so often drawn on in fantasy representations, including much of the Discworld series, was a violent one, in which conflicts of any kind were resolved violently. "His hands had closed automatically into fists because he had always been a man who thought with them" (26). This is still reality for far too many people; it was even more widespread in a time when insults were avenged by sword and spear. *I Shall Wear Midnight* appears to move us altogether away from the fantasy world that has beguiled the readers of the sequence, and into confrontation with an often sordid and brutal reality, in which danger is more likely to emerge from human conflict than from tangling with a magical entity like the Queen, the hiver, or the wintersmith.

Evil in *I Shall Wear Midnight* emerges not only through Pratchett's unflinching depiction of domestic violence—and its roots in prior violence—but also, returning us to Mrs Snapperly's fate in *The Wee Free Men*, evil as hatred, prejudice, even self-hatred. The Cunning Man, the enemy who stalks Tiffany in *I Shall Wear Midnight*, is a monster, but he is a monster bred of hatred and vengefulness and frustrated lust. The Cunning Man, Tiffany is told, is the remnant of a long-ago witchfinder who fell in love with one of his victims just as she was being set on fire.

> One simple deed and history will be different, and you are thinking it depends on what he does next. But you see, what he is thinking doesn't matter, because she knows what he is and what he has done and is

famous for [. . .] and [she] reaches with both hands smoothly through the wicker basket they've put around her to keep her upright, and grabs him, and holds him tight as the torch drops down into the oily wood and the flames spring up.

(191)

His origins are human, though his rage has energised him beyond death, but the acts he produces are inhuman as well as inhumane. Possession by the Cunning Man leads the prisoner to kill his pet bird, which nothing else would.

Tiffany has to deal with the effects of the Cunning Man in the world as well as facing it itself as a monster. But as in *A Hat Full of Sky* she also has to face the monster in herself. She despises herself for losing her boyfriend, she is afraid of what being a witch may mean, and those insecurities leave her a potential prey to the Cunning Man. Tiffany has to find an alternative way to centre herself. She confronts prejudice in the Other by showing it the reality of herself as an individual. She shows her community that she is a human being and is also the witch who helps her village; she shows her rival Letitia—and recognises herself—that they are very much alike. Throughout the sequence, Pratchett emphasises empathy, as he demonstrates that good and evil are not incompatible binaries but aspects of the human. But he also emphasises the ways in which an individual can combat evil. Tiffany perceives and transcends the cultural expectations that so readily constrain agency, in this case by recognising the insecurities that give those expectations their power.

This concept is particularly significant in the case of Mrs Proust, proprietor of the Boffo shop, which Tiffany discovers while visiting the city of Ankh-Morpork to inform the Baron's son, Roland, that his father is dead and he is needed at home. Aware of the suspicion of witches already aroused by the Cunning Man, Mrs Proust sticks a label on Tiffany's pointy hat: "It was a brightly coloured piece of cardboard on a piece of string, and it said: *Apprentice witch hat with evil glitter. Size 7. Price: $AM2.50. Boffo! A name to conjure with!!!*" (Pratchett, *I Shall* 138). Where Miss Tick disguised her pointy hat as a "stealth hat" with a retractable point (Pratchett, *Wee* 23), Mrs Proust has found an even more effective way to conceal Tiffany's witch identity. "The best disguise for a witch is a rather cheap witch's outfit! [. . .] It's boffo, my dear, pure unadulterated boffo! *Disguise, subterfuge and misdirection* are our watchwords" (Pratchett, *I Shall* 139). Mrs Proust's commercial enterprise is founded on the recognition that people desire not merely to bury their fears but to be reassured about them. By encouraging her customers to play with the concept of the witch in glitter-covered hats and hideous masks, she profits from their insecurities, but also promotes the idea that the wicked old witch is just a joke.

This is particularly important to Mrs Proust herself, as Tiffany recognises: "That really is *your* face, isn't it? The masks you sell are masks of *you*" (140). The concept of Boffo gets a final twist. The old woman with warts, a hooked nose, and clawed fingernails is not after all a complete fiction, whatever her associations with evil may be, and an ugly woman in a society that values appearance is likely to be rejected even without the waves of hatred stirred up by the Cunning Man. Mrs Proust has worked out that people will accept anything if it is presented as a game, a joke, a simple trick; she disguises her own frightening ugliness, like Tiffany's pointy hat, in plain sight, as a fake image of itself, and in so doing protects herself from the communal rage that destroyed Mrs Snapperly.

Mrs Proust's construction of Boffo points to Pratchett's own strategy throughout the sequence, in which often difficult messages are disguised as a mere children's fantasy. As Tiffany comments, the secret of Mrs Proust's identity is "another joke, and it's not really very funny" (Pratchett, *I Shall* 140). *I Shall Wear Midnight*, with its portrait of the brutal and brutalised Seth Petty and its acceptance of the ease with which human beings can turn against each other—Roland has not only dumped Tiffany, but for a while is suspicious that she has killed and robbed his dying father—presents its readers with a vision of life much more painful than the rather comic fairy tale the Tiffany Aching sequence has seemed to be. At the same time, Pratchett himself does not step too far beyond the game of Boffo, as he allows his readers a happy ending—even if not the one foreshadowed in *A Hat Full of Sky*, where Roland's gift of a horse pendant became central to Tiffany's sense of self and assisted her survival of the hiver, or *Wintersmith*, in which he served as her Hero. The final novel takes many turns, and readers' expectations are repeatedly aroused and disappointed.

Tiffany herself gets caught up in this experience. She shocks herself and Roland by blurting out, during a moment of reconciliation, that "[y]ou can trust me now when I say to you that *I will marry you*" (Pratchett, *I Shall* 317), but this prediction is fulfilled in an unexpected way. Appropriately for a sequence about a girl to whom words have always been important, we are reminded that the verb "marry" has a double meaning. At the climax, Tiffany lures the Cunning Man into the fire by running with Roland and Letitia and leaping across the flames so that none of the three is more than singed; as she explains to Letitia, in the process "I married you [. . .] Jumping over the flames together is a very ancient form of marriage" (393). As witch, Tiffany has married Roland to Letitia, shouting traditional words that have themselves changed their appearance over time—"*Leap, knave! Jump, whore!*" (389). Nothing is quite as it appears. But Tiffany, and the reader, do get the happy ending not only of Tiffany's eventual relationship with the intelligent Preston but, more importantly, of her relationship with herself and her community. The Mrs Snapperly problem is solved both externally, as the wedding guests take pride in the assembled witches' tribute to Tiffany's achievements, and internally, as Tiffany is reconciled to herself. "After all, she *was* the witch" (409).

Tiffany's self-recognition reflects, and reflects on, the title of the novel. This title in itself plays on the concept of appearances and the expectations they create. The reader of *A Hat Full of Sky* will remember Tiffany's eventual decision there to keep on wearing blue and green rather than black while she is young, "When I'm old I shall wear midnight" (Pratchett, *A Hat* 333), and the reminder provided by the title of the fourth book will arouse expectations of its content. But it also reminds us of Tiffany's own attitude to the attributes of the witch, the distinction she made at eleven between the old-woman trappings of the black dress, on the one hand, and the pointy hat as a badge of authority and indeed of identity, on the other. Granny Weatherwax, who lent Tiffany her own hat at the Witch Trials as a mark of respect, has told her that "There's no hat like the hat you make yourself" (Pratchett, *A Hat* 337), and Tiffany subsequently discards the grandiose Sky Scraper she has obtained from Zakzak's Emporium in favour of the hat she makes of the sky—as Granny Weatherwax says Tiffany's own Granny Aching had done (339)—on her beloved Chalk downland (350). The pointy hat becomes a mark of identity for Tiffany, but one the symbolic power of which may be understood by its reduction from the invisible reality Tiffany has relied on from the end of *The Wee Free Men* either to the commercial obviousness of the Sky Scraper, which impresses her Chalk community, or to a metaphor that, in the end, she makes herself. "Your own hat, for your own head. Your own future, not someone else's" (Pratchett, *A Hat* 350).

By contrast, the black dress has remained a contingent attribute, representing rather the practicality of garments chosen by old women than any quality intrinsic to the witch's identity or authority. Although Tiffany has recognised the glamour of the midnight Zephyr Billow cloak she also obtained from the shop in *A Hat Full of Sky*, she tells Granny Weatherwax that to wear such a thing requires "gravitas [. . .] dignity. Seniority. Wisdom" (Pratchett, 342), implicitly denying that she herself has reached such a stage. The attributes of the witch are being distinguished for us across the later books of the sequence. The pointy hat—real, imagined, or figurative—may be essential to the witch's identity, but her dress is contingent, whether on age or on its occasional accompaniment, gravitas, and her hooked nose may be absent, or cosmetically added, or, as for Mrs Proust, an unfortunate reality. Such distinctions underscore the extent to which stereotype and convention represent half-truths and untruths as well as possible truths, and encourage the reader to look always to the reality that they conceal, or expose, in developing a personal sense of identity and vision of the world.

Further, the fact that the fourth novel bears Tiffany's claim, as its title hints, either that the claim may be modified here or that its temporal condition, "[w]hen I'm old," may be in some way fulfilled. As it turns out, both these things are true. Tiffany wears midnight in the form of a gorgeous dress made for her at the end of the novel, when she is still in her teens, implicitly claiming for herself the maturity hinted at in her eleven-year-old view of old age; and across the novel she has visions of a mysterious black-clad old woman watching her, with whom she eventually speaks and whom she realises is indeed herself grown old. Pratchett's final novel thus fulfils the expectations created by appearance—its own title—while transforming these, as Tiffany's idea of who could or should wear midnight is transformed into herself as a young woman wearing a very sexy black dress. "I shall wear midnight, and I shall be good at it . . ." (Pratchett, *I Shall* 412). Pratchett concludes his witch sequence by encouraging the reader to reflect on just what "wearing midnight" both has meant and should mean. In so doing he invites his readers to develop, like Tiffany, a rich understanding of maturity—and so to attain it.

CONCLUSION

Both Pratchett and Jones deploy the figure of the witch to invite the child reader to recognize and critique the conventions of story as they reflect and shape the conventions of society, and especially to resist the constraints such conventions place on their own agency and development of individual identity. Jones portrays Sophie as trapped by her own expectations: she misrepresents herself as a "little grey mouse" (*Howl's* 21). However, when Sophie takes on a different role she recognises new strengths in herself and can move beyond the constraints of both roles. Jones at once depicts the limitations of accepting conventional structures and shows how an individual can use the conventions to produce an expanded sense of self and a greater degree of agency.

Pratchett's four Tiffany Aching novels all address the concept of the witch stereotype in different ways, from Tiffany's apparently simple reversal of the witch image from evil crone to responsible agent in *The Wee Free Men*, to acknowledgement of the glamour of the magical in *A Hat Full of Sky*, and to an idea of how the stereotype can be manipulated in *Wintersmith* and *I Shall Wear Midnight*. The concept of Boffo points to the extent to which group perceptions and preconceptions can themselves become fodder for the more sophisticated individual who can draw on them to create their own power within a community. *I Shall Wear Midnight* reminds readers, however, that evil is complex and pervasive; fantasy may represent it in a single figure, the Cunning Man or Lord Voldemort, but its real danger is the force of hatred and self-hatred within ordinary members of the community—potentially including readers themselves. Pratchett's Tiffany, though self-confident as a nine-year-old at the start of the sequence, risks falling prey to her own self-doubt. She discovers that combating these forces requires a mature and honest acceptance of her own complex identity.

Pratchett's Tiffany sequence develops a complex picture of human social interaction and places the witch at its heart. His analysis of the prejudices, both positive and negative, surrounding the figure of the witch exposes not only basic human anxieties but also the sophisticated strategies through which people can learn to survive and even exploit those anxieties. For both Jones and Pratchett, the figure of the witch provides a focus for a rich and complex revaluation of the operation of culture; their representations demonstrate that the witch can be not a figure to be feared but a powerful model. Through their enactment of the witch role, Tiffany and Sophie learn how to solve problems within their communities while fulfilling themselves.

Both writers also highlight the literary, both through their characters' explicit consciousness of fairy-tale conventions and through intertextual allusion, underscoring the significance of expectations in shaping our responses to situations and the need to transcend the limitations imposed by convention. They invite their readers to read actively, like Tiffany, and to draw on their reading to imagine possibility. Pratchett's demonstration of how the glamour of story may be deployed to warn against its constraints, like Jones's exuberant reshuffling of elements familiar from *The Wizard of Oz*, further provides a model for the creative imagination. Both authors teach readers how we too might play with as well as work against conventional assumptions to attain our personal goals. Their depiction of their protagonists as taking responsibility for the problems of those around them further encourages the development of a moral understanding of the world within which those goals may be articulated.

NOTES

1. Ximena Gallardo-C. and C. Jason Smith, arguing for Rowling's deconstruction of traditional gender roles, suggest that "[b]y far the most transgressive acceptance of the female other [in the early Harry Potter books] is Rowling's *de facto* redemption of the slanderous term 'witch'" (202).
2. Sophie later learns that the Witch has mistaken her for her sister Lettie (Jones, *Howl's* 256), but the Witch's recognition of the spells Sophie has unknowingly cast on the hats she has made appears to confirm her desire to punish Sophie: "No mistake, Miss Hatter" (32).
3. Since Fanny is comparatively young, we should infer that her old schoolfriend is too. Being a witch need not mean being a crone.
4. Is it an accident that Konigsburg's name translates as "Kingsbury," the name of a town in *Howl's Moving Castle*?
5. Pratchett points out in an author's note that our own world "had Witch Trials, too. They were not fun" (*A Hat* [352]).

5 Resisting "Destinarianism"

In Diana Wynne Jones's fifth Chrestomanci novel, *Conrad's Fate* (2005), twelve-year-old narrator Conrad's preoccupation with his Fate comes to dominate his understanding of himself so completely that when he is persuaded it is a lie he feels bereft not only of purpose but of identity itself: "If I didn't have a Fate, then what *was* I?" (Jones, *Conrad's* 246). Both Jones and J.K. Rowling consider the impact of ideas of destiny on the development of individual identity in the Chrestomanci series of novels (1977–2006) and the Harry Potter sequence (1997–2007) respectively. Both depict characters operating within contexts that evoke ideas of fate or destiny as affecting the central characters, although they do so in very different ways. In the Harry Potter novels, the idea that Harry's actions are subject to a predestined trajectory is repeatedly raised, especially through his identification as "Chosen One." The later stages of the sequence especially, with their previously discussed evocation of heroic fantasy conventions, may seem to cast doubt on the possibility that Harry has in fact any control over his eventual destiny. However, as we have seen in Chapter 2, that evocation is itself subverted within the sequence, and Rowling's treatment of Harry in fact demonstrates a commitment to an idea of moral responsibility that depends on individuals possessing agency. Rowling's sequence highlights the significance of moral choice throughout. Jones's Chrestomanci series, meanwhile, situates characters within a context of parallel worlds and personal analogues that in itself might seem to imply a notion of fate, but her plots repeatedly emphasise the importance of personal responsibility—framed as an ethical imperative— and of individual agency. Both writers undermine ideas of fate, although in strikingly different ways. This chapter examines attitudes to choice and destiny in the Harry Potter sequence and in the Chrestomanci novels, and explores their implications for characters' development of responsible agency.

Attitudes to human fate or destiny in fiction may be considered as falling into three categories, all of which I shall refer to as "destinarianism":

1) *Belief in Fate*: generally expressed by characters and implied by the operation of the narrative. On this view, the nature of the universe

is fundamentally deterministic; this determinism may be morally weighted or may be amoral in its operation. Fate in these texts may be considered a universal, affecting all individuals, although it may also be shaped by the prior actions of those individuals. Thus in *Conrad's Fate*, Uncle Alfred informs Conrad that his bad karma destines him to kill someone at Stallery Manor and that he must therefore become a servant there, and Conrad, at least initially, accepts and complies with this expectation.

2) *Belief in Personal Destiny*: explicitly articulated within a text in various forms. Although the implications of this are also deterministic, destinarian texts generally ignore day-to-day experience and highlight instead how destiny affects specific individuals to bring about historically significant events within the universe of the text. Garion, in David Eddings's Belgariad sequence (1982–84), is destined to take the Orb and become the Rivan King, Harry Potter is the Chosen One. It is this attitude that Farah Mendlesohn refers to as "destinarianism" (*Rhetorics* 137), and it is most notable in prophecy-driven narratives: a certain person will be born at midwinter, only a particular individual will be able to pull the sword from the stone, a climactic battle will take place on a given day and in specific circumstances, and Good will conquer Evil. In the worlds of such fictions, many details are not predestined and most lives, even of characters important in the world of the novel, can proceed without any visible interference by providential forces. The individuals affected, however, may struggle against the prophesied destiny, but it will take place anyway—even if not as inferred by interpreters of the prophecy, a common twist in recent fiction visible, for example, in Rick Riordan's *The Last Olympian* (2009). Fictions set in a destinarian universe of this type generally, although not always, imply that this destiny is driven by a conscious supernatural force—Providence, the gods—to deliberate ends, which are rarely morally neutral.

3) *Belief in Expected Outcomes*: rarely articulated within a given narrative, but shaped by genre patterns perceptible to the reader as structuring the narrative. Unlike the first two types of destinarianism, in which the reader's experience is created through the text's implicit mimesis of a more or less deterministic universe, this third type produces its effects through the reader's experience of texts themselves. Rather than affecting characters as representatives of ordinary human beings, this version of predestination affects characters as they represent known roles within a genre. The hero of the school story will meet his or her best friend and often worst foe on the train to the school or on the first day; will win victory for his or her side in the crucial sporting match; will be mistreated by a horrible teacher; will triumph. The hero of the detective story will discover the truth and, traditionally, will bring the evil-doer either to society's justice, in the

form of the law courts, or poetic justice, usually death. The hero of the heroic fantasy will be discovered to be a lost prince, will fight evil, regain his kingdom, and restore it to prosperity. The last of these may depend on the second type described above—with the protagonist visibly a "pawn of prophecy," as the first novel in Eddings's Belgariad puts it—but the reader will have the pattern in mind in any case. Jones mocks this convention and a host of its associated elements in her 1996 encyclopaedia and "tourist guide" *Tough Guide to Fantasyland* and its companion novel *The Dark Lord of Derkholm* (1998), both of which in different modes satirise the clichés of world-building in heroic fantasy to which readers have become accustomed.

Importantly, this third form of "destiny" may even be understood by characters within a novel themselves, if they are readers. As we shall see, Jones demonstrates in *The Lives of Christopher Chant* (1988) how this perception may be experienced not as subjection but as a structure deployed by an individual to achieve personal goals. Such a strategy provides a model to child readers of how they too might draw on ideas within their reading to shape their lives; it indicates a high degree of self-reflexivity in the novel. Both Jones and Rowling demonstrate such self-reflexivity in their depiction of choice and its relationship to fate or destiny.

HARRY POTTER: WHAT CHOICE DID HE HAVE?

The Harry Potter sequence engages at different stages with all three attitudes to fate or destiny. Much attention has been paid to the question of choice in the sequence, both as a general philosophical question and as evoked specifically by Dumbledore's emphasis on the importance of choice at the ends of both *Harry Potter and the Chamber of Secrets* and *Harry Potter and the Half-Blood Prince*. I do not propose to rehearse all these arguments here; among many others, a 2002 essay by Catherine Jack Deavel and David Paul Deavel covers material such as the implications of the Sorting Hat and the idea of character as destiny and demonstrates how this is refuted, while Patricia Donaher and James M. Okapal have provided a philosophical account of the text as Compatibilist in approach. Lisa Hopkins's 2009 analysis of how destiny is presented in the sequence moves from a rather overwhelming list of elements relating the sequence to the Arthurian cycle to a valuable explanation of the effects of these elements and of Rowling's response to them. Hopkins's approach indicates the importance of considering not only the text's pronouncements on the subject of fate and choice, determinism and free will, but also the reader's experiences of these across the sequence. We have already seen in Chapter 2 how the reader's perception of Harry both as hero of a school story and subsequently as hero of a heroic fantasy affects our understanding of his development. Here we shall see how Rowling invites her readers not only to perceive but to reflect on key moments in Harry's career in order more fully to comprehend the complex understanding of choice put forward in Rowling's novels.

Least important in the Harry Potter sequence, for most critics, is the idea of a universal fate (the first type of belief listed above). It is this that the subject of Divination seems to cover, as Sybill Trelawney interprets palm lines, tea leaves, and astronomical conjunctions to determine individual events, and it is Divination that, as has been widely noted, is continually undermined by the action especially of *Harry Potter and the Prisoner of Azkaban* (1999). Not only are Professor Trelawney's own predictions treated with scepticism, but her enthusiasm for the fraudulent predictions of Harry and Ron, to which she awards top marks, underscores the notion that her subject, and she, are fakes. It is nevertheless worth noting that neither Trelawney nor Divination is as readily dismissed as may appear. Although she does not know it, Sybill Trelawney has made two real predictions, one in Harry's infancy and one in the course of *Prisoner of Azkaban*, both of which are validated by the events of the novels. I shall return to these shortly. Moreover, the reader is introduced to an alternative form of divination, that practised by the centaurs and later taught to Harry and his classmates by the centaur Firenze after Trelawney's sacking in *Harry Potter and the Order of the Phoenix* (2003). The centaurs' version of divination is also represented primarily, though not solely, as astrological, but it does not rely on the association of constellations with local human experiences. As Firenze remarks, "Trivial hurts, tiny human accidents [. . .] are of no more significance than the scurryings of ants to the wide universe, and are unaffected by planetary movements" (Rowling, *Order* 663). In so saying, Firenze acknowledges a critique of astrology common in the mundane world outside the Harry Potter books, and gives more weight to his pronouncement that "the future may be glimpsed in the sky above us" (663), which he has already supported by suggesting that the centaurs' belief in this is based on centuries of study.

Firenze's exposition of the centaur practice of divination seems imbued with the authority notoriously lacking in Trelawney's version of the subject, rendering it more plausible, and he claims that centaur wisdom is "impersonal and impartial" (Rowling, *Order* 664). His teaching, however, does not involve either transmitting facts or training his human students to perceive what the centaurs can; although he demonstrates "the observation of fume and flame," he is unperturbed that the students can see nothing there, and Harry infers that his purpose is to teach them that "nothing, not even centaurs' knowledge, was foolproof" (664). Nevertheless, Firenze does inform the class that the centaurs' divination suggests that "wizardkind is living through nothing more than a brief period of calm between two wars. Mars, bringer of battles, shines brightly above us, suggesting that the fight must soon break out again" (664). Since Harry himself witnessed Voldemort's return at the end of *Harry Potter and the Goblet of Fire* (2000), this is hardly fresh news; what it does, however, is re-validate the notion, undermined by Trelawney's practice, that events have a recognisable and perhaps inevitable trajectory. As an observation it may recall evocations of destiny, in the narrow second sense described above; however, Firenze's critique of the local suggests that the centaurs' interpretations depend on a vision of time as causal at the broader level, rather than at the personal level most common to evocations of destiny in much heroic fantasy.

Firenze's words, like his presence in the fifth novel of the sequence, are likely to remind readers of his first appearance, in *Harry Potter and the Philosopher's Stone* (1997). In that novel, Harry's encounters with the centaurs were disturbing. Ronan and Bane were unresponsive when asked by Hagrid about whether they had seen anything odd in the forest, each commenting only "Mars is bright tonight" (Rowling, *Philosopher's* 274). In light of Firenze's remarks in *Order of the Phoenix*, this statement can be read as a direct, if unobvious, response to Hagrid's query. The odd thing in the forest that was killing unicorns in *Philosopher's Stone*—as Ronan sweepingly says, "Always the innocent are the first victims. So it has been for ages past, so now" (274)—turned out in fact to be the remnant of Voldemort, instigator of the previous war and planner of the next. That the centaurs frame this response as they do, however, depicts them as unhelpful to Harry and his allies, and their subsequent encounter with Firenze, who rescues Harry from the dangerous being in the Forest, locates them even as anti-human. Bane and Ronan upbraid Firenze for carrying Harry on his back, and although, based on what we learn in later novels, this objection may have significant historical roots in wizard treatment of other magical beings, at this point it is inevitable that the reader will reject Bane's hostility and be grateful to Firenze for his support of Harry. It is Bane who announces that "[c]entaurs are concerned with what has been foretold!"; Firenze who declares that "I set myself against what is in this forest, yes, with humans beside me if I must" (279). Firenze's declaration models Harry's own later decision to fight Voldemort. At this level of belief in fate, then, the centaur herd's passivity in the face of "what has been foretold" is implicitly rejected even before the reader fully understands it in *Order of the Phoenix*. If fate decrees a battle, it is at the least a battle in which Firenze, like Harry, feels able to choose and fight on one side. The eventual arrival of the centaurs to fight in the battle for Hogwarts in *Harry Potter and the Deathly Hallows* (2007) endorses the notion that all peoples of any value will join the fight against evil rather than remain passive. Thus the message of the sequence is implicitly to reject a belief in fate as deterministic—my first category above. There may be battles, but their outcome depends on the decisions of individuals to act; resistance to Voldemort may be painful, but it is not futile.

Whereas Professor Trelawney's version of Divination suggests a fated future that affects everything—even, according to Trelawney, a broken cup or a dead rabbit—Trelawney's own prophecies point to the second version of destinarianism described above, that in which a particular thread of history is destined and the career of one or more individuals is projected accordingly.

Trelawney's prophecies, unlike those of the centaurs, deal with individuals—
"The one with the power to vanquish the Dark Lord approaches" (Rowling,
Order 924), "Tonight, before midnight, the servant will break free and set
out to rejoin his master. The Dark Lord will rise again with his servant's
aid" (Rowling, *Prisoner* 238)—and it is these prophecies that receive the
most serious attention within the sequence. On this matter Dumbledore is
explicit in *Half-Blood Prince*: not all prophecies are fulfilled. He further
implies that their fulfilment depends at least in part on individuals choosing
to fulfil them: "If Voldemort had never heard of the prophecy, would it have
been fulfilled? Would it have meant anything? Of course not! Do you think
every prophecy in the Hall of Prophecy has been fulfilled?" (Rowling, *Half-
Blood* 476). Thus, according to Dumbledore, Voldemort not only chose to
act on the prophecy, but in doing so equipped his enemy with the tools necessary to ensure that "neither can live while the other survives" (Rowling,
Order 924); indeed, as we later discover, Voldemort in effect endows Harry
with the power to vanquish him.[1] What is important, on this interpretation
of events, is that it is Snape's overhearing and Dumbledore's hearing of the
prophecy that generate its fulfilment, as Snape's information makes Voldemort act and Dumbledore's inference from the result of that action enables
him to provide Harry with the necessary knowledge about what he must do,
including access to Dumbledore's memory of the prophecy itself. The fulfilment of the prophecy thus depends on the activities of at least four people
who have heard part or all of that prophecy; it rests not on an immutable
historical trajectory but on the decisions of those who have heard it to bring
it about. And the fact that Dumbledore firmly ascribes the validation of the
prophecy to Voldemort associates belief in destiny with a character who
not only represents evil in the sequence, but who is consistently accused of
failure to understand the reality of human experience as well as the operation of magic itself. This association, together with Dumbledore's insistence
that the fulfilling of a prophecy depends on individuals' decisions to fulfil it,
suggests that the sequence is dismissing destinarianism as expressed through
prophecy.

Two things complicate this interpretation, however. First, Professor Trelawney's prophecy may be her first but it is not the first the reader hears.
That first prophecy occurs in the course of *Prisoner of Azkaban*, and its fulfilment appears entirely independent of the fact that Harry hears it. The only
person to whom he manages to repeat it before its fulfilment is Professor
Trelawney herself, who disbelieves it; and Harry is not shown remembering
the prophecy either when he confronts Sirius Black, whom he believes to
be the Dark Lord's freed servant, or when he tells Sirius and Remus Lupin
to leave Peter Pettigrew alive, following which Pettigrew escapes to join his
master as foretold. This prophecy is fulfilled despite the fact that no one
who hears it cares to act either on it or against it, which somewhat undermines the effect of Dumbledore's vehemence—"Of course not!" (Rowling,
Half-Blood 476)—in his insistence on the fallibility of prophecy. We are left

to infer that this "real" prophecy (Rowling, *Prisoner* 311), like the astrology of the centaurs, does correspond to a predetermined trajectory of events.

Second, Dumbledore's argument for choice in *Half-Blood Prince* does not fully cohere with the reader's experience. In *Chamber of Secrets*, as has been much quoted, Dumbledore emphasises to Harry that choices define character. In *Half-Blood Prince* he announces that it is Harry's character that will determine his role in the drama, and even insists that this has been apparent through Harry's earlier actions:

> In spite of all the temptations you have endured, all the suffering, you remain pure of heart, just as pure as you were at the age of eleven, when you stared into a mirror that showed you your heart's desire and it showed you only the way to thwart Voldemort, and not immortality or riches. Harry, have you any idea how few wizards could have seen what you saw in that mirror?
>
> (Rowling, *Half-Blood* 477–78)

Dumbledore's words are intended to inspire Harry with understanding of himself and his strengths, but they also impel the reader to reflect on that moment in *Philosopher's Stone* when Harry was compelled by Professor Quirrell—himself, significantly, literally possessed by Voldemort and therefore with a much reduced personal agency—to look in the Mirror of Erised. Dumbledore's interpretation of that moment is that it was a signifier of Harry's rarity, even uniqueness. But the child reader of *Philosopher's Stone* is most likely to have read it in the opposite way. Harry in this moment is our representative, and he is our representative at least in part because he is constrained by events. First, he is coerced by Quirrell to look in the Mirror; compelled by a superior force, he is aware of his limited capacity for action. " 'I must lie,' [Harry] thought desperately. 'I must look and lie about what I see, that's all' " (Rowling, *Philosopher's* 314). In taking this decision, Harry is our hero, determined to do what a hero must to achieve the longstanding goal of the novel and thwart Voldemort, but he is also a child placed in an impossible situation by a powerful and dangerous adult. Second, what Harry sees comes as a surprise to him and to the reader: any sense of agency, or even desire, is absent here. "Harry felt something heavy drop into his real pocket. Somehow—incredibly—*he'd got the Stone*" (314).

The notion that Harry might have seen riches in the Mirror at this crucial stage in his experience, as Dumbledore suggests in *Half-Blood Prince*, is risible; the chance that he might have seen immortality—however one does see immortality—is scarcely less remote. At most, the reader, and Harry, might have expected that he would see the faces of his lost parents and other family, as in his previous encounters with the Mirror. But the pace of events in the last section of the novel has left no room for personal desires, as has already been demonstrated in the text. Although Hermione comments on Harry's decision to go forward alone that "you're a great wizard, you know" (Rowling, *Philosopher's* 308), Harry's decision—shaped for the reader by Rowling's construction of the novel as part-quest, part-detective story—seems inevitable, rather than chosen. The reader's experience of the text invites us to expect a trajectory, as in the third category of destinarianism I described above, that implicitly reduces Harry's agency.

Dumbledore's comments, then, may at first seem unconvincing as an attempt to recast the climactic events of *Philosopher's Stone* as a demonstration of Harry's purity of heart. They point to a tension between the sequence's moral trajectory and its literary development. The climax of *Philosopher's Stone* can be read retrospectively as an early stage of Harry's journey to become the Chosen One, the boy whose destiny is to confront and kill the evil Lord Voldemort: in that sense, which is probably dominant for readers of the sequence as a whole, it is therefore an early phase in a heroic fantasy. Yet, as we have seen in Chapter 2, the sequence seems insistently to undermine its own operation as heroic fantasy. In this case, it is important to pay attention to Dumbledore's comments in *Half-Blood Prince*, ridiculous as they may seem, as an attempt to alter both Harry's and the reader's understanding of the meaning of events: Dumbledore's words implicitly provide a critique of the climax of *Philosopher's Stone* as heroic fantasy. What seemed inevitable, both to Harry and to the reader, was not.

This may be supported by consideration of another moment in *Philosopher's Stone* where Harry appeared to respond without choice. Not many pages before his passage through the black flames to confront Quirrell, Draco Malfoy and Fang had both fled at the sight of a hooded figure drinking the blood of a unicorn in the Forbidden Forest. A moment before, "Harry, Malfoy and Fang stood transfixed" at the sight (Rowling, *Philosopher's* 277): it is not Harry who acts, but Malfoy. We are not told of Harry's behaviour, only of his experience as "a pain pierced his head [. . .] half-blinded, he staggered backwards" (277). Here, as on many occasions throughout the sequence, events seem to take place around Harry and he reacts as to physical compulsion: he "stagger[s] backwards" because of what he experiences as a blow to the forehead. What the engaged reader takes away from Harry's experience is his suffering of it; what the analytic reader, Dumbledore, might take from it is that it does not occur to him to flee. Malfoy and even the dog Fang take to their heels; Harry stands his ground. The fact that this is not represented as in any way a conscious choice works two ways. On the one hand it locates Harry as plaything of events, the future pawn of prophecy, but on the other it casts him, more simply, as the child whose behaviours spring from his inherent qualities, unmediated by conscious choice—in other words, as the child who is "pure of heart," as Dumbledore claims. At the climax of *Philosopher's Stone* Harry is revealed as the hero of fairy tale, not now a male Cinderella but the hero to whom it does not occur to run away. This may make him less brave than the more imaginative Hermione, but his very unreflectiveness can be taken as "purity of heart," a model for right action.

Critics such as Mendlesohn have pointed out that Harry is in fact inactive in the early novels, and gets credit for achievements for which his friends are mostly responsible; this is not unusual in heroic fantasy. It is arguable, however, that Harry is portrayed in the early novels as possessing a strong will. He twice speaks "coolly" to Malfoy, an adverb by which Rowling deftly directs her readers to respect him (*Philosopher's* 120, 167), and he insists on pursuing actions he sees as right or necessary even at personal cost, such as dropping down the pipe to find the Chamber of Secrets or following the troll into the bathroom where Hermione is hiding in *Philosopher's Stone*. The narratorial question "what choice did they have?" (190) invites the reader to consider the extent to which Harry and Ron do in fact have a choice at this moment, as Julia Pond observes in her analysis of choice in the novels, but its rhetorical structure underlines how that choice is constrained by their own sense of ethical responsibility—a key concern of the sequence that could be taken to summarise its position on the nature of choice.

It is hard not to feel that Rowling is having it both ways in relation to destiny and choice. Harry is free and not free, destined and choosing. But this is perhaps the message of the sequence. Pond's analysis includes an account of a variety of characters as "enactors of fate [who] unknowingly drive him towards his destiny by attempting to control his life, while themselves controlled and directed by fate" (193). Since Pond's list includes not only the adults, and Dobby, who attempt to intervene to protect Harry, but also the Dursleys, who control him "by keeping from him knowledge of his past and understanding of his identity" (Pond 193), this argument risks becoming one about determinism as a mechanical process of causality rather than fate or destiny in the grand sense, and about the extent to which we are all, heroes or not, constrained and shaped by our environments. For Dumbledore in *Half-Blood Prince*, that shaping is a crucial part not of the fulfilment of destiny but of the production of choice:

> "[. . .] Imagine, please, that you had never heard about that prophecy? How would you feel about Voldemort now? Think!"
> Harry [. . .] thought of his mother, his father and Sirius. He thought of Cedric Diggory. He thought of all the terrible deeds he knew Lord Voldemort had done. A flame seemed to leap inside his chest, searing his throat.
> "I'd want him finished," said Harry quietly. "And I'd want to do it."
> (Rowling, *Half-Blood* 478)

Dumbledore's words impel Harry to reflect on his own motivations, to take responsibility for his future actions. He can no longer be the child responding instinctively to the needs of the moment; if he remains that child he lacks agency whether the prophecy is fulfilled or not. Maturation involves recognising reality to the full and accepting it.

Thus in *Order of the Phoenix* Harry learns that his life is constrained by Trelawney's prophecy; in *Half-Blood Prince* this is modified significantly to the recognition that he has a choice in relation to the prophecy and action on it; in *Deathly Hallows* he accepts that the only possible way to kill Voldemort is to offer himself to be killed, as Voldemort's seventh Horcrux. He is not "dragged into the arena" (Rowling, *Half-Blood* 479), nor offered to it as a pig for slaughter, as Snape suggests in *Deathly Hallows* (551), but "walks into it, head held high" (Rowling, *Half-Blood* 479) even when he finally understands that the fight not only might but must encompass his own death. This is choice as it operates in the real world, neither strict determinism nor the action of fate nor the unfettered freedom of a philosophic ideal, but the reality of human beings acting on the basis of their individual, biologically and socially shaped humanity within a specific context. It is the kind of choice implicit in the question "What choice did they have?": at that early stage the question could only be rhetorical, as it does not occur to Harry or Ron as "pure" eleven-year-olds that they could choose not to enter the bathroom where Hermione is trapped. By the end of the sequence Harry has learned to reflect on the consequences of his choices—hence he is able to say, in *Deathly Hallows*, "Forget Dumbledore. This is my choice, nobody else's" (Rowling, 193), just as later he will throw away the stone that gives him access to the illusory protection of his parents and their classmates.

On this model, destiny is dynamic, not static, because people grow and change. Like the centaurs who can choose to fight, Harry can choose whether and how to deal with Voldemort. Rowling implicitly rejects all three versions of destinarianism: fate can be contested, destiny can be chosen—and readers can revise and reflect on their own expectations of a fictional trajectory. We should remember here Dumbledore's belated comment to Snape that "sometimes I think we Sort too soon" (Rowling, *Deathly* 545). This undermines the simplicity of character as destiny that some, especially noting characters' names, have criticised in the early novels. Snape's development, as retrospectively revealed in "The Prince's Tale" chapter of *Deathly Hallows*, shows how the strength of a single attachment can result in an otherwise unpromising character's decades-long display of loyalty, bravery, and self-sacrifice even for someone—Harry—for whom Snape feels no love at all. Snape, who grows away from the youth who seemed destined to follow the Dark Lord, and Harry, who seemed constrained by prophecy, are both shown exercising real choice as adults on the basis of emotional growth and understanding. The "pure" child Harry who reacted automatically becomes the adult Harry who accepts that his death is inevitable not because an abstract destiny binds him to Voldemort but because his body is a Horcrux tying Voldemort to life. The message of the sequence depends on Harry's recognition that he does have choice, even if that choice is limited to the only choice anyone in the real world can hope to get—not whether to die but when and how.

THE RELATED WORLDS OF CHRESTOMANCI:
A DESTINARIAN UNIVERSE?

Whereas Harry Potter's experiences take place apparently in our own world, if mostly within what Colin Manlove calls a "bubble" world concealed within it (*From Alice* 180), Jones's six Chrestomanci novels are set in worlds parallel to and apparently including our own known as the Related Worlds. The novels are known as the Chrestomanci series, although they are neither a series in the strict sense—a set of novels repeating a specific formula—nor a sequence like the Harry Potter novels. Rather, they are connected by the Related Worlds setting and by featuring, sometimes prominently, sometimes not, a figure known as Chrestomanci. As with the Dalemark quartet, the fact that these novels neither follow a formula nor develop a visible trajectory is appropriate to Jones's image of the universe as plural and varied rather than fixed.

A key feature of the Related Worlds, articulated in the first novel, *Charmed Life* (1977), is that they themselves come in twelve Series, each world within a Series of nine sharing key geographical features and all worlds speaking the same languages—and, it is intimated, possessing some degree of magic. People within the worlds of a given Series have analogues within other worlds of the Series (Jones, *Charmed* 156); in most cases they will have an analogue in every world, but very rarely an individual is born who has no analogues at all. In this case, that person has all the magic that would be possessed not only by himself but by his eight non-existent analogues, and is therefore known as a "nine-lifed enchanter" (247).

The very existence of parallel worlds and personal analogues evokes questions about agency and destiny, as it arouses the expectation that personal analogues will possess the same identity and desires—and therefore have a similar fate. These ideas are particularly at issue in the novels *Charmed Life*, *Witch Week* (1982), and *Conrad's Fate*. The latter represents Jones's most complex and precisely metaphorical study of the nature of identity. I have examined elsewhere how she demonstrates the importance of socialisation and performance in the construction of identity in *Conrad's Fate* (Webb, "False"): surrounded by actors both overt and covert, Conrad learns the various ways by which identity may be performed while still expressing personal desires. The idea of fate in this novel is articulated through Conrad's belief in a karma that will deny him the chance to choose his own future. His narrative is imbued with speculation: the word "if" appears frequently—including in the phrase "if only," as Conrad muses on alternative ways of living from which he believes he is barred (Jones, *Conrad's* 167). Phrases such as "as if" and "like" are still more common, indicating that analogies, if not analogues, are central to Conrad's understanding of the world.

Although it emerges that Conrad's alleged fate was a lie of his Uncle Alfred's, Jones does not entirely reject the idea of fate in this novel. Karma itself turns out to be real—its agent punishes Uncle Alfred—and the activities of the butler/landowner Mr Amos in "pulling the possibilities" (18), distorting probability so as to earn sufficient wealth to pay for his aristocratic mansion to be sustained in ideal splendour, are revealed to be both destructive and futile. Jones suggests in *Conrad's Fate* that there may be a limit to human choice, but that limit emerges from the conditions and context of individual existence, not from an overarching destiny. These concepts of choice and its limitations, and particularly the idea that there are ways for a child to exercise choice and develop an individual identity through recognition of social and ethical constraints, emerge in the earlier Chrestomanci novels as well.

Charmed Life, Jones's earliest Chrestomanci novel, centres on a boy called Cat Chant who for much of the novel appears contented to be dominated by his precocious and ambitious elder sister Gwendolen. Following the deaths of their parents, Cat and Gwendolen are taken to live at the peculiar Chrestomanci Castle by the authoritative Chrestomanci. Here Gwendolen, annoyed by the apparent indifference of the castle's inhabitants, casts an escalating series of malevolent spells designed to upset the inhabitants and especially Chrestomanci himself. Thwarted, and finally stripped of her witchcraft, Gwendolen nevertheless manages to escape to another world, leaving her brother to cope not only with her absence but with the unwilling presence of Janet, one of her analogues who has been pulled into Cat's world by Gwendolen's departure. The events Gwendolen has conspired to set in motion, however, proceed, resulting in Cat making some quite surprising discoveries about both Gwendolen and himself.

Janet turns out to be quite unlike Gwendolen not only in her lack of magic but in personality. Her characterisation thus becomes one focus of Jones's investigation in this novel of the nature of choice and responsibility. When she first appears, dressed back-to-front and oddly seeming "astonished, and rather frightened" unlike the perennially confident Gwendolen, Cat decides that "when people lost their witchcraft, they also lost their memories" (Jones, *Charmed* 216); but when she reveals her ignorance of where she is he notices not only slight physical differences but also that "the downright look on [her face] was not right" (217). Despite her physical similarity to Gwendolen, Janet has a different expression that turns out to express a different set of values. Janet and Gwendolen themselves do not initially recognise this. When she accepts the situation, Janet expects Gwendolen to think as she does, and initially seems correct, quickly unearthing Gwendolen's hidden letter to herself with the comment "She's got the same secretive mind as I have" (122). Gwendolen, too, assumes that "[s]ome other Gwendolen will move into your place and pretend to be you because we are all so clever. You can carry on here making Chrestomanci's life a misery and I shall be greatful [sic], knowing it is in good hands" (123). So, finding a spell on the back of the mirror, her own favourite hiding place, Janet concludes that "it's hell having a double! You both get the same ideas" (125). It is eventually revealed, however, that the spell is Chrestomanci's, not Gwendolen's—and

Janet proves herself quite uninterested in making Chrestomanci's life a misery. Moreover, despite Gwendolen and Janet's assumptions that their analogues are clever, Janet soon decides that Gwendolen is stupid because of her poor classroom performance. It is ironic that Janet accidentally blackens Gwendolen's reputation by getting wrong questions she is posed about the history of Cat's world; but Janet is obviously quite well-informed about the history of her own world, giving answers that though wrong in Cat's world would be right in ours.[2]

Later, following a brief return to her own world in which she read her replacement Romillia's diary, Janet reports that Romillia was "utterly terrified of being sent back. She'd had a dreadful life as an orphan in her own world" (Jones, *Charmed* 244), while Chrestomanci has discovered that "Jennifer, who came after Romillia, is as tough as Gwendolen and had always wished she was an orphan; whereas Queen Caroline, whom Gwendolen displaced, was as miserable as Romillia and had run away three times already" (245). Gwendolen, as we already know, "was in her element" (245) as ruler in Caroline's place. Although they are analogues, then, their actual lives in the different worlds are dramatically different, and—importantly—so are their personalities, in ways with which the influence of context seems to have little to do. Gwendolen, after all, has been manipulating Cat's magic to her own ends since both were very small children in ways unacceptable to their parents as well as unimaginable in Janet. This first Chrestomanci novel evokes a universe that could appear to involve ideas of fate through the concept of personal analogues, but in fact does not.

The point is underlined by Mr Saunders's explanation of the role of Chrestomanci himself:

> "Post?" said Janet. "Isn't it a hereditary title then?"
>
> Mr Saunders laughed [. . .] "Heavens no! We're all Government employees here. The job Chrestomanci has is to make sure this world isn't run entirely by witches. Ordinary people have rights too. And he has to make sure witches don't get out into worlds where there isn't so much magic and play havoc there. It's a big job. And we're the staff that helps him."
>
> (Jones, *Charmed* 247)

Where Janet assumes that Chrestomanci's title is hereditary, and thus to some extent destined—an idea supported by the fact that Cat, himself a nine-lifed enchanter, turns out to be related to him—Mr Saunders's explanation transforms the Chrestomanci role into just another government job, presumably with its own official salaries, perquisites, and regulatory constraints. Such a vision seems very remote from ideas of destiny.

Jones thus disables a genre convention that might seem to be shaping *Charmed Life* as well as the later *Lives of Christopher Chant*: the classic fantasy of the lost heir destined to take his place at the apex of his society. This subgenre of the heroic fantasy not only invokes stereotypes, and therefore invites reader expectations of likely outcomes (type 3 above), similar to the school story, but specifically engages with notions of destiny (type 2) itself. David Eddings's Garion (*Enchanter's End Game*, in the Belgariad sequence), Tad Williams's Simon (*To Green Angel Tower: Storm*, in the Memory, Sorrow, and Thorn sequence [1988–93]), and a host of others discover, often to their dismay, that despite their apparently humble and peripheral origins they are actually heirs to a long-unfilled throne and must defeat a hereditary enemy and take up kingship. In *Charmed Life*, Cat's discovery that he is a nine-lifed enchanter is, like Garion's and Simon's discoveries of their inherited identities, belated; a reader accustomed to such narratives might expect certain responses and consequences. But Jones strips the convention of the panoply of prophecy—Chrestomanci, in fact, reveals that he had ignored one of the few documents referred to in the novel, a letter in which Cat's father had appealed to him to intervene in his daughter's manipulation of her brother. The letter carries neither prophetic weight for the reader nor any sense of urgency for the characters; it is exactly what it seems, a man's expression of concern over puzzling behaviour he is witnessing at the time.[3] Chrestomanci's own later concerns in the situation are not about Cat's identity but about his agency: "Does Cat know what he is doing? If he doesn't, why doesn't he? And if he does know, what is he up to?" (Jones, *Charmed* 249).

Thus Cat's eventual discovery is accompanied not by a sense either of awe or of inadequacy in the face of "destiny," but by a fear of his motives being misunderstood.

> "Stop treating me so carefully!" he said. "I'm not a fool or a baby. You're all afraid of me, aren't you? You didn't tell me things and you didn't punish me because you were afraid I'd do something dreadful. And I haven't. I don't know how to. I didn't know I could."
>
> (Jones, *Charmed* 249)

Cat's ignorance is framed very differently from that of the predestined hero; the focus of the novel is on his acceptance that he must take conscious action, of whatever kind, as an individual in his own right. He cannot act as an instrument of Gwendolen—or of destiny—but must develop his own sense of identity and learn to exercise personal agency. Chrestomanci's implication that Cat is to some extent responsible for Gwendolen's abuse of his powers emphasises that even inaction can be seen as a form of moral choice; Jones's dismantling of destiny carries ethical force.

Witch Week, the second Chrestomanci novel, raises questions of destiny and its relationship to individual identity in a very different way. This novel is set in a world that seems substantially similar to our own contemporary world, with the focal characters, Charles Morgan and Nan Pilgrim, resentful outsiders at a co-educational boarding school. The primary difference between the novel's world and our own turns out to be that in this England, magic is real and witches are still being persecuted. The school contains a high number of "witch-orphans" (Jones, *Witch* 8)—children whose parents have been executed as witches—and the novel opens with a teacher's discovery of an anonymous note declaring that "SOMEONE IN THIS CLASS IS A WITCH" (7). However, most of the events of the novel, magical or otherwise, are based firmly in the mundane. Charles's first attempt at magic pulls every shoe in the school into a vast heap, while Nan is anxious not to wake the others when a broomstick takes her for a ride. Eventually a number of the children grow desperate enough to flee the school in ones and twos; Nan and Estelle Green seek out a "witches' escape route," apparently similar to the routes for escaped slaves in the American South (174), but the route has been shut down and instead they are given a mysterious name to call on. Chrestomanci, summoned by his name, is identifiably the Chrestomanci of *Charmed Life*. He is puzzled by what he learns of their world, and eventually declares that it ought not to exist (Jones, *Witch* 224).

The idea that a world could be "all wrong" (Jones, *Witch* 216) is a new one in the Chrestomanci series, and could imply that there is after all some kind of shaping force, or fate, at work in their universe. However, other elements seem to contradict this; again Jones's concern is ethical, and practical. Instead of assisting the children's flight, Chrestomanci shocks them by pointing out their own responsibility for having caused trouble in the school (205). As elsewhere in this series, personal responsibility, even in a child, is heavily emphasised. Further, Chrestomanci states that "[y]ou shouldn't get a civilised world where witches are burnt" (224). The reader is to infer that "civilisation" is too far at odds with the superstitions and fears involved in witch burning, a practical problem with the world's functioning rather than a moral or cosmic one. This is not an objection made on the basis of an idea of a fated order in the world.

The resolution of the novel, meanwhile, paradoxically emphasises both the integrity of individual action and the powerful effect of context on character. Earlier, Nirupam Singh had remarked that he had thought another outsider, Brian Wentworth, was nasty just because "it was his situation," and Charles had reflected that "he was not sure that a person's character could be separated from their situation in quite this way" (Jones, *Witch* 189). The novel's ending bears out the idea that character is affected by situation. Nan, the storyteller, narrates her version of what has gone wrong with their world and persuades her classmates that it must be fixed through the use of an existing "Simon Says" spell that Charles had earlier placed on the irritating Simon Silverson—everything Simon said immediately came true—and that Nirupam had reversed. Everything Simon says now becomes untrue, so that his statement "Guy Fawkes blew up the Houses of Parliament" turns that into a lie and restores the world to unity with our own prosaic world, in which Guy Fawkes failed (264). The final chapter then gives us a brief glimpse of the school not only transformed to an ordinary comprehensive high school, but reconfigured socially. Charles and Nirupam are now friends with Charles's earlier tormentor Dan Smith; Brian sits happily with Simon.[4] But Mr Crossley is still interested in Miss Hodge, and Dan, who had stolen Charles's spiked shoes and unknowingly eaten them when Nirupam had transformed them to cake, has in the changed world eaten tin-tacks for a bet with Nirupam. In this novel, character is shown to be shaped much more powerfully by context than by fate, but it is the choices that people make within those contexts that define who they are.

The latter point is made particularly evident through the characterisation of Charles Morgan. It is significant that the reader is given narrative glimpses of the past only through Charles's memories: he is the only character whose past experiences are represented as being crucial in determining his present behaviour, in an important deviation from the operation of traditional school stories. Charles has been affected by specific experiences, and his decisions are shown to be powerfully based on his reactions to those experiences. Unlike those of the other children, which deal with their present situations, Charles's school journal encodes his daily reflections on two childhood encounters with witches. In the first he saw a fat man burnt at the stake for witchcraft; in the second he allowed a young woman who confessed herself to be a witch to escape through his house. Charles's fascination with the witches, his horror at the burning, and his fear of himself being burnt as a witch dominate his responses to nearly every situation in the novel. He even burns his own finger in order to stop himself working magic accidentally by reminding himself that "*it hurts to be burnt*" (Jones, *Witch* 87). His obsession with witches, and his resentment of those who have made him afraid, are such that when Chrestomanci rebukes him for his failure to recognise the dangers of the "Simon Says" spell he is angry, and initially refuses to assist Chrestomanci to alter the world—especially because Chrestomanci informs him that he will probably lose his high level of magic in the new world and have a talent for something else. For Charles, witchcraft is power: at worst it is the power to suffer, but it is also the power to cause suffering. The mischievous spell Charles had cast, a malicious response to a bully, was, as Chrestomanci had pointed out to him, powerful enough to change the world.[5] Charles does not want to surrender the power to avenge himself on people like Simon or Dan.

Charles decides after all to act, to help Chrestomanci change the world, only partly because of Nan's story. As Sarah Fiona Winters points out, "Charles has to realize the complex connection between fear and hatred, between his culture's victimization of him and his own anger, before he can exorcise the evil from his own personality" (91). He is impressed by the physical effort Chrestomanci must make magically to give Nan time to persuade the class, but the main reason for his change of heart is his view of the Inquisitor who belatedly arrives, Inspector Littleton. "The fat man had been so astonished at being burnt. And [Charles] suddenly understood the witch's amazement. It was because someone so ordinary, so plain stupid as Inspector Littleton had the power to burn him. And that was all wrong" (Jones, *Witch* 262). This is a different kind of statement from Chrestomanci's statement about the wrongness of the world, even though it seems similar: Charles is making a moral decision to make a moral change. He believes in the power of the Inquisitors—it is great enough to burn witches, maybe even to burn Charles himself—and he rejects that power as "wrong." Charles works to change the world so that it will not be a world where such things happen. For most of the class, the decision to aid Chrestomanci is produced by Nan's power to tell a story that convinces them that the world is physically in error; for Charles it is generated by his recognition of his own responsibility. Charles acts to ensure that people like himself and the fat man and the fleeing woman will not be burnt by fools like Littleton. His apology to Chrestomanci acknowledges his responsibility; in so doing it underlines the fact that in the Chrestomanci universe, whatever world people live in, however powerful the influences of context, their decisions are their own. This is not a destinarian universe, but one where individual choice and moral consciousness are paramount.

CHRISTOPHER AND THE SCHOOL STORY: CHOOSING DESTINY

In *The Lives of Christopher Chant: The Childhood of Chrestomanci*, the emphasis falls less on the parallels between the worlds than on their differences, as the child Christopher explores what he thinks of as the Anywheres he can reach from the Place Between in his dreams. The idea of fate, as a universal determinant of events, is not evoked in this narrative. Unlike in *Charmed Life*, Christopher does not meet anyone who seems to be an analogue of someone else; although he does see people who remind him of others, these similarities are represented as shared personality traits, so the effect is rather like Agatha Christie's Miss Marple deducing people's probable actions by comparison with the actions of similar people she has known in the past. Thus, although near the end of the book Christopher recognises that his spirit-friend Tacroy has seen Christopher's Uncle Ralph as like the Dright, the ruler of the single World Eleven, Christopher also sees himself in the Dright—and he is not an analogue for the Dright, although he suggests that he is the Dright for his world. It is their approaches to power that make them similar as personalities, while it is Uncle Ralph's selfishness and willingness to use people that make him like the Dright. These are of course individual characteristics that may result in widely different activities, as the action of the novel makes clear. Thus the existence of the Related Worlds in this novel emphasises the multiple possibilities available to characters and indeed worlds, but the action of the novel highlights individual lives and their trajectories. It is the way in which Jones positions the individual life as operating within a set of personal expectations and choices that I examine here. Interestingly, in *The Lives of Christopher Chant* Jones represents how these expectations may be formed not only by real-life experience, but by the process of reading itself. Through reading, the reader may imbibe fictional conventions of how life works; we have seen in Chapter 2 how Jones and Rowling work to dismantle these. In *The Lives of Christopher Chant*, Jones both comments on certain genre conventions and demonstrates how an agile reader can deploy those conventions to her own benefit.

In *The Lives of Christopher Chant*, we are introduced to the child who a reader of the prior Chrestomanci novels will recognise from the subtitle is to become the adult Chrestomanci of *Charmed Life*, *Witch Week*, and *The Magicians of Caprona* (1980). This anticipated future, however, is not structured by ideas of a fixed fate or destiny but, as in *Charmed Life*, by a concern with how children, as beings generally governed by the rules and expectations of adults, may acquire individual agency. In this novel, Christopher's mother has her own plans for him—he is to enter "Society," which as a young child Christopher thinks means he must become a missionary— and his father, we learn, is a maker of horoscopes who believes that Christopher is destined to be a powerful enchanter and who has taken his own steps to circumvent a fate he has discovered in Christopher's horoscope.[6] When his Uncle Ralph discovers Christopher's ability to travel between worlds, he sets him tasks that an alert reader will recognise have to do with Uncle Ralph's goals rather than Christopher's; the concern here is not with destiny, despite the views of Christopher's father, but with the ready compliance of the child with the expectations of its elders, even where those expectations involve exploitation.

It is early clear to the reader, if not to Christopher, that Christopher's gifts are unusual even within the fictional setting, and when he turns out to be able to return to life after being killed on several occasions it is obvious that he must be very important indeed—that being a talent we customarily associate only with gods, or with Harry Potter. When it is belatedly established that Christopher is indeed a nine-lifed enchanter he is told that this means he must become Chrestomanci, as the present one is very old and has been searching for a successor for some time. It is here that destinarianism enters the novel in an explicit way: Christopher's Papa declares, "You will become a very important man" (Jones, *Lives* 140), and Christopher realises to his fury that "[i]t was all settled" (139). Christopher's subsequent resistance to this notion is very much in the heroic fantasy tradition, and readers of such fantasies—not just of the other Chrestomanci novels—will not be surprised to learn not only that he is forced to act within the role before the end of the novel but that he discovers that he is good at it and enjoys it. However, Jones does not allow this fulfilment of narrative expectation to go unchallenged. She complicates and interrogates ideas of destiny and personal choice, and she does so in part by evoking expectations from another genre, the school story.

Jones's interrogation of destinarianism in *The Lives of Christopher Chant* operates in several ways. First, she makes it clear that Chrestomanci is a role, in fact a job, as previously indicated in *Charmed Life*. In other words, being the Chrestomanci is like being the head of a research institution where only a few individuals will have the required relatively rare attributes that are needed to do the job, as opposed to being the Dalai Lama, who is born to his position—or being the lost heir of a fantasy kingdom. This is brought out through the contrast between the role of Chrestomanci and the incarnation of the Goddess Asheth. While travelling in Series Ten, Christopher meets a girl known as the Goddess because a birthmark on the sole of her foot has revealed that she is the Living Asheth, an incarnation of her world's goddess. This identification is never challenged within the novel. What is challenged, however, is the girl's destiny. She knows that the Living Asheth is always a little girl, but a question from Christopher makes her realise that this means that she cannot both grow up and remain the Living Asheth. Seeking a portent of her future, the Goddess infers that she must be intended to become a Dead Asheth. Like Christopher, however, the Goddess is reluctant to accept what she sees as a destined future, and takes direct action, running away to Christopher's world for protection.

There are two points to be learned from the Goddess's story within the novel. First, it turns out that she is wrong. Although the goddess Asheth does indeed demand a life when the new Living Asheth takes over, her high priestess Mother Proudfoot is in the habit of taking a life from one of the Temple cats—cats of course also have nine lives—and setting up the ex-goddess girls in a different life. She has always planned that this particular girl will be properly educated, and comes to ask the current Chrestomanci, Gabriel de Witt, for help with this. Thus destiny, even at its most explicit and official, can be circumvented, if only through a loophole in Asheth's expectations. Second, the Goddess's decision to run away is energised by her reading of school stories from Christopher's world that give her an idea of an alternative future, and of how to get it. "When Millie's friend Cora Hope-fforbes's father broke his neck hunting, she had to borrow her school fees" (242). The Goddess's awareness of the pattern of story provides her with a model on which she deliberately draws to shape her future.

The references to the school story in *The Lives of Christopher Chant* are sustained by the Goddess's frequent allusions to it, which dominate the closing pages, and draw our attention to the elements of the school story within Christopher's own story. Christopher himself is sent to school part way through the narrative; unlike the Goddess, he does not perceive his experience in genre terms, although the reader might do so. It is significant that it is at school that Christopher starts to acquire agency. In the earlier part of the novel he is presented as a lonely and naïve child with few formulated desires of his own: "It was wonderful that Uncle Ralph thought him important. He was so glad and delighted that he would have done far more for Uncle Ralph than just not tell anyone" (Jones, *Lives* 30–31). However, his insertion into the social world of the school, in which he has peers rather than guardians, swiftly teaches him a wider set of values. He recognises his responsibility for his past actions, realising that as an honourable schoolboy he must pay the Goddess back for a stolen cat—which he does by taking her the school stories. He also acquires the very traditional schoolboy esteem for sport, dreaming like his friend Oneir—whose name in fact means "dream"—of becoming a professional cricketer.

Christopher, like Harry Potter, experiences school without the mediation of his own readerly expectations. But whereas Harry in many ways fulfils the expectations of the school story genre, with the repeated outwitting of Snape and Filch, the enmity with Malfoy, and above all success at Quidditch, Christopher's brief experience of school just sketches in what we expect—he has two inseparable friends he meets on the train, there are no midnight feasts but midnight reading of the *Arabian Nights*, and instead of hated French lessons he has boring magic lessons—because the focus is on how it relates to the rest of his life. In particular, Christopher's belief that he is a brilliant cricketer, an expectation that coheres with reader expectations of school story protagonists, is largely unsupported within the text. He does in fact win a cricket match despite the expectations of those around, the stereotypical achievement of the underdog hero, but the match occurs *after* he has left school. His victory depends on a single stroke, which in itself could be dramatic but in context is not: he just has to make two runs, and the fact that he makes them on his first stroke may indeed show clever play but does not demonstrate brilliance or indeed that quality of the miraculous that is usually seen in the underdog hero in this situation. What is important about the school experience within Christopher's life is quite simply that it portrays how a child is socialised to value and desire. This is not evidence for destinarianism nor for determinism, but represents a process undergone by every human being within a society. Christopher emerges from his brief time at school dreaming of a future that is at odds with his father's plan—he has become a typical teenager.

Whereas school itself mediates Christopher's experience and teaches him desire, the Goddess uses the school story to mediate her own desires. The Goddess chooses to invoke the conventions of the school story to shape her own destiny. That is, although her birth-destiny is first to be the Living Asheth and then to become a Dead Asheth, she rejects that destiny and chooses instead to be a schoolgirl, with all the constraints that implies. She insists not only on behaving in accordance with the ethics of the school novels but indeed on invoking the schoolgirl story even at the possible cost of losing the schoolgirl life. Thus she suggests to Gabriel de Witt that "I have to own up, like they do in the books. I don't *deserve* to go to school!" (Jones, *Lives* 318). In this statement she simultaneously invokes the code of the school stories as applying to her, asserting her identity as schoolgirl, and risks that that code will prevent her from actually entering the school story world.

It is unsurprising to the reader—and perhaps also to the Goddess, as astute reader of school stories—that the Goddess's "wickedness" will be pardoned and that her "punishment" in fact will help her get her way (Jones, *Lives* 318). Gabriel rebukes her,

> Stop crying, young lady. You will have to go to school because I should be misusing your chest of diamonds if you do not. Regard that as your punishment. You may come and live in the Castle with the rest of the young enchanters during the holidays.
>
> (318)

As so often happens to the heroes and heroines of the school stories, the punishment the Goddess receives is in fact what she desires. Small wonder then that "[t]he Goddess's blissful smile came back and diverted the tears on her face round her ears and into her hair" (318–19), a description of an extremely wide smile that also underlines the extent to which her destiny of being the Dead Asheth has also been diverted, or rather averted. Her success empowers her to correct Gabriel, "Hols . . . The books always call them the hols" (319), a statement asserting not only her knowledge of the system but her right to maintain it. The Goddess has drawn on the school stories to shape her own identity and values as well as her sense of a desirable future, in a conscious exploitation of the third type of "destinarianism" identified above. Her thorough identification with the school story heroine—which leads to her actually taking the heroine's name, "Millie," as readers of other Chrestomanci novels will realise—operates even at the potential cost of any actual school experience, and Gabriel's acceptance of the code as applying to her— "Regard that as your punishment"—confirms her in her chosen identity.[7]

Jones's emphasis on the Goddess's investment in the values learned from the school story, by contrast with Christopher's investment in the values learned at school, signals her awareness of the importance of literary genre and of reading generally in shaping reader understanding of the world and of themselves. Jones's portrayal of Christopher's enactment of the lost heir story is therefore crucial to her education of her own readers. By the end of the novel we have been shown that gifts of personality and destiny can be separable and destiny itself can be diminished. If Christopher determines to trap Uncle Ralph, it is because he feels partly responsible for having helped Uncle Ralph gain his power, rather than because he is destined to be Uncle Ralph's doom—capturing Uncle Ralph is the equivalent of a police job rather than a destined battle, as is shown by the behaviour of the inhabitants of Chrestomanci Castle prior to the capture of Tacroy. It is Christopher's values, that is his own choices, that make him take on the task of being Chrestomanci. And even though one of Christopher's actions in his final battle, like Harry Potter's, is deliberately to sacrifice a life in order to save his friends, that battle turns out not to be with Uncle Ralph but with the Dright, the ruler of Tacroy's home world in Series Eleven, about whom neither Christopher nor the reader even knows until the penultimate chapter of twenty-one in the novel. Like so many of Jones's novels, *The Lives of*

Christopher Chant does not provide a neat story in which everything can be predicted. Instead of a trajectory of destiny, therefore, what we are shown is how young people like Christopher and the Goddess imbibe both values and ideas of their future lives from their environment—whether that environment be real or fictional—and engage with those values according both to what is socially possible and to what is appropriate to their personalities. Jones provides her readers not with destinarianism but with an image of socially constrained choice.

CONCLUSION

The desire to escape the burden of individual responsibility may manifest in belief in the forces of Fate, or of individual destiny. The former empowers the universe, the latter dignifies the hero, but both effectively exculpate the individual from the need to choose and act independently. Rowling and Jones both deny their characters and their readers this escape from personal responsibility. Rowling's sequence engages the reader in a debate about the nature of destiny and of choice: the very existence of the debate points to the requirement for any reader, any individual, to choose a position—and in so doing to accept the responsibility to make personal choices in the world. Harry's acceptance of the necessity to die is represented as a conscious decision, not a submission to fate; in the process of making that decision, as well as in the acceptance of the requirements of his situation, he acts as an exemplar to the readers who have engaged with his experiences across the seven books.

While characters within the sequence—primarily Dumbledore—frequently voice a belief in the overriding importance of personal choice, this belief may seem undermined by the frequent reference to divination and prophecy. However, Rowling invites her readers to critique destinarian accounts. The reader is emotionally drawn into engagement with characters, primarily Harry, in ways that invite positive or negative responses to certain attitudes and behaviours; in the course of this process we learn to distrust ideas of destiny whether acquiesced to by the centaurs or acted on by Voldemort. Moreover, Rowling's late account through Dumbledore of Harry's actions early in the sequence invites a re-examination of his behaviour not as reactive but as generated by his powerful moral sense. By the end, Harry's decision to die at Voldemort's hands is represented as an act of conscious moral choice— a choice that includes acknowledgement of the almost unbearable constraints imposed not by an abstract fate but by the circumstances in which he finds himself.

Jones's novels, meanwhile, locate her characters within a universe that may seem destinarian in structure, but in which individuals are repeatedly compelled to take personal responsibility for their actions. These characters do after all choose, but their freedom to do so does not mean the freedom to flee consequences and ignore guilt. Jones's Chrestomanci makes this point in rebuking the children of *Witch Week* for their attempt to flee a situation their own behaviour has worsened; Charles Morgan recognises that he has the responsibility as well as the capacity not only to atone for his own errors, like Christopher Chant, but to make his world a better place. Jones places ideas of fate in tension with a more nuanced view of the complexities of personal context to suggest that identity is constructed through actions taken within those contexts. The analogues of *Charmed Life* may look similar, but their choices are very different. Christopher Chant appears to have a destined future; however, he develops a sense of identity, shaped by the values of his school environment, that extends beyond what may be required of him in his role as Chrestomanci. It is that sense of himself that directs his decision to act and to atone for his past mistakes.

In *The Lives of Christopher Chant* Jones not only evokes the spectre of a genre-driven narrative only to dismiss it, but also represents the character of the Goddess as consciously modelling her identity and her future trajectory on what she has learned from school stories. Jones's representation of characters as gaining agency from appropriative reading underscores the importance of her own activity as a writer. Her novels show how even children like Cat, Charles, and Christopher can and must take responsibility for themselves and their worlds; like Harry, they become examples for readers to follow. Both Jones and Rowling emphasise the importance of choosing consciously and of accepting the moral consequences of choice.

NOTES

1. This may make sense of the language of the prophecy statement that Voldemort's nemesis "approaches": since Voldemort apparently acts on it immediately, Harry is already one year old at the time of the prophecy, so his "approach," read retrospectively, refers to his acquisition of power, including becoming a Horcrux of Voldemort.

2. As in *Howl's Moving Castle* (1986), that is, what is in the novel a portal world—in this case never seen within the text—is our own ordinary world; the story itself is set in what is to the reader a fantastic space. Janet's arrival in Cat's world is an inversion of traditional portal fantasy, since Janet's home world is unmistakably our own. Mendlesohn has also commented on the effect of Janet's appearance as portal traveller being depicted from the point of view of the receiving world: "unusually, the reader sees what it is like for the portal world to receive a traveller who is not the locus of the disturbance" (*Diana* 82). Technically, Janet's arrival should make the novel an intrusion fantasy, in Mendlesohn's terms—but in an intrusion fantasy the intruder *is* normally the locus of the disturbance.

3. Gwendolen's ambitious and self-serving witch allies attempt to take power not from Frank Chant's letter but from Chrestomanci's reply, which bears his signature, but are foiled because, with a rationality rare in heroic fantasy, Chrestomanci has "sign[ed] his name under unbreakable protections" (Jones, *Charmed* 175).

4. Sarah Fiona Winters points out that "Jones leaves unresolved the question of whether Brian is indeed inherently nasty, whatever his situation, or whether Simon, given a new situation, is much nicer" (91). Mendlesohn suggests that Brian has learned to be a "real boy," as Nan would put it, but observes that "Nan's 'real boys' are not nice" (*Diana* 31).

5. As observed in the Introduction, Deborah Kaplan and Debbie Gascoyne have each discussed the importance of language as performative in Jones's fiction.

6. As is typical of such endeavours in literary texts, his father's intervention has unintended and problematic consequences for Christopher.

7. In *Conrad's Fate*, Millie (the Goddess) has discovered that the Swiss school to which she has been sent does not meet her expectations and run away from it, but although this discovery indicates a disjunction between real schools and storybook schools the disjunction is not emphasised: Gabriel de Witt acknowledges that the Swiss school was not a good one and plans to send her elsewhere.

Conclusion

Diana Wynne Jones, Terry Pratchett, and J.K. Rowling write narratives for children that delight their readers. Their fictions are absorbing and playful, attracting readers to enter a complex and imaginative realm of fantasy. But for these writers, fantasy is more than entertainment: it is an important way for readers to learn about the real world, to interpret and critique expectations within that world, to imagine new possibilities, and to develop the capacity for agency. Characters such as Rowling's Harry, Pratchett's Tiffany, and Jones's Sophie exemplify this process.

All these novelists exhibit a profound commitment to fiction as an object of pleasure in its own right, but also as a means of promoting an ethical awareness in their readers. While they demonstrate ways in which children may develop their own identities and capacities for agency, all three writers frame that demonstration within a moral vision of individual action. This ethical impulse is reflected across their work in their approaches to conventional concepts, such as the figure of the witch. Pratchett's Tiffany becomes, and remains, a witch in order to prevent the unthinking victimisation of the helpless by those too caught up in their own fears to see clearly. His account of her development focuses on community attitudes to the witch, both positive and negative; he explores how both those attitudes and the anxieties that foster them may be confronted. As we saw in Chapter 4, Tiffany learns to manipulate community expectations in order to gain authority within her society, an authority she can then use to re-work those expectations themselves.

The importance of an ethical framework is also visible in Rowling's interrogation of ideas of fate and destiny in the Harry Potter sequence (1997–2007): the sequence insists on the primacy of individual choice, but Rowling highlights the fact that the choice Harry finally makes is impelled by love and self-sacrifice. As we saw in Chapter 2, the resistance to traditionally heroic virtues visible across the later novels demonstrates a concern with those virtues as impractical and even dangerous, like Jones's briefer sketch of those virtues in *Cart and Cwidder* (1975). While we admire Harry for his "daring, nerve, and chivalry" (Rowling, *Philosopher's* 130), Rowling suggests that these qualities must be sustained within a broader moral framework of care for others and a comprehensive understanding of the real world. Jones's account of individual choice as opposed to a destinarian attitude to experience, as we observed in Chapter 5, likewise emphasises personal responsibility. The Chrestomanci novels (1977–2006) at once invoke and dismiss ideas of fate through the concept of Related Worlds and personal analogues, as they emphasise not identity but individual difference, and her child characters learn to take responsibility not just for their own actions but for the shape of the society in which they live.

As can be seen from Jones's use of the concept of Related Worlds, the use of fantasy is central to the ethical strategies of these writers. Pratchett and Jones both deploy the fantastic trope of the wainscot society to highlight the importance of moving beyond limiting assumptions, whether these derive from social convention or habits of reading. Pratchett's nomes and Jones's people/Lymen provide a fresh perspective on the humans they see, but through their own behaviour we can also reflect on the habits of human social groups. Both writers play with fantasy genres to engage readers with their ethical messages. The Bromeliad (1989–90) crosses the wainscot fantasy with the "lost colony" trope to encourage us to look beyond what we know, while Jones's *Power of Three* (1976) disguises a wainscot fantasy as an immersive fantasy to encourage the importance of interrogating what we think we know, and especially to look past the mental barriers of race prejudice. Both texts endorse a resistance to cultural givens and an openness to other possible modes of being. Rowling evokes the concept of prophecy and the Chosen One in order to encourage an evaluation of the nature of human choice, and like Jones, draws on heroic fantasy conventions while compelling the reader to recognise the imaginative and moral limitations of the formula fantasy. All three novelists thus demonstrate a preoccupation with the power of story itself; their sophisticated treatment of genre conventions encourages a critical awareness in their readers.

Unsurprisingly, given her investment in the power of language, narrative strategy is crucial to Jones's approach to heroic fantasy, as discussed in Chapter 2. In the novels of the Dalemark quartet (1975–93) she provides immersive fantasy in which divergences from the heroic-fantasy conventions are comparatively subtle, yet point to the inadequacy even in a fantasy "real life" of the values endorsed by those conventions. In *Hexwood* (1993), she challenges the reader much more directly, presenting a narrative trajectory that can be very hard to follow that mixes features of stereotypical heroic fantasy in unexpected ways. As with the allusions to Donne's "Song" and *The Wizard of Oz* (1900) in *Howl's Moving Castle* (1986), Jones plays with literary elements, mixing these together to produce new literary ideas that challenge the reader to think beyond their literary expectations. *The Dark Lord of Derkholm* (1998) engages its readers with dragons and griffins, heroic quests, and a struggle against evil, but inverts our expectations of these: the novel impels readers to reflect on the nature and values of heroic fantasy itself. Thus Jones's writing presents a narrative surface that sometimes seems straightforward, as in *Charmed Life* (1977), sometimes confusing, as in *Hexwood*, but effectively challenges the reader to think in complex ways: the lessons that may be drawn from her fiction are rarely straightforward. The reader posited within these fictions is an engaged one, ready to invest time and energy in a complex story, to ponder the experiences of her characters, and to question the conventional operation of genre.

Pratchett's fiction also posits an intelligent and active reader. Although his diction is generally simple, we saw in Chapter 1 how he invites readers of *The Wee Free Men* (2003) to admire and empathise with a character who is self-consciously intelligent and critical not only of her community but even of her reading. Through Tiffany, Pratchett critiques the conventions of fairy tale even while engaging the reader through fairy tale itself. His framing of the Bromeliad novels also implies an expectation that his readers will be acquainted with works such as the Bible or an encyclopaedia and able to perceive the disjunction between the discourses within his imagined versions. As we saw in Chapter 4, Pratchett even invites readers to critique the method of his own fiction and their pleasure in it: the ironic contrast between Mistress Weatherwax's mundane message and its magical delivery in *A Hat Full of Sky* (2004) invites interrogation of Pratchett's own engagement of his readers with magic and fantasy. The accessibility of most of his narrative language belies the sophisticated and self-reflexive nature of his writing.

Rowling's approach to fantasy presents a far simpler surface than those of either Pratchett or Jones. In *Harry Potter and the Philosopher's Stone*, she represents her protagonist as a naïve and vulnerable child of no particular insight, encouraging identification or sympathy from a wide range of possible readers. Whereas Jones and Pratchett appeal to what Mendlesohn calls the "Reading Child" (*Diana* 194), the beginning of *Philosopher's Stone*, at least, is available to a comparatively inexperienced reader. Rowling's model is evolutionary. Her strategy is therefore very unlike Pratchett's in the Tiffany sequence (2003–10) or Jones's in her parodic *The Dark Lord of Derkholm*, as she embeds traditional plots or situations subtly rather than drawing attention to these—few readers notice the "Cinderella" plot in *Philosopher's Stone*. Nevertheless, the Harry Potter sequence emerges as highly sophisticated in its literary project. As we saw in Chapter 1, the first novel draws readers in through its portrait of Harry as the child caught in cartoonishly unpleasant circumstances and then discovering the pleasures of a magical school, but also through a narrative style that develops gradually from simplicity to grammatical complexity. Moreover, the gratifyingly repetitive structure of the early novels, which draw on the successful tradition of the school story, gives way to an increasingly dramatic evocation of the heroic that, as we saw in Chapter 2, nevertheless resists the values of heroic fantasy.

Pratchett refers frequently to stories themselves—the stories read by Malicia and by the rats in *The Amazing Maurice and His Educated Rodents*

(2001), *The Goode Childe's Book of Faerie Tales* so resented by Tiffany in *The Wee Free Men*, the cultural stories the nomes have woven into rigid authority in *Truckers* (1989). His account of story demonstrates that stories have enormous power to shape expectations of the world—sometimes damagingly so, as with the stories of witches that result in the death of Mrs Snapperly and the hatred, even self-hatred, faced by Tiffany in *I Shall Wear Midnight* (2010). But Pratchett's characters can also take positive messages from stories. Dorcas gains insight into his own situation from the metaphor of the frogs in the bromeliad, and even the simplistic story of *Mr Bunnsy* can be become more than either a lie about utopia or a book "some silly woman wrote [. . .] for ickle kids" (Pratchett, *The Amazing* 189) if properly read by Dangerous Beans and Darktan. Tiffany can see how Miss Treason and Mrs Proust manipulate cultural stories and in *Wintersmith* (2006) learns to do so herself. Tiffany, the rats, and the nomes all learn from story about what the world is like: the fact that *The Goode Childe's Book of Faerie Tales* does not tell the truth about life is less important than the fact that it, and books like it, encode and transmit what people think is the truth. Fantasy in this sense can be more powerful than realism: in its simplest form it depicts basic cultural attitudes to life with astonishing clarity, as Tiffany perceives. Used adroitly by writers such as Pratchett it can direct readers' critical attention to assumptions about the world, and provide new ways of imagining a possible future. Pratchett depicts readers like Tiffany developing a conscious critique of the lessons and constraints imposed by cultural stories and using this critique as a basis for development of a coherent sense of individual identity.

Prior to *Harry Potter and the Deathly Hallows* (2007), Rowling appears to ignore fiction as a subject; even when the issue of art is addressed, she represents it as functional, as are the paintings and statues of Hogwarts. By the time Harry and Hermione read "The Tale of the Three Brothers," they are seeking messages, not pleasure. Yet children famously enjoy the Harry Potter sequence: Rowling's practice demonstrates the capacity of story-telling to engage, even as she represents various approaches to reading and exposes their weaknesses and strengths. Jones's Goddess, meanwhile, learns how to direct her future not from her narrow personal experience but from her reading. School stories provide her with a model, if a limited one, of another way of living. The Goddess, like the rat Darktan, like Sophie Hatter, finally like Harry in his reading of "The Tale of the Three Brothers," has learned how to use story as a map, a way to chart a path to a possible future.

All these characters are drawing not just on fiction but on fantasy. Mimesis of the mundane may be instructive, but as Sir Philip Sidney pointed out, it is limited to the "brazen" reality of the ordinary world (216). Fantasy fiction allows for a wider imagination of the possible and invites us to interrogate our understanding of the "impossible." Like Jones's Polly, readers can discover "true, strange fact[s]" in fairy tale (*Fire* 171); like Pratchett's Tiffany, they can learn to recognise what they say about cultural preconceptions. Harry Potter eventually learns both these things from "The Tale of the Three Brothers," and is finally able to take from that story an understanding and acceptance of death as a natural human experience. Jones, Pratchett, and Rowling educate their readers in the process of reading the world. They provide their readers with fantasies that are pleasurable and imaginative, but far from encouraging escape from reality, they convey important lessons about the complexities and challenges of the real world—and how these may be faced and solved. All three writers deploy the tropes and imaginative possibilities of fantasy to disturb, challenge, and enlarge the world of their readers.

Works Cited

Alton, Anne Hiebert. "Generic Fusion and the Mosaic of Harry Potter." Whited 141–62.

Anatol, Giselle Liza, ed. *Reading Harry Potter: Critical Essays*. Westport, CT: Praeger, 2003. Print.

———. *Reading Harry Potter Again*. Santa Barbara: Praeger, 2009. Print.

Anstey, F. *Vice Versa, or A Lesson to Fathers*. 1882. *Project Gutenberg*. Web. Accessed 10 March 2013.

Attebery, Brian. *Strategies of Fantasy*. Bloomington: Indiana UP, 1992. Print.

Bar-Hillel, Gili. "Of Moving Castles and Flying Houses: *The Wizard of Oz* and *Howl's Moving Castle* as Interconnected Milestones in Children's Fantasy Literature." *Crossing Textual Boundaries in International Children's Literature*. Ed. Lance Weldy. Newcastle upon Tyne: Cambridge Scholars, 2011. 382–97. Print.

Baum, L. Frank. *The Wonderful Wizard of Oz*. 1900. *Project Gutenberg*. Web. Accessed 18 March 2012.

Beaumont, Mme leprince de. "Beauty and the Beast." *The Young Misses Magazine*. London, 1783. Rpt. in *Merveilles et contes* 3.1 (1989): 127–36. JSTOR. Web. Accessed 6 August 2014. Trans. of "*La Belle et la bête*." By Beaumont. *Le Magasin des enfants, ou dialogues entre une sage gouvernante et plusieurs de ses élèves*. 1756.

Bloom, Harold. "Can 35 Million Book Buyers Be Wrong? Yes." *Wall Street Journal* 11 July 2000. Web. Accessed 27 August 2012.

Breebart, Leo, ed. "*Diggers*." *The Annotated Pratchett v9.0*. Web. Accessed 18 April 2012.

Burroughs, Edgar Rice. *The Chessmen of Mars*. 1922. *Project Gutenberg*. Web. Accessed 3 June 2013.

Butler, Andrew M., Edward James, and Farah Mendlesohn, eds. *Terry Pratchett: Guilty of Literature*. 2nd ed. Baltimore: Old Earth, 2004. Print.

Butler, Charles. *Four British Fantasists: Place and Culture in the Children's Fantasies of Penelope Lively, Alan Garner, Diana Wynne Jones, and Susan Cooper*. Lanham, MD: Scarecrow, 2006. Print.

———. "Now Here: Where Now? Magic as Metaphor and as Reality in the Writing of Diana Wynne Jones." Rosenberg, Hixon, Scapple, and White 66–78.

Byatt, A.S. "Harry Potter and the Childish Adult." *The New York Times* 7 July 2003. [A13.] Web. Accessed 27 August 2012.

Campbell, Joseph. *The Hero with a Thousand Faces*. 3rd ed. San Francisco: New World, 2008. Print.

Carroll, Lewis. *Alice in Wonderland*. 1865. Gray 1–99.

———. *Through the Looking Glass*. 1872. Gray 101–209.

"Childe Rowland." Jacobs n.p.

Cleaver, Hylton. *The Forbidden Study*. Chicago: Childrens, 1961. Print.

Clueless. Dir. Amy Heckerling. Paramount, 1995. Film.

Clute, John. "Wainscots." *The Encyclopaedia of Fantasy*. Eds. John Clute and John Grant. London: Orbit, 1997. 991–92. Print.

Cooper, Susan. *Seaward*. 1983. New York: Collier, 1987. Print.

Deavel, Catherine Jack and David Paul Deavel. "Character and Choice in Harry Potter." *Logos* 5.4 (2002): 49–64. Web. Accessed 13 June 2008.

Defoe, Daniel. *Robinson Crusoe*. 1719. *Robinson Crusoe: An Authoritative Text; Backgrounds and Sources; Criticism*. Ed. Michael Shinagel. New York: Norton, 1975. 1–237. Print.

Donaher, Patricia, and James M. Okapal. "Causation, Prophetic Visions, and the Free Will Question in Harry Potter." Anatol, *Reading Harry Potter Again* 47–62.

Donne, John. "Song." *Poetical Works*. Ed. Sir Herbert Grierson. London: Oxford UP, 1933. 8–9. Print.

Eccleshare, Julia. *A Guide to the Harry Potter Novels*. London: Continuum, 2002. Print.

Eddings, David. *Enchanters' End Game*. New York: Ballantine-Del Rey, 1984. Print.

———. *Pawn of Prophecy*. New York: Ballantine-Del Rey, 1982. Print.

Ende, Michael. *The Neverending Story*. 1979. Trans. Ralph Mannheim. Harmondsworth: Penguin, 1984. Print.

Fleischbein, René. "New Hero: Metafictive Female Heroism in *Fire and Hemlock*." *Journal of the Fantastic in the Arts* 21.2 (2010): 233–45. Print.

Fredericks, Casey. "In Defense of Heroic Fantasy." *The Future of Eternity: Mythologies of Science Fiction and Fantasy*. By Casey Fredericks. Bloomington: Indiana UP, 1982. 91–120. Print.

Freeman, Don. *Tilly Witch*. New York: Puffin, 1969. Print.

Furlong, Monica. *Wise Child*. 1987. New York: Knopf, 1989. Print.

Galbraith, Robert [J.K. Rowling]. *The Cuckoo's Calling*. London: Sphere, 2013. Print.

———. *The Silkworm*. London: Sphere, 2014. Print.

Gallardo-C., Ximena, and C. Jason Smith. "Cinderfella: J.K. Rowling's Wily Web of Gender." Anatol, *Reading Harry Potter* 191–205.

Gascoyne, Debbie. "'Why Don't You Be a Tiger?' The Performative, Transformative, Creative Power of the Word in the Universes of Diana Wynne Jones." *Journal of the Fantastic in the Arts* 21.2 (2010): 210–20. Print.

Gray, Donald J., ed. *Alice in Wonderland: Authoritative Texts of Alice in Wonderland, Through the Looking-Glass, The Hunting of the Snark; Backgrounds; Essays and Criticism*. 2nd ed. New York: Norton, 1992. Print.

Griesinger, Emily. "Why Read Harry Potter? J.K. Rowling and the Christian Debate." *Christian Scholars Review* 32.3 (2003): 297–316. *ProQuest*. Web. Accessed 13 June 2008.

Grimes, M. Katherine. "Harry Potter: Fairy Tale Prince, Real Boy, and Archetypal Hero." Whited 89–122.

Grimm, Jacob and Wilhelm Grimm. "The Worn-Out Dancing Shoes." *The Complete Fairy Tales of the Brothers Grimm*. Trans. and introd. Jack Zipes. New York: Bantam, 1987. 470–73. Print.

Gruner, Elisabeth Rose. "Teach the Children: Education and Knowledge in Recent Children's Fantasy." *Children's Literature* 37 (2009): 216–35. *Project Muse*. Web. Accessed 7 April 2014.

Gupta, Sunan. *Re-Reading Harry Potter*. 2nd ed. London: Palgrave, 2009. Print.

Harry Potter and the Chamber of Secrets. Dir. Chris Columbus. Warner Bros, 2002. DVD.

Harry Potter and the Deathly Hallows, Part 1. Dir. David Yates. Warner Bros, 2010. DVD.

Harry Potter and the Deathly Hallows, Part 2. Dir. David Yates. Warner Bros, 2011. DVD.

Harry Potter and the Goblet of Fire. Dir. Mike Newell. Warner Bros, 2005. DVD.

Harry Potter and the Order of the Phoenix. Dir. David Yates. Warner Bros, 2007. DVD.

Harry Potter and the Philosopher's Stone (also released as *Harry Potter and the Sorcerer's Stone*). Dir. Chris Columbus. Warner Bros, 2001. DVD.

Heilman, Elizabeth E., ed. *Harry Potter's World: Multidisciplinary Critical Perspectives*. New York: RoutledgeFalmer, 2003. Print.

———. Introduction. Heilman 1–10.

Herbert, Frank. *Dune*. 1965. New York: Berkley, 1977. Print.

Hixon, Martha P. "The Importance of Being Nowhere: Narrative Dimensions and Their Interplay in *Fire and Hemlock*." Rosenberg, Hixon, Scapple, and White 96–107.

Homer. *The Iliad*. Trans. Richmond Lattimore. Chicago: U of Chicago P, 1951. Print.

Hopkins, Lisa. "Harry Potter and Narratives of Destiny." Anatol, *Reading Harry Potter Again* 63–75.

Hughes, Thomas. *Tom Brown's School Days: By an Old Boy*. 1857. London: Humphrey Milford, 1928. Print.

Jacobs, Joseph. *English Fairy Tales*. 1890. *Project Gutenberg*. Web. Accessed 16 October 2012.

John Carter. Dir. Andrew Stanton. Disney, 2012. Film.

Jones, Diana Wynne. *Black Maria*. 1991. London: HarperCollins, 2000. Print.

———. *Cart and Cwidder*. 1975. London: Reed-Mandarin, 1993.

———. *Castle in the Air*. 1990. London: Collins, 2000. Print.

———. *Charmed Life*. 1977. London: HarperCollins, 2000. Print.

———. *Conrad's Fate*. London: HarperCollins, 2005. Print.

———. *The Crown of Dalemark*. 1993. Oxford: Oxford UP, 2001. Print.

———. *The Dark Lord of Derkholm*. London: Gollancz-Millennium, 1998. Print.

———. *Deep Secret*. New York: Starscape, 1997. Print.

———. *Drowned Ammet*. 1977. London: Reed-Mammoth, 1993. Print.

———. *Eight Days of Luke*. 1975. London: Collins, 2000. Print.

———. *Fire and Hemlock*. 1985. London: HarperCollins, 2000. Print.

———. *The Game*. 2007. London: HarperCollins, 2008. Print.

———. "The Heroic Ideal." *The Lion and the Unicorn* 13.1 (1989): 121–40. *Project Muse*. Web. Accessed 25 May 2010.

———. *Hexwood*. 1993. London: HarperCollins-Collins, 2000. Print.

———. *The Homeward Bounders*. 1981. New York: Greenwillow, 2002. Print.

———. *House of Many Ways*. 2008. London: HarperCollins, 2009. Print.

———. *Howl's Moving Castle*. 1986. London: HarperCollins, 2000. Print.

———. *The Lives of Christopher Chant: The Childhood of Chrestomanci*. 1988. London: HarperCollins, 2000. Print.

———. *The Magicians of Caprona*. 1980. London: Collins, 2000. Print.

———. *The Merlin Conspiracy*. London: Collins, 2003. Print.

———. *The Pinhoe Egg*. London: HarperCollins, 2006. Print.

———. "The Plague of Peacocks." 1984. *Unexpected Magic: Collected Stories*. New York: Greenwillow, 2004. 42–57. Print.

———. *Power of Three*. 1976. London: CollinsVoyager, 2001. Print.

———. *The Spellcoats*. 1979. London: Reed-Mammoth, 1993. Print.

———. "Stealer of Souls." *Mixed Magics*. London: Collins, 2000. 33–99. Print.

———. *The Tough Guide to Fantasyland*. 1996. London: DAW, 1998. Print.

———. *Witch Week*. 1982. London: HarperCollins, 2000. Print.

Kaplan, Deborah. "Diana Wynne Jones and the World-Shaping Power of Language." Rosenberg, Hixon, Scapple, and White 53–65.

"Kate Crackernuts." Jacobs n.p.

Kingsley, Charles. *The Water Babies: A Fairy Tale for a Land Baby*. 1863. Ware: Wordsworth, 1994. Print.

Klaus, Anne. "A Fairy-Tale Crew? J.K. Rowling's Characters Under Scrutiny." *J.K. Rowling Harry Potter*. Eds. Cynthia J. Hallett and Peggy J. Huey. London: Palgrave, 2012. 22–35. Print.

Konigsburg, E.L. *Jennifer, Hecate, Macbeth, and Me*. 1967. Harmondsworth: Penguin, 1973. Print.

Kurtz, Katherine. *Deryni Rising*. New York: Ballantine, 1970. Print.

Lang, Andrew. *Blue Fairy Book*. 1889. New York: Longmans, 1949. Print.

Le Guin, Ursula K. *A Wizard of Earthsea*. 1968. *The Earthsea Trilogy*. By Ursula K. Le Guin. Harmondsworth: Penguin, 1979. 9–167. Print.

Le Lievre, Kerrie Anne. "Wizards and Wainscots: Generic Structures and Genre Themes in the Harry Potter Series." *Mythlore* 24.1 (Summer 2003): 25–36. *Literature Online*. Web. Accessed 13 June 2008.

Lewis, C.S. *The Allegory of Love: A Study in Medieval Tradition*. 1936. London: Oxford UP, 1958. Print.

Lieberman, Marcia R. "'Some Day My Prince Will Come': Female Acculturation Through the Fairy Tale." *College English* 34.3 (1972): 383–95. Print.

Lurie, Alison. *Boys and Girls Forever: Children's Classics from Cinderella to Harry Potter*. 2003. London: Vintage, 2004. Print.

McCaffrey, Anne. *The White Dragon*. New York: Ballantine, 1978. Print.

MacDonald, George. *The Princess and the Goblin*. 1872. *Project Gutenberg*. Web. Accessed 3 February 2013.

Man of Steel. Dir Zack Snyder. Warner Bros, 2013. Film.

Manlove, Colin. *From Alice to Harry Potter: Children's Fantasy in England*. Christchurch: Cybereditions, 2003. Print.

———. *The Order of Harry Potter: Literary Skill in the Hogwarts Epic*. Cheshire, CT: Winged Lion, 2010. Print.

Mendlesohn, Farah. "Crowning the King: Harry Potter and the Construction of Authority." Whited 159–81.

———. *Diana Wynne Jones: Children's Literature and the Fantastic Tradition*. London: Routledge, 2005. Print.

———. *Rhetorics of Fantasy*. Middletown, CT: Wesleyan, 2008. Print.

Moody, Nickianne. "Death and Work." Butler, James, and Mendlesohn 153–70.

Moon, Christine. "I Must Not Tell Lies: Truth Telling and the Reliability of the Word in Harry Potter." 2012 Biennial Conference of the Australasian Children's Literature Association for Research, National Library of Australia, Canberra, Australia, 20–22 June 2012. Unpublished conference paper.

Murphy, Jill. *The Worst Witch*. 1970. *The Worst Witch at School*. By Jill Murphy. Cambridge, MA: Candlewick, 2007. 1–87. Print.

Nesbit, E. *The Story of the Amulet*. 1906. Harmondsworth: Puffin, 1959. Print.

———. *The Story of the Treasure Seekers*. 1899. *Project Gutenberg*. Web. Accessed 3 July 2013.

———. *The Wouldbegoods: Being the Further Adventures of the Treasure Seekers*. 1901. Harmondsworth: Puffin, 1958. Print.

The Neverending Story. Dir. Wolfgang Petersen. Warner Bros, 1984. Film.

The Neverending Story II: The Next Chapter. Dir. George T. Miller. Warner Bros, 1990. Film.

Nikolajeva, Maria. "*Harry Potter*—A Return to the Romantic Hero." Heilman 125–40.

———. "Heterotopia as a Reflection of Postmodern Consciousness in the Works of Diana Wynne Jones." Rosenberg, Hixon, Scapple, and White 25–39.

Norton, Mary. *The Borrowers*. 1952. London, Penguin, 1958. Print.

———. *The Borrowers Afield*. 1955. London: Penguin, 1960. Print.

———. *The Borrowers Afloat*. 1959. London: Penguin, 1970. Print.

———. *The Borrowers Aloft*. 1961. London: Penguin, 1970. Print.

———. *The Borrowers Avenged*. 1982. Norton, *The Complete Borrowers* 501–700. Print.

———. *The Complete Borrowers*. Rev. ed. London: Penguin, 2002. Print.

———. Introduction. 1966. Norton, *The Complete Borrowers* 3–6. Print.

Oxenham, Elsie J. *The Girls of the Abbey School*. Glasgow: Collins, 1921. Print.

Panshin, Alexei. *Rite of Passage*. 1968. London: Magnum, 1980. Print.

Pennington, John. "From Elfland to Hogwarts, or the Aesthetic Trouble with Harry Potter." *The Lion and the Unicorn* 26.1 (2002): 78–97. *Project Muse*. Web. Accessed 13 June 2008.

Perrault, Charles. "Cinderella or: The Little Glass Slipper." *The Fairy Tales of Charles Perrault*. Trans. and introd. Geoffrey Brereton. Harmondsworth: Penguin, 1957. 53–64. Print.

Pinsent, Pat. "The Education of a Wizard: Harry Potter and His Predecessors." Whited 27–50.

Pond, Julia. "A Story of the Exceptional: Fate and Free Will in the Harry Potter Sequence." *Children's Literature* 38 (2010): 181–206. *Project Muse*. Web. Accessed 10 June 2011.

Porter, Roy. "Culture and the Supernatural c.1680–1800." *Witchcraft and Magic in Europe: The Eighteenth and Nineteenth Centuries. The Athlone History of Witchcraft and Magic in Europe*. Eds. Marijke Gijswijt-Hofstra, Brian P. Levack, and Roy Porter. Vol. 5. London: Athlone, 1999. 191–274. Print.

Pratchett, Terry. *The Amazing Maurice and His Educated Rodents*. 2001. London: Corgi, 2004. Print.

——. *Carpe Jugulum*. 1998. London: Corgi, 1999. Print.

——. *The Carpet People*. Rev. ed. 1992. London: Corgi, 1993. Print.

——. *The Colour of Magic*. 1983. London: Corgi, 1985. Print.

——. *Diggers: The Second Book of the Nomes*. 1990. London: Corgi, 1991. Print.

——. *Guards! Guards!* 1989. London: Corgi, 1990. Print.

——. *A Hat Full of Sky: A Story of Discworld*. 2004. London: Corgi, 2005. Print.

——. *I Shall Wear Midnight*. 2010. London: Corgi, 2011. Print.

——. "Imaginary Worlds, Real Stories." The Eighteenth Katharine Briggs Memorial Lecture, November 1999. *Folklore* 111.2 (2000): 154–68. *JSTOR*. Web. Accessed 2 April 2012.

——. *Johnny and the Bomb*. 1996. London: Corgi, 2004. Print.

——. *Johnny and the Dead*. 1993. London: Corgi, 2004. Print.

——. *Lords and Ladies*. 1992. London: Corgi, 1993. Print.

——. *Nation*. 2008. London: Corgi, 2009. Print.

——. *Only You Can Save Mankind*. 1992. London: Corgi, 2004. Print.

——. *Truckers: The First Book of the Nomes*. 1989. London: Corgi, 1990. Print.

——. *The Wee Free Men: A Story of Discworld*. 2003. London: Corgi, 2004. Print.

——. *Wings: The Third Book of the Nomes*. 1990. London: Corgi, 2004. Print.

——. *Wintersmith: A Story of Discworld*. 2006. London: Corgi, 2007. Print.

——. *Witches Abroad*. 1991. London: Corgi, 1992. Print.

——. *Wyrd Sisters*. 1988. London: Corgi, 1989. Print.

Pratchett, Terry, and Neil Gaiman. *Good Omens: The Nice and Accurate Prophecies of Agnes Nutter, Witch*. 1990. London: Corgi, 1991. Print.

Preussler, Otfried. *The Little Witch*. Illus. Winnie Gayler. Trans. Anthea Bell. London, Abelard-Schuman, 1961. Print.

Pullman, Philip. *His Dark Materials*. London: Scholastic, 2002. Print.

Purkiss, Diane. *The Witch in History: Early Modern and Twentieth-Century Representations*. London: Routledge, 1996. Print.

Ransome, Arthur. *Swallows and Amazons*. 1930. Harmondsworth: Puffin, 1962.

Riordan, Rick. *The Last Olympian*. New York: Hyperion, 2009. Print.

Rosenberg, Teya, Martha P. Hixon, Sharon M. Scapple, and Donna R. White, eds. *Diana Wynne Jones: An Exciting and Exacting Wisdom*. New York: Peter Lang, 2002. Print.

Rowson, Martin. *The Waste Land*. New York: Harper, 1990. Print.

Rowling, J.K. *The Casual Vacancy*. London: Sphere, 2012. Print.

———. *Fantastic Beasts and Where to Find Them*. London: Bloomsbury, 2001. Print.

———. *Harry Potter and the Chamber of Secrets*. 1998. London: Bloomsbury, 2007. Print.

———. *Harry Potter and the Deathly Hallows*. London: Bloomsbury, 2007. Print.

———. *Harry Potter and the Goblet of Fire*. 2000. London: Bloomsbury, 2007. Print.

———. *Harry Potter and the Half-Blood Prince*. London: Bloomsbury, 2005. Print.

———. *Harry Potter and the Order of the Phoenix*. 2003. London: Bloomsbury, 2004. Print.

———. *Harry Potter and the Philosopher's Stone*. 1997. London: Bloomsbury, 2004. Print.

———. *Harry Potter and the Prisoner of Azkaban*. 1999. London: Bloomsbury, 2004. Print.

———. *Quidditch Through the Ages*. London: Bloomsbury, 2001. Print.

———. *The Tales of Beedle the Bard*. London: Bloomsbury, 2008. Print.

Sanders, Andrew. *A Deed Without a Name: The Witch in Society and History*. Oxford: Berg, 1995. Print.

Sayers, Dorothy L. *Murder Must Advertise*. 1933. New York: Avon, 1967. Print.

Schanoes, Veronica L. "Cruel Heroes and Treacherous Texts: Educating the Reader in Moral Complexity and Critical Reading in J.K. Rowling's Harry Potter Books." Anatol, *Reading Harry Potter* 131–45.

Sidney, Sir Philip. "The Defence of Poesy." 1595. *Sir Philip Sidney*. Ed. Katherine Duncan-Jones. Oxford: Oxford UP, 1989. 212–50. Print.

Simpson, Jacqueline. "Terry Pratchett, Tiffany Aching, and the Wee Free Men." *Gramarye* 4 (2013): 7–16. Print.

Smith, Karen Manners. "Harry Potter's Schooldays: J.K. Rowling and the British Boarding School Novel." Anatol, *Reading Harry Potter* 69–87.

Speare, Elizabeth George. *The Witch of Blackbird Pond*. 1958. Harmondsworth: Penguin, 1967. Print.

Star Wars. Dir. George Lucas. 20th Century Fox, 1977. Film.

Steege, David K. "Harry Potter, Tom Brown, and the British School Story: Lost in Transit?" Whited 140–56.

Stephens, John. *Language and Ideology in Children's Fiction*. New York: Longman, 1992. Print.

———. "Witch-Figures in Recent Children's Fiction: The Subaltern and the Subversive." *The Presence of the Past in Children's Literature*. Ed. Anne Lawson Lucas. Westport, Praeger, 2003. 195–202. Print.

Stevenson, James. *Yuck!* 1984. London: Gollancz, 1985. Print.

Swinfen, Ann. *In Defence of Fantasy: A Study of the Genre in English and American Literature Since 1945*. London: Routledge, 1984. Print.

"Tam Lin." *The Oxford Book of Ballads*. Ed. Arthur Quiller-Couch. Oxford: Clarendon, 1910. 4–13. Print.

Tepper, Sheri S. *The True Game*. 1983–84. London: Corgi, 1985. Print.

Tolkien, J.R.R. *The Fellowship of the Ring: Being the First Part of The Lord of the Rings*. 1954. Rev. ed. London: George Allen, 1966. Print.

———. *The Hobbit*. 1937. Rev ed. New York: Ballantine Books, 1966. Print.

———. *The Return of the King: Being the Third Part of The Lord of the Rings*. 1955. Rev. ed. London: George Allen, 1966. Print.

———. *The Two Towers: Being the Second Part of The Lord of the Rings*. 1954. Rev. ed. London: George Allen, 1966. Print.

Tyler. "Harry Potter Turned a Generation of Kids into Readers, Data Shows." *On Our Minds @Scholastic: The Official Blog of Scholastic Inc*. 19 July 2011. Web. Accessed 29 October 2012.

Virgil. *The Aeneid*. 19BC. Trans. Robert Fitzgerald. New York: Vintage, 1984. Print.

Webb, Caroline. "'Abandoned Boys' and 'Pampered Princes': Fantasy as the Journey to Reality in the Harry Potter Sequence." *Papers: Explorations into Children's Literature* 18.2 (2008): 15–21. Print.

———. "'Change the Story, Change the World': *Papers: Explorations into Children's Literature* 16.2 (2006): 156–61. Print.

———. "'False Pretences' and the 'Real Show': Identity, Performance, and the Nature of Fiction in *Conrad's Fate*." *Journal of the Fantastic in the Arts* 21.2 (2010): 21–32. Print.

———. "Pottered Morality Nourishes a Generation." *Newcastle Herald*. 14 July 2011. [11.] Print.

Westman, Karin E. "Perspective, Memory, and Moral Authority: The Legacy of Jane Austen in J.K. Rowling's Harry Potter." *Children's Literature* 35 (2007): 145–65. *Project Muse*. Web. Accessed 13 June 2008.

Whited, Lana A., ed. *The Ivory Tower and Harry Potter: Perspectives on a Literary Phenomenon*. Columbia, MO: U of Missouri P, 2002. Print.

Wilcox, Carolynn E. "Everyday Magic: *Howl's Moving Castle* and Fantasy as Sociopolitical Commentary." *Welsh Mythology and Folklore in Popular Culture*. Ed. Audrey L. Becker, Kristin Noone, and Donald E. Palumbo. Jefferson: McFarland, 2011. 160–70. Print.

Williams, Tad. *To Green Angel Tower: Storm*. 1993. London: Orbit, 1997. Print.

Winters, Sarah Fiona. "Good and Evil in the Works of Diana Wynne Jones and J.K. Rowling." Rosenberg, Hixon, Scapple, and White 79–95. Print.

Woolf, Virginia. *Jacob's Room*. 1922. Oxford: Oxford UP, 1992. Print.

Yamazaki, Akiko. "*Fire and Hemlock*: A Text as a Spellcoat." Rosenberg, Hixon, Scapple, and White 108–16. Print.

Index

Aching, Tiffany 7, 19, 23–4, 26–8,
    29–33, 34, 37, 38, 39, 44, 45–6,
    46n3, 47n5, 47n6, 47n7, 101,
    106–17, 143, 145, 146; as adult
    19, 32–3, 37, 45; and agency 26,
    28, 29–32, 35–6, 45, 46, 114;
    and critique of stereotype 30, 38,
    45, 47n6, 101, 107, 108, 146;
    and fairy tale 19, 24, 29, 30,
    32, 33, 47n6, 145; and identity
    32, 37, 106, 107, 116, 117; and
    responsibility 28, 34, 109
agency 12, 13, 17, 19, 21, 24, 25–6,
    28, 29–32, 34, 35–6, 37, 45, 46,
    96n4, 97, 100, 101–4, 105–6,
    114, 117, 119–21, 123–8, 132,
    133, 135–7, 140, 141, 143, 144,
    146; *see also* destiny
Alton, Anne Hiebert 7, 33
*Amazing Maurice and His Educated
    Rodents, The* 7, 8–11, 76, 77,
    145, 146
analogues 21, 119, 129–31, 135, 140,
    144
Anstey, F. 102
"Aschenputtel" 46n2
Attebery, Brian 76–7
Aunt Maria see Black Maria

Bar-Hillel, Gili 105
Baum, L. Frank 105–6
Beaumont, Mme le prince de 47n8
"Beauty and the Beast" 47n8
Belgariad *see* Eddings, David
Black Maria 17
Bloom, Harold 4, 42
Blyton, Enid 4, 12
Borrowers, The 78–82, 84, 88, 89, 91,
    96n1–2

Borrowers Afield, The 81, 96n1
Borrowers Afloat, The 80, 96n1
Borrowers Aloft, The 79, 81
Borrowers Avenged, The 82, 83
Borrowers sequence 20, 76, 77–83, 84,
    85, 86, 88; *see also individual
    novels*
Bromeliad 7, 20, 22n2, 76–80, 83–8,
    144, 145; and *Aeneid* 86; and
    Borrowers sequence 20, 76,
    77–80, 83–8; and *Iliad* 86; and
    Lord of the Rings 85; and "lost
    colony" trope 85, 144
Browning, Robert 8–9
Burroughs, Edgar Rice 74n3
Butler, Charles 5, 17, 67
Byatt, A. S. 41

Campbell, Joseph 49
Carroll, Lewis 1
Cart and Cwidder 16, 60–1, 75n9, 143
Casual Vacancy, The 5
centaurs: version of divination 122–3
Charmed Life 5, 6, 129, 130–2, 135,
    136, 141, 141n2, 141n3, 145
"Childe Rowland" 27
Childe Rowland (character) 27, 28,
    47n4
choice 21, 34, 54, 104, 119, 121–2,
    125, 126–8, 130, 132, 134,
    135–6, 139, 140, 141; *see also*
    agency
Chrestomanci series 6, 21, 23, 119,
    129, 131, 133, 144; and fate 21,
    119, 129, 131, 133, 144; *see also
    individual works*
Christie, Agatha 135
"Cinderella" 12, 24–6, 27, 30, 33, 38,
    45, 46n1, 46n2, 49, 145

Grimes, M. Katherine 11, 24, 25, 29
Grimm, Brothers 27, 46n2
Gruner, Elisabeth Rose 33, 47n6, 47n7,
47n9, 108
Guards, Guards! 21, 31
Gupta, Sunan 4

Hagrid, Rubeus: as fairy godmother 25,
46n2
Harry Potter (character) *see* Potter,
Harry
Harry Potter (films) 48, 49, 52, 59,
75n7
*Harry Potter and the Chamber of
Secrets* (film) *see* Columbus,
Chris
*Harry Potter and the Chamber of
Secrets* (novel) 11, 13, 50–1, 58,
121, 125, 127
Harry Potter and the Deathly Hallows
(novel) 5, 11, 12, 14–16, 35, 38,
39, 41, 57–9, 61, 73, 128, 146;
epilogue 59; and heroic fantasy
57–9, 61, 73; and reading 14–16
*Harry Potter and the Deathly Hallows
Part 2* (film) 59
Harry Potter and the Goblet of Fire
(film) *see* Newell, Mike
Harry Potter and the Goblet of Fire
(novel) 12, 52–3, 54, 122
Harry Potter and the Half-Blood Prince
(novel) 13–14, 34, 47n10, 55–7,
121, 124–5, 127, 128
*Harry Potter and the Order of the
Phoenix* (film) 75n7
*Harry Potter and the Order of the
Phoenix* (novel) 35, 39, 40,
41, 42, 53, 54, 55–6, 59, 70,
75n7, 122–3, 124, 128; and
language 41
*Harry Potter and the Philosopher's
Stone* (film) *see* Columbus, Chris
*Harry Potter and the Philosopher's
Stone* (novel) 5, 11, 12, 15,
23–6, 29, 32, 33–5, 38–40,
41–2, 43, 44–5, 46, 49, 123,
125–6, 127, 128, 143, 145;
and agency 24, 38, 126–7; and
"Cinderella" 12, 24–6, 29, 33,
38, 45, 46n2, 49, 145; and fairy
tale 11, 12, 19, 24–6, 27, 29,
32, 38, 39, 42, 45, 46, 126;
and heroic fantasy 51, 126; and

language 41–3, 45, 46; and
positioning of reader 24, 38, 40,
42–3, 44, 45, 46, 60, 145; and
school story 33, 50–1; and wish-
fulfilment 15
*Harry Potter and the Prisoner of
Azkaban* (novel) 12, 52, 53,
122, 124
Harry Potter and the Sorcerer's Stone
(novel) *see Harry Potter and the
Philosopher's Stone* (novel)
Harry Potter sequence (novels) 4–5,
11–16, 19–20, 21, 23, 44–5,
46, 49, 50–9, 72–3, 74, 76, 77,
99, 110, 119, 121–8, 143, 145,
146; Christian message 59; and
destiny 54, 119, 121–8, 143; and
development 20, 24, 35, 44–5,
46, 127; and heroic fantasy
20, 44–5, 46, 53–8, 61, 72–3,
119, 126, 145; and positioning
of reader 24, 29, 41, 42, 145,
146; and school story 20, 33,
50–3, 121, 145; and wainscot
21, 76, 77; and witches 21; *see
also* centaurs; Dumbledore,
Professor; Dursleys; Granger,
Hermione; Hagrid, Rubeus;
individual works; Longbottom,
Neville; Lovegood, Xenophilius;
McGonagall, Professor; Mirror
of Erised, the; Potter, Harry;
Snape, Professor; Trelawney,
Professor; Voldemort, Lord;
Weasley, Ron
Hat Full of Sky, A 2, 36, 37, 107–10,
112, 114, 115–16, 117,
118n4, 145
Heilman, Elizabeth E. 23
Herbert, Frank 48
heroic fantasy 48–50, 52–4, 55, 57–9,
60–74, 141n3, 144–5; and
bildungsroman 48, 54, 71; and
cliché 70, 72, 121; conventions
58, 59, 61, 62–5, 66, 67–8,
71, 74, 76, 77, 96n4, 113,
119, 121, 131–2, 136–7; and
destiny 48, 54, 59, 123, 126,
131–2; and escapism 48–9, 60;
heroic qualities in 51, 56; and
inadequacy to experience 55, 57,
144; parodied 65; and prophecy
54, 96n4, 121; and reader 54–5,

Printed by PGSTL